HOWIE MORENZ

HOWIE MORENZ

The Greatest Season in the Life of Hockey's First Legend

DONALD MURRAY

sh.
SUTHERLAND HOUSE

TORONTO, 2025

Sutherland House
416 Moore Ave., Suite 304
Toronto, ON M4G 1C9

First edition, October 2025

If you are interested in inviting one of our authors to a live event or media appearance, please contact sranasinghe@sutherlandhousebooks.com and visit our website at sutherlandhousebooks.com for more information about our authors and their schedules..

We acknowledge the support of the Government of Canada.

Manufactured in Canada
Cover by Lena Yang
Book composed by Karl Hunt

Library and Archives Canada Cataloguing in Publication
Title: Howie Morenz : the greatest season in the life of hockey's first legend / Donald Murray.
Names: Murray, Donald (Lawyer), author.
Description: Includes bibliographical references.
Identifiers: Canadiana (print) 20250248050 | Canadiana (ebook) 20250248174 | ISBN 9781998365791 (hardcover) | ISBN 9781998365807 (EPUB)
Subjects: LCSH: Morenz, Howard William, 1902-1937. | LCSH: Montreal Canadiens (Hockey team)—History—20th century. | LCSH: Hockey players—Québec (Province)—Biography. | LCGFT: Biographies.
Classification: LCC GV848.5.M67 M87 2025 | DDC 796.962092—dc23

ISBN 978-1-998365-79-1
eBook 978-1-998365-80-7

Contents

PREFACE

Opportunity

HOWIE MORENZ HAD been in hospital for eight of the past ten nights. Just being able to be dressed for tonight's game involved the collective efforts of Dr. Sir Henry Gray, Dr. James Corrigan, hospital nursing staff, and trainers Jim McKenna and Eddie Dufour. All that, plus Morenz's own determination to be on the ice when the puck dropped.

The Montreal Canadiens and Chicago Black Hawks were about to begin the fifth and final game of the 1931 Stanley Cup final at the Montreal Forum. Each team had two wins. The first period started dangerously for the Canadiens, with the Hawks creating a deserved 10-3 shot advantage. Morenz tried to establish a pace for the Canadiens. Instead, held by Chicago's Tommy Cook, he wrestled him to the ice with a snarl. When they separated, Cook was bleeding from a cut to his head. Both were penalized.

Drawing blood had become a feature of Morenz's physical confrontations with younger challengers. Was it impatience with their lack of respect, distress at his own increasing difficulty in skating away from them, or, in this instance, a marker of his own concern for the outcome of the game? After the penalty time expired, Cook created a partial breakaway. Morenz overtook him and blocked the shot attempt.

Thirteen thousand fans filled the Forum, as many as half a million more were listening to the game's radio broadcast across Canada and into the United States. Even more stood anxiously outside newspaper and telegraph offices, waiting to surge forward when the next bulletin would be announced with a megaphone, and details posted in the window.

These were Morenz's followers. For nearly a decade he personified a new professional version of the game. He was acknowledged in North America as the incomparable hockey player, the best of his era. His renown carried outside of the hockey arena via the imaginative, evocative vocabulary of radio and newspapers, into magazines and novels. He was woven into the cultural fabric of the Jazz Age, an inspiration to his own generation and generations to come.

As Morenz got his feet under him in the second period, he seemed to hover above the ice, forcing his opponents to make decisions, bending their responses with a nod of his head, a dip of a shoulder, the lift of a skate. Each gesture could intimidate his opponents and spark the imaginations of teammates and fans alike. He did it all with the instincts he acquired as a boy. He learned early to appreciate the extra half-second of time he gained through his uncanny ability to anticipate, to see the game as a whole. The respect of his opponents gave him yet another moment of opportunity. Their hesitation opened a space for his creativity—allowing him to play more imaginatively than anyone else, commanding the whole of the ice. He had achieved an excellence where he really had no peers. He had made himself the nonpareil.

On a Canadiens power play near the midpoint of the second period, Johnny Gottselig of the Hawks was defending, wasting time with the puck when Morenz trapped him by the boards at centre ice. The puck came free, allowing Canadien Aurèle Joliat to fling it to an open Johnny Gagnon on the far side of the ice. Given the room to dash into the Hawk zone on his own, Gagnon scored the game's first goal.

The Hawks stormed back. While everyone knew Morenz was playing hurt, no one could carry the team like him, so Coach Cecil Hart would play him at centre, wing, sometimes even defence. Morenz would jump into the net to stop shots. He was the best player in the league at making the rest of his teammates better, magnifying their greatness while burnishing his own renown. Hart now turned to him to kill a teammate's penalty, with every expectation that he would succeed. Morenz had made himself into *the* go-to player, always responsible for devising the attacks, blunting the threats, and leading the winning efforts. At the end of the second period, the Canadiens maintained their precarious one-goal lead.

As soon as the third period began, the Hawks began drumming relentlessly against the Canadiens' defence. Morenz broke away with the puck from the bedlam in his own end. His rink-length dashes were truly awesome—their speed and creativity compelled crowds in every NHL city to rise and roar.

Nowhere were the roars of his followers louder than here, at home in Montreal's Forum. Here he was among the people who adopted and celebrated him as their own. He represented the people of this city and their causes as his own. The boy from southwestern Ontario, this international star, was a Québécois champion.

Morenz's rushing, hopeful burst toward the Chicago net stopped short when he was pulled down by a hook. The Hawks survived the ensuing penalty and resumed their attack with extra urgency, but Morenz's effort pushed Chicago two minutes closer to defeat.

Now he circled through the middle of the ice, focusing on the patterns he was seeing in the Hawks' attack, the open ice revealed by their defence, and the imperturbable, immovable presence of Charlie Gardiner in the Chicago goal. Somewhere in the mix of all those elements lay his next opportunity. Before he could strike, his teammate Pit Lepine took two stick penalties. Morenz stayed on the ice with his friend Joliat to kill each of them. During one stretch, the Hawks controlled the puck in the Canadiens' end for a full thirty seconds without finding a shot. The Hawks broke through after the penalties; Mush March carried the puck right to the Canadiens' net but was halted at the last inch by Canadien goaltender George Hainsworth. The game appeared to be going down to the final whistle.

Despite each of his necessary moments on the ice, Morenz and his fans, teammates and opponents all knew that it had been exactly a month since he had scored a goal. In eleven games since March 14, including three overtime losses, his team needed him to score, and he had not. It was a stellar run, the greatest regular season of his career with a thousand sparkling moments. But all the glory and accolades would fade to nothing if, in this final game, he couldn't do a little more. He knew he had to do something more.

He bent to another faceoff in his own end.

PART I

The Beginning

CHAPTER 1

Expectation

HOWIE MORENZ FIRST played in the village where he was born in 1902, in Mitchell, Ontario. He hadn't been a particularly remarkable player at first, but Mitchell's frozen Thames River allowed him to discover his unquenchable need to play.

He still had that now, at the age of 27. He told a *Montreal Star* reporter: "A fellow doesn't know what to do with himself for the first couple of weeks after hockey ends and before the golf season starts seriously. You go downtown, find nowhere to go, and then go home again. Another forty-four games for the summer wouldn't be bad at all."[1]

By the time his family relocated 20 kilometres down the road from Mitchell to Stratford in 1916, there were also glimmers of his superior ability to see, imagine, and manage the game on the ice.

Howie was the youngest of six children, but few of his siblings were still around for his annual visit to Stratford in the summer of 1930. His oldest brother Wilfred described by Howie as the goaltender in the family, now lived in Feltz Mills, New York (just south of Kingston, Ontario). Howie's other brother Ezra, who taught him some stickhandling skills, had died unexpectedly from diabetes, when Howie was thirteen. Two of his three sisters had married and moved away: Erma to Toronto, and Freda to Wisconsin. Gertrude remained in Stratford and still lived in the family's Wellington Street home with their father, William. She had become an avid archivist of Howie's hockey career, saving innumerable newspaper clippings and mementos that chronicled the achievements and experiences of her littlest brother.

Morenz enjoyed immersing himself in that local celebrity. His former coach, Dick Thorne, still had a shoe store in Mitchell where Morenz and another early coach, Dave Eizerman, could reflect on how their efforts continued to show in his NHL performances. The former left winger on the Mitchell Juveniles' 1917 Western Ontario Championship team, Arthur W. Blowes, was now the town clerk. Right winger Leslie Gatenby and defenceman Layton Sawyer were other teammates from that championship who remained local friends.

In Stratford, Morenz could point out the cigar store and billiard hall where George Bulucon would claim to have become his self-appointed "patron," giving him his first job. Dr. Robertson was still prominent in town, both as the local physician and the hockey executive who arranged for Morenz's apprenticeship in the Grand Trunk Railway's repair shops. "Father Bill" Gerby was still active in developing Stratford's next generation of hockey talent. Gerby was the coach who promoted the uniqueness of Morenz's talent, playing him simultaneously as a midget and a senior between 1917 and 1921, and then between 1919 and 1922 at the junior Ontario Hockey Association (OHA) and senior levels.

Morenz's fame also elevated the importance of Stratford's summertime events—the opening of a new road or a new park. Hundreds of his friends inevitably appeared to shake his hand and to applaud when he was introduced as the world's greatest hockey player. The towns of both Mitchell and Stratford commemorated his participation in these events with impromptu awards—such as being the visitor having come the greatest distance.

Morenz cultivated those hometown relationships wherever and whenever he could—jumping over the boards at training camp for a word with someone he recognized; visiting a Stratford buddy working the night shift at the CNR plant in Point St. Charles after a game at the Forum; chatting with a couple of friends who were worried about losing a bet between periods during a game in Toronto; and making time to accompany visiting acquaintances to the races in Montreal. He generated a sense of warm and genuine attachment with each, which they would recall with enduring satisfaction.

Arriving home after his first Stanley Cup in the summer of 1924, he was confronted with the sudden death of former Stratford Midgets teammate Larry Berger. He responded generously, and privately, to the Berger family. Years later they remembered and "looked up to Howie as a personal friend."[2]

In the summer of 1930, Morenz's father had just retired from the Grand Trunk Railway shops. Time was passing. Expectations had seemed so simple before he became an NHL star. He'd led the Montreal Canadiens to an unexpected Stanley Cup championship in his rookie season of 1923–24. This summer he returned to Stratford as the leader, again, of an unexpected Stanley Cup championship team.

There was a more pressing destination in this summer's pilgrimage—his mother's grave. Rose Pauli Morenz died suddenly in 1922 while Howie was in Guelph, Ontario, for a hockey game. Her death at age fifty-three had been province-wide news. The newspaper said she suffered from mental illness, although the circumstances in which her body was found suggested an accident at home.

No matter the fame, glory, and prestige that hockey gave him, Morenz would forever associate the demands of the game with the loss of his mother. She had been the one to nurse him back to health when his legs were scalded in a kitchen accident. She had gone all the way to Toronto to rescue him from running off to join the army when he was fifteen. She tried to protect him from the consequences of every youthful passion and risk that had threatened to consume him.

Rose Morenz had also deliberately avoided the very thing that became most important to her son. She would not watch him play hockey. She didn't want to see him hurt. She had wanted him to love music. But she couldn't protect him from his consuming desire to play the game. When she died, he was on the cusp of becoming an internationally famous professional hockey star.

Standing in front of her grave as a one-time Stanley Cup champion, then as a husband and father, and now as a two-time Cup champion, he understood that those achievements could never make up for not having her with him. Sportswriter James C. Hendy claimed that Morenz's demeanour changed after Rose died in 1922, that the player "had always been happy and carefree up to this time," but that "when he returned to competition after a short absence, he was more brilliant than ever."[3]

Since then he had played as if hockey needed to compensate him, pay him back for that irreparable loss. Two unexpected Stanley Cup victories were not enough. He wanted another because of everything he had given up to play the game.

He knew that between exhibitions, the regular season, and then playoffs, it would take about fifty games. The summit of his personal dreams would require teammates, and depend on his relationship with each of them. Each game, each moment, each turn on the ice, would demand a demonstration of his best as a player, both physically and emotionally, always against a vigorous and often antagonistic opponent. If his body allowed him to meet those challenges, the games would ultimately reveal a cumulative exposition of hockey performance excellence. He would create the definitive archetype of the hockey player for future generations in his own image.

CHAPTER 2

Training Camp

HOWIE MORENZ TOOK to the ice at the Montreal Forum, alone, on the evening of October 28, 1930. It was two weeks before the start of the NHL season. He hadn't skated or taken a shot on goal for more than six months. That had been in Atlantic City, in mid-April, for an NHL promotional series. This night's solo skate not only gave him a jump on his teammates but it also set an example for them.

Morenz was active over the summer. In addition to playing in the Atlantic City series, he renewed his youthful affection for baseball with a couple of outfield appearances in charity games at Montreal's Delormier Park in late July against Chappie Johnson's Chappies, a team of local Black players, and then in early August against Johnson's former professional club, the Brooklyn Royal Giants. Morenz occasionally played tennis to keep his reactions sharp and cycled to maintain knee and ankle mobility.

The main focus of his off-season training was golf. It helped him manage stress. It fed his competitiveness. NHL president Frank Calder, one of his occasional golf partners, observed how Morenz was an enthusiastic player, but his athletic dedication didn't exactly translate from the ice to the fairway: "He was a pretty fair golfer, and if he had taken the game seriously he might have developed into quite a good one."[1]

Instead of a casual excuse to be outside on a summer afternoon, golf was a near daily devotion that would leave him exhausted—sometimes even exasperated or short-tempered—after a round. He played as often as he could, in good weather and bad, favouring the Forest Hills course in the Montreal Island suburb of Lachine.

The depth of his obsession was on display a couple of years earlier, when a lightning storm hit the course. Instead of pausing his round, he chose to play through. The *Globe* reported: "Fortunately Morenz was using a wooden-shafted club, for as he was swinging it, there was a sharp crackle and a flash, the club was knocked from his hands, the steel twisted and the wood split by the force of the electric current, which was running through the air. Morenz got a jolt and so did his caddy."[2]

Despite his efforts, Morenz struggled to achieve golfing success. He sometimes broke 80, but no better. His own assessment of his game was that he was "about 85,"[3] but always determined to improve.

Morenz's twenty-eighth birthday on September 21 marked the true end of summer. Now back in the city after time with his wife and son at a summer place in Coteau Landing, he began to hang around the Canadiens' offices in the Windsor Hotel, with the three men who'd owned the Canadiens for the past decade: Joe Cattarinich, Leo Dandurand, and Louis Letourneau—the *trois mousquetaires*. Over his eight years with the team, Morenz's relationship with the owners became close. He sat in on their meetings, they included him in their business discussions, and occasionally provided him with financial advice.

After spending a few weeks together, and just as the Canadiens were to begin serious physical training, Morenz and the owners settled the terms of his new contract. Negotiations were amicable and brief. It was his first-ever two-year contract.

Leo Dandurand often proclaimed that the Canadiens paid the league's highest salaries. The Canadiens' owners, unlike those of the Rangers, were not using the Depression as bargaining leverage to reduce the payroll. The previous spring's Stanley Cup championship meant that the hockey business in Montreal was booming. After seven full seasons, it remained clear to all that Morenz was the main reason for that boom.

In 1930–31, salaries for near peers such as the Bruins' Eddie Shore ($10,000),[4] and the Leafs' King Clancy ($8,000)[5] and Charlie Conacher ($10,000),[6] suggest that Morenz's contract would not have been lower than the $11,500 eventually acknowledged by Dandurand.[7] Regardless, Morenz was committed to the Canadiens. The club provided him with a level of security that allowed him to concentrate fully on his hockey responsibilities.

Now it was time to train. There were two Montreal NHL teams at the time, the Maroons being the other. They were the first league team to begin training that year, having assembled for off-ice workouts on October 6.

Canadiens' coach Cecil Hart thought that was much too early, waiting until October 18 to begin physical assessments.

Morenz's first professional training camp back in 1923 had involved some limbering up, some skating in the "old, dilapidated fruit-warehouse with an outmoded refrigeration system" arena in Grimsby, Ontario, and then a few exhibition games against other NHL clubs.[8] Few physical demands were imposed. That continued to be the style of camp favoured by the New York teams, who did little more in 1930 than throw a puck on the ice and give the veterans and prospects an opportunity to play.

The Canadiens were not as advanced as either the Maroons or Chicago Black Hawks in terms of training techniques, but there had been some training improvements during Morenz's first seven years in the league. This year the veterans and prospects were called to report on October 18 for physical assessment. Morenz would then lead the Canadiens in their first real day of training on October 21. Participants were expected to remain in the gym, out on the field, or on the road, for about ten days before hitting the ice on November 1. That was too much of a delay for Morenz, which was why he went solo as soon as the Forum ice was ready.

Morenz reported to camp at 166.5 lb., between five and ten pounds heavier than his usual playing weight. Team watchers told themselves that he needed to carry a little extra physical heft in order to maintain his expected pace of play.

Morenz also arrived in camp mentally prepared. He exuded confidence, a belief that he remained the best and most valuable hockey player in the world. Aurèle Joliat predicted that Howie was going to have his best season ever. The writer George Sullivan described him simply "as unstoppable as falling water."[9]

Morenz had not joined the Canadiens by accident. They had pursued him incessantly in 1923 until he was signed. There were stories that he had been discovered when he played against Ernie Sauve, or was refereed by Sauve in Montreal or Stratford, or had been scouted by Cecil Hart at a CNR hockey tournament in Montreal early in 1923. These tales were inflated, if not entirely fabricated, by writers such as Milt Dunnell in Toronto.

Mike Rodden of the Toronto *Globe* identified Morenz as a burgeoning hockey star in a 1919 Ontario series between the Stratford Juniors and Woodstock's team of future NHLers. The *Globe*'s story about Stratford's 6-3 victory over Collingwood in the OHA junior playoffs on March 3, 1921, was headlined by Morenz's two goals and four assists. The same paper's story about the Memorial Cup games later that month also included headline coverage about Morenz.[10] His excellence on the ice was already known throughout the province, if not more widely.

When Morenz's mother died in January 1922, she was identified as the mother of the "star centre of the Stratford Midgets."[11] Six weeks later, on March 1, 1922, the Canadiens were playing in Hamilton at the same time Morenz was playing a CNR game in Guelph. Two columns over from its report of the Canadiens' victory, the *Globe*'s readers learned that Morenz had scored ten goals in Stratford's 14-6 pasting of Toronto in the Grand Trunk Apprentice League championship semifinal. It was then that he went to Montreal and played against Ernie Sauve, and was no doubt scouted in person by Hart—possibly Dandurand as well. More publicity ensued.

In March 1923, the *Globe* gave detailed coverage to Morenz and his Stratford team as they played Sault Ste. Marie in the Allan Cup playdowns. In addition to commenting that the team would move easily into senior competition the next season, the *Globe* also said that Morenz, and his opposing centre Bill Phillips, "have been offered professional contracts."[12] In that waning winter of 1923, Morenz "was already a can't-miss prospect and every amateur club with Allan Cup ambitions wanted him," wrote Brian McFarlane. "Along with Babe Siebert of Kitchener, it is said that Morenz actually arrived in Sudbury before the signing deadline with every intention of playing for the great Sudbury Wolves but changed his mind."[13]

Stratford sportswriter "Chick" Appel confirmed that Morenz was no hidden treasure in the spring of 1923. NHL teams knew they needed to compete for his services. Leo Dandurand claimed that all four NHL clubs were in the running with offers. Morenz's sister recalled that offers were turned down from Toronto, Victoria, and Saskatoon. There was another offer from Wesley Champ to sign with Regina of the Western Hockey League.

The logical NHL destination may have been Toronto. OHA coach Frank Selke had seen Morenz play and recommended him to the St. Pats—the team that wouldn't be renamed the Maple Leafs until 1927. Although one of the St. Pats owners viewed Morenz as a mere "intermediate" prospect, owner Charlie Querrie still offered him $1,000 for the five games remaining in the Pats 1923 NHL season.[14] Riley Hearn, a former Stanley Cup-winning goalie with the Montreal Wanderers, made a pitch for Morenz to sign with the Canadiens at about the same time, but was turned down. Either Lou Marsh or Mike Rodden (or perhaps both sportswriters) persuaded Dandurand to make another overture during the summer of 1923, which is when Cec Hart went to Stratford and signed a contract with William Morenz.

Howie was confirmed as the newest member of the Canadiens in a short note in both *La Patrie* and *La Presse* on July 10, 1923. Despite Howie's temporary second thoughts a few weeks later, the July 2023 signing by the Canadiens secured the rare opportunity to build a team around the most talented player of his generation.

Arriving at his first NHL camp that December, Morenz competed for the role of starting centre against two veterans: the Canadiens' starting centre, Odie Cleghorn, and the famous Joe Malone, who was looking for one more year of professional hockey after a couple of years with the Hamilton Tigers. Morenz understood that other veteran roster players were waiting to be convinced he deserved a starting spot. These included Sprague Cleghorn, Odie's brother, generally regarded and known as a "disgrace to hockey," and Billy Coutu, a defenceman who would soon be banned for life from the NHL for physically attacking a referee.[15]

The first time Morenz had wondered about making a team was in Stratford, just after turning fifteen. In December 1917 he had designs on making a midget team that played in a league with an upper age limit of twenty. After one practice, he was left bleeding, bruised, in tears, and dismissed. After the team's disastrous first outing, Morenz was invited back to centre their forward line. He played his first Ontario Hockey Association game on January 1, 1918, and never had to worry about making a hockey team again—even the Canadiens in 1923.

Morenz quickly convinced Sprague Cleghorn and the rest of the Canadiens that he could make a difference at their level of hockey. He was two months past his twenty-first birthday when he captured the starting centre position for the Canadiens out of that first training camp, a highly unusual and almost miraculous accomplishment. Veteran Joe Malone was blunt: "I took a look at a new kid and I knew right then I was ready for the easy chair. In practice, he moved past me so fast I thought I was standing still."[16]

The *New York Times* observed that Howie's transition to the NHL was as natural as putting on his skates, and "that he never was regarded in the light of a substitute player."[17]

The Canadiens embraced Morenz as an immediate star. Morenz became so comfortable that he had made the team at that first camp that he persuaded Dandurand to let him skip off home in the middle to spend time with a girlfriend. Morenz then delayed his scheduled return, teasing the team's owner with the idea that he might prefer time with the girlfriend to an NHL career.[18]

Morenz's first solo skate on the fresh Forum ice on October 28, 1930, made an impact on his teammates. The next night, ten other members of the team snagged some ice time for themselves to get their own starts on the season.

There was time on the morning of October 30 for a quick team photo of the players, fully dressed in their colours, on the sidewalk outside the Forum. The only player smiling was the one standing off to the far left, as ten others sat. Howie Morenz had not been interested in sitting. The Canadiens' first official on-ice practice of the season had arrived. Within days the *Montreal Star* reported that "Morenz, the ever reliable, is going as fast as ever."[19]

Morenz repaid his own experience of arrival, acceptance, and support from the Canadiens' organization with an unstinting professional generosity to all those who came after him. His sense of security, and perhaps a lingering recollection of when older players in Stratford physically abused him at his midget tryout, allowed him to empathize with each of the prospects who had their own professional dreams.

Pete Pelangio, one of the prospects who already had short peeks at the NHL game with the Canadiens and Detroit Cougars, recalled: "When I signed with Canadiens, I was a real yokel. In that kind of company, you can imagine how green I must have looked. The fellow who was the most help was Howie Morenz. He spent all kinds of time trying to teach me. Those are the things a young player won't forget."[20]

Johnny Sorrell had a similar experience in the fall of 1927: "I only lasted three weeks. There were a lot of rookies out that year, and among ourselves we all agreed that the only possible way to attract attention would be to catch

Howie. Howie would take the puck and let us chase him. A few caught him, but I always thought Howie was just teasing or maybe giving the kids a little encouragement."[21]

On November 5, with snow already on the ground, the Canadiens lined up for their first organized game of the year against the Providence Reds. More than five thousand fans showed up. Coach Hart started the players who had started the Cup final win against Boston: Morenz, Joliat, and Nick Wasnie up front; Sylvio Mantha and Marty Burke on defence; George Hainsworth in goal. It was a wise choice: there was no shortage of action, with a final score of 8-4 for the Canadiens.

"The game served as a medium to show new and old Canadiens in their setting as world champions. It illustrated that Morenz and Joliat have the same excessive speed, that the team has balance and condition," wrote the *Montreal Star*. "Morenz and Joliat looked impressive with dazzling forays."[22]

A couple of nights later, coach Hart changed the lineups. The game was tighter, and Providence led 3-2 going into the third period. Hart had limited Morenz's shifts, but after the Canadiens tied the score in the third, Hart opened the door to him again.

For Morenz, proving himself as the best meant that winning was always important, even in an exhibition game. The *Star* described how, with less than a minute left to play, Morenz "whipped an angle shot from the corner that saw the puck *spin in*" the net.[23]

The Canadiens concluded their training camp on November 11 with a 7-1 exhibition victory in London, Ontario, against the Tecumsehs of the International League. Morenz assisted Joliat on the first goal of the game, but didn't play much after Joliat's winning goal a few minutes later. He was more interested in visiting with several familiar faces and voices in the crowd—fans visiting from Stratford. He took time after the game to speak with each of them. A few surprised him with the gift of a silver tea service. Initially at a loss for words, he responded with generosity, thanking his friends and promising to return to London whenever circumstances allowed.[24]

Jean Pusie and Art Lesieur had hoped to make the Canadiens as defencemen, but old Bert McCaffrey had shown enough strength in camp to retain his place. Despite Morenz's encouragement, Pete Pelangio would not make the opening night cut either. The only rookie added to the Canadiens out of training camp would be right winger Johnny Gagnon.

By Friday night, resting in his own bed, lying on his back with wife, Mary, beside him, Morenz caught his breath. The Stanley Cup had reappeared in the Canadiens' club offices. The names from last spring were now stamped into its metal. There were still some who said the win over Boston had been a fluke. To prove it wasn't, the Canadiens were going to have to win again. He felt healthy. He felt young. He felt eager. He believed it would be a season of great opportunity.

PART II

Regular Season

CHAPTER 1

Saturday, November 15, 1930

Canadiens vs. Senators in Montreal

The Leader and the Captain: Howie Morenz and Sylvio Mantha

ON OPENING NIGHT, the streets around the Forum were full, the fans crowding for entry at the Ste-Catherine Street doors. From Atwater Park, it looked like a theatre premiere. Anticipation energized the fans as much as the players. While hockey fans around the rest of the league hoped their local team would be better than last year, Canadiens fans expected their team to be the best once again. It was the only way Howie Morenz ever knew how to think about a new season: "The old gang is together again . . . Just watch us go this year," he told the *Gazette*, with pride in his voice. "We can't miss."[1]

Despite the expectations, this Canadiens' dressing room was relaxed. Sylvio Mantha was beginning his eighth NHL season, fifth as captain. He was one of the players who made the Canadiens different from many other NHL clubs. He had played all his youth hockey in the city. He was among the first of a core who had either learned their hockey in Montreal or lived in the city year-round. Though sometimes identified as having Italian heritage, Mantha was clear: "We're proud to be pure French-Canadiens."[2]

Mantha was initially a forward until his first Canadiens training camp in 1923. Like Joe Malone, he saw Howie Morenz sweep by him at full speed.

Joliat was chasing, trying to keep up. In that moment, Mantha decided that his career as a forward was over. Morenz acknowledged that Mantha was even slower than the veteran King Clancy.

Morenz was quick to notice Mantha's other elite qualities: "Sylvio is one of the hardest men to get past," he told *La Patrie*. "His arms are so strong that it's a real problem to get the puck from him."[3] Another of the captain's unique skills was using his skates to hold a puck against the boards when necessary. So Mantha became a defenceman, protective of his home end of the ice.

It was Mantha's ability to quickly recognize and appreciate his place that soon had him in charge: both in the dressing room and on the ice. He was anointed as *père Mantha*, a nickname that became even more apt when his younger "brother" Georges joined the club. As captain Sylvio did not need to score important goals for the team, although he could. He did not need to establish the speed or manner of play, although he could occasionally do that, too. What he really needed to do was nurture the soul of the team as a vehicle to demonstrate the pride of French Canadiens. It was a role he embraced.

Howie Morenz, the other leader in the room, was already in motion. "He'd like to walk around before a game," said Aurèle Joliat. "He always had so much energy. He just couldn't get out on that ice fast enough. He was the leader, he'd pep up a team. Just to watch him, hell, you'd want to jump out of your boots almost."[4]

Goalkeeper George Hainsworth was always first on the ice, followed by Morenz, who had his own routine—some even called it superstition. "When Canadiens appear on the ice," wrote the *Montreal Star*, "you will see Howie follow George Hainsworth out, drop the puck and drive it into the open cage at the north end. Howie has been following that habit for years and now it's all part of his night's work."[5]

After the national anthem, and a ceremonial faceoff collected by Morenz, Howie moved into his "familiar crouch," and then leapt into action when the puck dropped.

Within a couple of minutes, Mantha picked up a loose puck on his side of the ice, inside his own blueline and with no opponent close. The *Montreal*

Star reported how "he bounded down centre, straightened up as he raced by the thinned-out Ottawa defence, made for the right corner and then reversed in at express-train speed to sweep a shot across the mouth of the net into the cords. It was his second rush of the night."[6]

Mantha sometimes scored statement goals, like the first goal ever in the Boston Garden. Although he would only score four times this season, this goal at 3:30 of the first period of the Canadiens' first game of the season was another.

Mantha continued to push the Canadiens' attack. He put Wil Larochelle into the clear for Montreal's second goal. Then Morenz took command.

His goal twenty seconds after the Larochelle score ignited a chorus of "*Les canayens sont la!*" and "*Il gagne ses épaulettes!*" from the crowd. Midway through the period, Morenz got another that the *Gazette* called "the most brilliant individual effort of the evening. Streaking down the left lane, Howie swung around the Ottawa defence and went in unmolested on [goalie Alex] Connell. Alex moved off his inner post, fearing a drive to the far corner, and Morenz victimized him with deadly accuracy. There were only inches between Alex and that latter upright, but Morenz's shot whistled through like an arrow."[7]

Connell admitted later that he'd never even seen the shot. Referee Bobby Hewitson had been absorbed watching Morenz, too: "The big kick in handling a Canadiens game in those days," he said, "was to watch the great Howie Morenz in action."[8]

Those successive Morenz goals to boost the Canadiens' lead to 4-0 demonstrated the contrast between his style of leadership and that of *père* Mantha. The latter was solid and stable and dependable. Morenz would lift fans to their feet and make them want to sing.

The third period was almost perfunctory. Art Gagné, a linemate on the Stanley Cup-winning Canadiens of 1924, but now playing for the Senators, scored for Ottawa. Aurèle Joliat responded, closing out a 5-1 Canadiens victory.

It had been an impressive and confident display by the Canadiens. Sylvio Mantha, with a goal, an assist, and two penalties, was content with how everything worked out. He had set the tone for the season. The Canadiens had been victorious. Four of the six goals (the ones not scored by Morenz) came from French-Canadians. For Mantha, and his city, it was essential to express the identity of the team by who was actually on the ice—to have men from his city and his province in the NHL uniform. Leo Dandurand agreed.

Both Dandurand and Manta were aware that the fans recognized not just who was on the ice, but an equivalent importance of how the game was played. Even as père Mantha's signature was his longer commitment to establishing and keeping a place for French-Canadians, and the Montrealais, among the world's best hockey players, Howie Morenz would inevitably be recognized and remembered as the team's *game* leader. Morenz, not Mantha, was the recognizable individual star to whom the fans would look in hope. It was he who could be expected, at any moment, to illuminate any game with a personal, breathless, and electric brilliance.

Ottawa **1** at ***Canadiens*** **5**

Morenz: 2 goals

Game 1	GP	G	A	Pts	PiM	HG	AG	HA	AA	GWG	GWA
Season Total:	1	2	-	2	-	2	-	-	-	-	-

CHAPTER 2

Tuesday, November 18, 1930

Canadiens vs. Bruins in Boston

Morenz's Adoring "Gods" of Boston

BOSTON'S MADISON SQUARE Garden was built on top of the city's North Station. The train traffic underneath would regularly cause the walls, seats, and even the ice surface to tremble. The stacked balconies "seemed to hang almost over the ice surface,"[1] with bars between every three rows to prevent any unexpected tumbles among the occupants. The fans were truly on top of every play, seeing everywhere Morenz could come from, and everywhere he had the chance to go. Fans were close enough to see the players' facial expressions, to hear their shouts, and to ensure every player heard their shouts, too. For some players, that alone made the Boston Garden a most hateful place to play, even into the 1990s.

The boisterous, noisy, and profane "gods" in the gallery always set the tone. Benevolent in their attitude toward any honest effort put forward by men wearing Bruins sweaters, the "gods" were also ready with harsh sarcasm for anyone—Bruin or opponent or referee—who failed to perform with energy or demonstrate a proper sense of sportsmanship. That was why they loved watching Howie Morenz play.

With the unnecessary help of a Santa Claus Charity promotion, the building this night was banged out with about sixteen thousand customers. The morning newspapers still referred to the Bruins as the "uncrowned champions" after last spring's playoff loss to the Canadiens.[2] The "gods" saw the game as a revenge match, the true beginning of the Bruins' effort to reverse April's embarrassment. Morenz knew that he would be expected to respond.

At 3:41 of the first period, the Bruins' Dit Clapper scored over a falling Hainsworth with a bullet. Shortly after, Clapper found Pit Lepine vulnerable and threw the Canadien hard against the boards, clipping him in the head with his stick. Even though Lepine was only out for a few seconds, he was bleeding. A new rule required a major penalty.

Howie Morenz returned to the ice in place of the staggered Lepine. Bruin defenceman Lionel Hitchman "was the first to be tricked as the puck slid underneath him to be collected again by Morenz," wrote the *Boston Post.* "[Percy] Galbraith received similar treatment as Howie skated like mad toward the goal and finally [Bruins goalie] Tiny Thompson was baffled as an unexpected snap shot scaled beneath him before he could drop full way to save, and the score was tied as the generous Bruin fans applauded deservingly."[3]

Morenz had gone through three Bruins to score the equalizer unassisted. It was precisely the kind of goal the NHL's American fans wanted to see. It was the kind of performance that allowed the league to expand from a four-team eastern Canadian pro circuit in 1917 to the dominant ten-team North American league that the NHL had become. The Toronto *Globe* explained the phenomenon: "The fans want to see Canadiens and the secret is not hard to find. The answer is supplied by Howie Morenz. Recognized as the outstanding hockey player of the present generation, he is to hockey what Babe Ruth is to baseball. . . . In his position he has no equal in the NHL. There may be better goal-getters, players with as much speed and stickhandling ability, but for all-round performance the Mitchell meteor tops them all. That is why the fans flock to see him."[4]

"Morenz has the biggest asset you can have in any sport," said hockey legend Jack Adams. "In my opinion, he's the Babe Ruth, Ty Cobb, and 'Danny' Vance of hockey, all rolled into one."[5]

Sportswriter Trent Frayne explained the phenomenon as Morenz being "a fairy-tale figure who could do things no one else could do, against greater odds. When Morenz duped a defenceman, it was David slaying Goliath."[6]

Attraction to the Morenz style superseded team loyalty, mesmerizing both Boston fans and the *Boston Post* alike: "If there is any one hockey player in the business the fans delight in watching it is Howie Morenz, and for some reason Howie likes to show at his best against the Bruins. The Boston fans have always taken a fancy to the 'comet' . . . and when he gets peeved he can put on a terrific hustle, and away he goes, skating like sixty, with his black hair streaming out straight in the breeze and with the puck as much under his control as though it were a part of his stick."[7]

It was the way he played, willing himself to the edge of recklessness to get to the net, that rivetted their attention. "Time and again he'd go down with bone-rattling bodychecks, often he'd get caught squarely in the 'sandwich,'" Montreal sportswriter Andy O'Brien explained. "But he'd come back and leave the crowd aghast as he'd hurtle through, pick up the puck and score—or nearly score. On several occasions, I saw this meteoric Morenz bowl over both defencemen with sheer, reckless savagery. Like the Babe, who used to pack a thrill even [when] striking out, Morenz in missing was an experience."[8]

After the initial exchange of goals, the game became more physical. The Canadiens found themselves with a four-on-three power play, but the Bruins' Cooney Weiland intercepted a pass in the Boston zone and was away for a solo toward Hainsworth. The Canadiens' defencemen were caught too far forward. In a glance, the "gods" in the Boston gallery saw Morenz chasing, even though he had been deepest in the Bruin zone. They leaned forward. He closed the gap on Weiland. The "gods" stood and roared as Weiland readied to shoot. Morenz left his feet and caught Weiland from behind with a flying rugby-style tackle to nullify Weiland's chance. It saved a goal, but earned Morenz the first major penalty of his career.

The "gods" did not begrudge Morenz his penalty. The desperate, but athletically magnificent, act of flinging himself through the air to prevent an unchallenged shot on goal brought simultaneous thrills and groans and cheers. It was the kind of commitment to the game that earned fans' respect. The best offensive player in the league was still willing to do the hard defensive stuff to help his team and to do it in a way to evoke awe, even in the first period of the second game of a long season.

Morenz tried to give the Canadiens a lead in the middle period on yet another power play. He was behind the Boston skaters by about a stride, but goalie Tiny Thompson charged out to meet him. The collision crumpled Morenz and the puck skittered off the back boards.

The Canadiens' chances ebbed after that. The Bruins scored two quick goals early in the third period and added two more later for a 5-1 lead with less than five minutes left.

If the audience felt the game was over, Howie Morenz did not. He continued to carry plays into the Boston zone, and, with three minutes left, assisted on Johnny Gagnon's first NHL goal.

The *Gazette* was muted in acknowledging just "another stellar display" by Morenz.[9] The *Boston Globe* was more effusive, recognizing what the "gods" had seen in Morenz: the most "outstanding" player in the Garden that night. It had been "exhilarating to watch the best player in the world pushing himself to extremes."[10] It would become both the aspiration and pattern for his whole season.

***Canadiens* 2** at Boston **5**

Morenz: 1 goal, 1 assist
1 major penalty (5 minutes)

Game 2	GP	G	A	Pts	PiM	HG	AG	HA	AA	GWG	GWA
Season Total:	2	3	1	4	5	2	1	-	1	-	-

CHAPTER 3

Thursday, November 20, 1930

Canadiens vs. Maroons in Montreal

The Morenz Homes in Montreal

WHEN THE CANADIENS returned to Montreal, both Howie Morenz and Pit Lepine had been complaining of sore backs. After a stop for both at Dr. Henry Gray's hospital, Morenz was quickly excused and spent his Wednesday night at home.

Home for Morenz, wife Mary, and Howie Jr. was at 4114 Girouard Avenue in Montreal's Notre Dame de Grace (NDG) neighbourhood. It was just west of Decarie, and a little south of Monkland Avenue. Howie and Mary had first moved onto Girouard in 1928, just after Howie Jr. was ready to walk. They had lived at 588 then, further south and nearer to St-Jacques. The neighbourhood around 4114 boasted the most spacious of the residences Morenz rented during his career. The two-storey building contained two units: one up, one down. There was a front lawn, backyard, a solid-looking stone facade, and a proper (not shared) front door.

NDG was an egalitarian, cosmopolitan neighbourhood, like the Plateau, where his first apartment in Montreal had been. While the Plateau was a community of working-class renters, a milieu in which he fit easily as a former machinist apprentice, NDG represented a higher class of upwardly mobile office people, but who still lived with the instability and uncertainty of being temporary occupants. During his time in Montreal, he had still never lived in any one place for more than a couple of years.

His other home, the Montreal Forum at the corner of Atwater and Ste-Catherine Street, was about a forty-five-minute walk from there. The most direct route from Girouard to the Forum was through Westmount, a separate, decidedly Anglo city where inherited or acquired wealth was obligatory, and its social boundaries were as clearly defined as its streets.

Howie Morenz only ever qualified to hover near Westmount's boundaries. People with significant hockey pedigrees, such as Lester Patrick and Art Ross, had grown up in Westmount. Men connected with the birth of professional hockey in Canada, like the Wanderers' Sam Lichtenhein and the Maroons' James Strachan, were domiciled there. The men who were important in the history and current operations of the Canadiens, such as the surviving family of George Kendall, Leo Dandurand, and Cecil Hart, lived there, too.

On the farther boundary of Westmount from NDG, the Forum represented a more accessible home for Howie Morenz. When he first arrived in the city, he played out of Mount Royal Arena. Then, on November 29, 1924, the Canadiens opened the Canadian Arena Company's new Forum. That night Morenz and the Canadiens played as if they owned the building themselves, overwhelming the Toronto St. Pats 7-1.

Even as the Canadiens christened the Forum, a new tenant had already moved in as the building's primary occupant. "The Montreal Professional Hockey Club," playing under the name of the Montreal Maroons, was largely financed by Westmount interests. The Maroons were also managed exclusively by men from Westmount. The management group saw themselves as the rightful heirs to the hockey heritage of Lichtenhein's Wanderers, for a time recognized as the best, and most important, professional team in the game.

The primary challenge to the Maroons' conceits always came from the Canadiens. Each game between the clubs represented a struggle to see which would occupy the Forum as its rightful home. It was a battle that remained as insoluble as the shifting control of the Alsace-Lorraine region between France and Germany. The struggle was often violent. Their games stood as a proxy for the social divides in the seats and on the city's streets. The games became frank linguistic contests, with the Maroons' lineup consistently featuring English-stock players. This season, the Maroons qualified just two French-Canadians on a seventeen-man roster, both from Ontario.

On this Thursday night, the Maroons were already surly, having lost their first three games of the season and having failed to score a single goal. The Canadiens, as expected, took the lead. The Maroons managed to tie the game 1-1 shortly after. The Canadiens recaptured the lead just thirty-five seconds later, with a goal by Johnny Gagnon.

The Maroons' Bill Phillips was the kind of player that the team's management had always preferred. Solid if not heavy, he had been a scoring forward like Morenz, but his best offensive days were now behind him. He was thirty-four years old, playing now as a defenceman rather than as a forward. His job was confined to slowing down smaller and swifter players, roughing them up as necessary. Phillips had been flat-footed, slow to react, and embarrassed on the Gagnon scoring play.

Phillips was still on the ice when the Canadiens returned to the Maroons' end. He joined a scrum in front of the Maroons' net and hacked Canadien Armand Mondou in the head with his stick. There was blood, earning Phillips a ten-minute major penalty. The game turned.

The Canadiens scored three times, like "chain lightning," during the disastrous Phillips penalty. Morenz got the first of them on a passing sequence started by Joliat, through Larochelle to Morenz. It was "a beautiful piece of combination play," wrote the *Gazette*. "The scoring line worked into position with the precision of a well-trained basketball team."[1]

Morenz scored the third power-play goal with a burst of speed, vaulting the Canadiens into a 5-1 lead. They would later add two more.

The undoing of the Maroons had been emphatic. The sequence of violence, the penalty, and the three goals confirmed that the Forum was the Canadiens' home. It was as much *la maison* for Morenz and his teammates, as it would become, decades later, for the Canadiens' Yvan Cournoyer, who said: "It wasn't my second home, it was my first."[2]

It was, in fact, the most permanent home of any sort that Morenz had during the whole of his time in Montreal.

Maroons **1** at ***Canadiens* 7**

Morenz: 2 goals, 1 assist

Game 3	GP	G	A	Pts	PiM	HG	AG	HA	AA	GWG	GWA
Season Total:	3	5	2	7	5	4	1	1	1	-	1

CHAPTER 4

Sunday, November 23, 1930

Canadiens vs. Black Hawks in Chicago

Getting Shut Out: The Value of a Reputation

THE STANLEY CUP champion Canadiens were still basking in the glow of their 7-1 dismantling of the Maroons when they headed west to Chicago. They were cocky about having scored sixteen goals in their first three games. Better yet, they hadn't lost to the Chicago club since February 11, 1927—a string of fourteen wins and one draw. Howie Morenz and the Canadiens felt indomitable.

Morenz was personally buoyed by his start to the season: five goals and two assists in three games. He remembered scoring the very first time he had played in Chicago, at the Coliseum, on December 22, 1926. Since then, he'd enjoyed multi-goal and multi-point games against the Hawks, once accumulating five points in a single game. Last spring, it had been his goals that eliminated the Hawks from the playoffs and launched the Canadiens into the Stanley Cup final.

All of that had earned him the reputation as "the Nemesis," not just once but over and over again in Chicago.[1] Reputations were important in the city. They could make you an important person. They gave you access to the city's other important people. But a failure to live up to your reputation could mean immediate social exile.

Chicago's still-new Union Station, with its imposing Great Hall, served notice to each of the Canadiens how small they were. That Chicago sense of dimension was reinforced at the Stadium. Paddy Harmon, who liked people to think of him as the "Tex Rickard of the West,"[2] had built the Stadium in hope of luring the National Hockey League to his city. The league had sold the franchise instead to someone with higher social status, leading directly to Harmon's financial ruin. Within months of the Stadium's opening on March 28, 1929, Harmon lost control of the building to wealthy grain-dealer James Norris and died the following year.

The Stadium remained a tribute to Harmon's vision. It had the largest capacity in the league from the time it was built until it was replaced. With no barriers separating the team benches from the paying public, players felt "the fans are leaning right over your shoulder."[3] Where the Boston Garden made that kind of close intimacy feel personal, the Stadium's size made the relationship feel impersonal and menacing.

The Stadium was also the noisiest place in the league. Supported by an organ played at thunderous volume, the fan noise became its own presence. Sometimes players could barely hear themselves breathe. Each player's heart beat to the combined rhythms of the crowd's threat, the organ, and the game on the ice.

Often seated amid that cacophony were some larger-than-life figures, including Al Capone. "Scarface" had been the leading criminal boss in the city since 1925, primarily in the business of what he referred to as the "light pleasures"—gambling, sex, and alcohol. Like Tex Rickard in New York, Capone engaged in both local and national fight promotions. He enjoyed visits to the ballpark. He regularly befriended important athletes and sports figures, from Jack Dempsey and Barney Ross to the writer Damon Runyon.

Capone had a more than casual interest in hockey. He befriended Howie Morenz when the twenty-four-year-old arrived in town in 1926. The press would report, as an incidental social note, how Capone attended Hawks games when the Canadiens were in town. There is reputed to be a picture of them together in a Capone roadster. Capone's public affinity for athletes gave him a public aura of legitimacy, even innocence. Morenz and Dempsey had served the same purpose as the soup kitchens that Capone ran in downtown Chicago in late 1930—props in Capone's image-maintenance strategy. However, now under indictment, Capone had no time to spend with Morenz, or even to watch hockey games.

Another dominant Chicago presence at the Stadium was the Black Hawks' owner, Major Fred McLaughlin. The major was a native Chicagoan from a wealthy coffee family. After a short military career with the 85th Division of the United States Army, McLaughlin promoted sporting events with New York's Rickard, who in turn got McLaughlin involved with the National Hockey League.

Originally regarded as a know-nothing owner, McLaughlin proved himself to be an interested and active learner. He had ideas and was willing to test them with his team, even when his ideas offended traditional "hockey people," or were resisted by his string of coaches. He attended his team's games at home and on the road, visited the dressing room, and sat with his players on the bench. He wasn't there to share any *esprit de corps* with his employees. He was there to supervise and direct, with a harsh temper.

McLaughlin soon became an impulsive and impatient hockey executive. He developed an out-sized sense of competence after a five-year association with the game. He assumed he could bend the game to his will. He believed he could be financially successful without owning his own arena. Eventually, all this would contribute to his downfall. But tonight, he would feel rewarded by his team's dominance over their traditional tormentors, and the end of Howie Morenz as "the Nemesis."

Morenz's expectation that he and the Canadiens would give Chicago a show was disrupted early. About fourteen minutes in, the Hawks' Teddy Graham and Tommy Cook cuffed at the puck in a pile-up that was sliding toward George Hainsworth. The puck ended up in the Canadiens' net. Objections by the Canadiens went for naught. A similar tangle of players led to another goal for the Hawks early in the second period. The Canadiens had trouble developing any effective offence. Morenz became irritated at the interference coming from Duke Dutkowski on the Chicago defence. The two began mixing things up behind the Chicago net, and both were penalized for roughing.

Late in the third period, Vic Ripley picked up the puck again in his own zone and found an opening. He skated toward Hainsworth all alone. Morenz was the only Canadien chasing, but tonight could not catch up. He had to watch as Ripley scored the Hawks' third goal. Morenz's reputation as "the

Nemesis" had proven as worthless in Chicago as the reputations of Harmon and Capone. Morenz and McLaughlin would renew their engagement with each other in the months and years to come.

***Canadiens* 0** at Chicago **3**

Morenz: 1 penalty

Game 4	GP	G	A	Pts	PiM	HG	AG	HA	AA	GWG	GWA
Season Total:	4	5	2	7	7	4	1	1	1	-	1

CHAPTER 5

Thursday, November 27, 1930

Canadiens vs. Falcons in Detroit

The Buddies: Howie Morenz and Marty Burke

COACH CECIL HART responded to the Canadiens' second consecutive road loss of the young season by holding practices both Tuesday and Wednesday at the Detroit Olympia. Four of the five Ontarians on the Canadiens' roster came from close by, but the extra practices discouraged any ideas about skipping away for an off-day with family. Instead, this early gap in the schedule gave the Canadiens four consecutive days to get reacquainted with their teammates.

On the road, Howie Morenz was regularly part of a quartet that included the French-speaking Albert Leduc, the reclusive George Hainsworth, and defenceman Marty Burke. Leo Dandurand referred to them as "the Four Musketeers."[1]

Morenz and Burke were even more constant companions. They were road-trip roommates for seven of Burke's eleven seasons in the league. They shared competitive off-ice interests in golf and baseball. Burke had a clear advantage as a ball player. But though he had a lifelong devotion to golf and sometimes worked as a golf pro, it was a rare round when Burke could beat Morenz.

How they became such good friends is difficult to discern. Burke grew up as a butcher's son in Toronto and wasn't particularly committed to hockey as a youngster. After playing outdoors at the Perth Square Rink in a Toronto church league, and then OHA junior, he took a year off when he was fifteen. He came back to hockey by playing a couple of years with the St. Mary's

Juniors before moving to Stratford for senior hockey. That was when his aspirations suddenly seemed to expand.

By the time Burke arrived in Stratford, Morenz had already been gone for a year, but Burke still had the chance to play with, and against, many of Howie's former teammates. After another year as a senior with the Port Arthur Bear Cats, the twenty-two-year-old Burke showed up in Montreal in the fall of 1927 and asked for a tryout with the Canadiens.

Perhaps intrigued by Burke's brash self-confidence, Dandurand gave him his tryout. This was the year Johnny Sorrell described the true test at training camp: who could catch Howie Morenz?[2] Burke impressed Dandurand enough that he was signed to a contract.

Had Morenz been tipped off from Stratford that Burke was coming to Montreal? Had he heard a whisper that Burke was a hidden gem? Did Morenz, in turn, give Burke a bit of a break and let him show well, as he was known to do for other prospects? Any answers remain secrets. What is known is that after eleven games with the Canadiens, Burke was loaned to the NHL's Pittsburgh Pirates for the balance of that 1927–28 season. By the start of the 1928 playoffs, Morenz said, "In my opinion, Marty is the defensive player whose future promise is brighter than that of any rookie of the year."[3] Burke was recalled to the Canadiens and began his real career and destiny as Howie Morenz's on- and off-ice companion.

By the summer of 1930, the Montreal Maroons, Detroit Falcons, and New York Rangers had all been making offers to acquire Burke. The Falcons' interest came from coach Jack Adams, who believed that "hockey was a simple game with only two basic manoeuvres: either you knock the puck away from the man or you knock the man away from the puck."[4] It was an approach to the game that characterized Adams's own career, and one that Burke embraced. The *Gazette* described him as "small for a defenceman, but he packs a hefty bodycheck and his steadying qualities have proved an inspiration to his team."[5]

Despite being a small man on a small team, Burke accumulated over five hundred minutes in penalties in just over five hundred regular season NHL games. For five successive seasons he was the Canadiens' penalty leader. In the 1929–30 season, Burke had set a career high of seventy-one minutes in penalties.

Instead of being physically intimidating, the *Montreal Star* described Burke's approach to defence as "hard-bitten" and "durable."[6] He was also "dynamite" when he connected on a check.[7] The previous season he checked a rushing Hap Day in Toronto and came out of the play with a broken bone in his shoulder. Two months later, he hit Frank Boucher of the Rangers and broke Boucher's collarbone. His tenacity was also well-known around the league. "He fears no foe," wrote the *Globe and Mail*, "and he'll bodycheck a man like Charlie Conacher just as surely as he will the lightest player in the league."[8]

His physical attitude on the ice was an important aspect of his relationship with Morenz. As Burke increased his physical engagement with opponents, the offensive productivity of his friend Howie increased as well. This game at Detroit's Olympia provided a vivid example of that.

On the Falcons' initial rush of the game, Burke forced puck-carrier Tommy Filmore deep into the corner. However, the puck took a strange bounce from them into the Canadiens' net. Just twenty-three seconds had passed from the opening faceoff. That misadventure animated Burke's next check, resulting in a penalty for charging. As soon as the penalty expired, Morenz evened the score with a classic but extended give and go.

The *Gazette* described it as "a typical Morenz–Joliat goal, as the centre player dashed down the middle, passed to Joliat, who stickhandled his way through two players, and then passed the puck down to Morenz who was waiting. The Detroit team dashed down at Howie but he had already slapped the rubber into the nets and equalized the score."[9]

The game remained tied into the third period, when play became scrappier. Morenz was anxious to grab the lead, but he drew a charging penalty just as the period began. A major penalty to Joliat followed. The Canadiens extinguished the Morenz penalty, but then Burke's abrasive checking style again caught the attention of referee Mickey Ion. Burke took Morenz's place on the bench for slashing, restoring Detroit's two-man advantage. Burke returned, but took another slashing minor. His absences made the critical difference in the game, with Herbie Lewis scoring twice, pushing Detroit ahead 3-1.

The Canadiens had been short-handed for nearly nine minutes of the third period. When all of them finally vacated the penalty bench, Morenz scored an unassisted goal out of a scramble. Despite further effort, the Canadiens could not pull even.

When the game was over, Marty Burke was recognized in the Detroit press as having played a strong game, despite his three penalties, despite having been directly involved in the first Falcons goal, and for leaving his teammates short-handed for Detroit's two other scores. He could not be ignored. In addition to roughing it up on the ice, he had been vocally involved, both in English and stilted French. The *Globe* said his "roars of encouragement can be heard all over the arena."[10]

Burke wasn't much interested in his reputation as a "Rock of Gibraltar" in the NHL. What was important to him was that Howie Morenz's final goal the previous spring had put his name on the Stanley Cup. He knew that if that were to happen again, it would also be thanks to Morenz. Burke understood that it was his role to support Morenz on the ice by whatever means he could.

Despite trades that sometimes left them on different teams, Burke remained perpetually loyal to Morenz, his friend and road companion. Whenever asked, Burke would polish his friend's virtues, defend against comparisons, and object to even the most subtle criticisms of Howie's play. Being able to play on the Canadiens with Morenz had given Burke everything he wanted out of his career.

Morenz also understood the value of his relationship with Burke, on and off the ice. Their relationship meant that no matter how hard it would get for either of them, Marty Burke would always be ready to share every struggle with him. Even now as the Canadiens remained winless on the road.

***Canadiens* 2** at Detroit **3**

Morenz: 2 goals
1 penalty

Game 5	GP	G	A	Pts	PiM	HG	AG	HA	AA	GWG	GWA
Season Total:	5	7	2	9	9	4	3	1	1	-	1

CHAPTER 6

Saturday, November 29, 1930

Canadiens vs. Bruins in Montreal

The Agility of Morenz

WHEN THE CANADIENS scurried through Windsor Station on Friday afternoon, everyone in Montreal was wondering about the team's three-game road losing streak, all against American Division teams. The next time the Canadiens were seen, they stepped onto the Forum ice in front of nearly 12,500 supporters for their Saturday night game against the Boston Bruins. The Canadiens had only twelve players available, while the Bruins had thirteen.

Howie Morenz started the game anxiously and was soon penalized for tripping. The teams traded early goals, one on a Canadiens power play by Nick Wasnie, with the other by Dit Clapper short-handed for the Bruins. With the teams still playing careful and unproductive hockey early in the second period, Cec Hart leaned over the boards and hollered to his players that they needed to "skate till it hurts."[1]

If anyone could answer Hart's call to action, it was Morenz. He could be the fastest. He had more control of shift and pace than his opponents. He was more agile. He was also more adventurous, more courageous, and more innovative on skates than anyone else in the league, perhaps in the whole hockey world. Most important, he was willing to test his own limits at any moment, whatever the risk.

Like the rest of the Canadiens, Morenz played on CCM skates. They had been sourced through Joseph Choquette's sports equipment store on rue Hotel de Ville, where the Canadiens also obtained their handmade sticks.

Before attending the Canadiens' training camp for the first time, Morenz played using "Automobile C" skates that had been invented, and then manufactured, by the Canada Cycle and Motor (CCM) Company in Weston, Ontario. The blades were fabricated of chrome nickel steel. When he arrived in Grimsby in December 1923 with those worn "wheelbarrows," he was fitted by Leo Dandurand with a more up-to-date pair.[2]

This new equipment introduced Morenz to the value of a shorter blade—shorter, at least, than ones used by most of his teammates. The short blade provided initial traction, some glide, and a forward balance point. Short blades also enabled sharper turning. The point at the toe, instead of a smooth forward rocker, facilitated his unique ability to jump and hurdle.

While there was some snide criticism of players who indulged in "Sonja" skating, referring to world figure skating champion Sonja Henie,[3] no one derided Morenz on that basis. Players, fans, and writers understood that Morenz's style was the expression of superior abilities, combining speed, pace, turn, and particularly lift for each new offensive challenge.

It was this facility in coaxing advantages from his skates that allowed him to play a different game than that of his opponents. The *Montreal Star*'s Andy O'Brien recalled, "In his first three seasons, Morenz faced defences that were seldom caught far away from their nets. Usually they were side-by-side out front . . . Sometimes he'd be stopped cold by the human 'sandwich' but often he'd shove the puck by the dour duo and hurtle through the barrier, crowbarring them apart to recover the puck and deke the goaler out of the net."[4]

Trent Frayne, in *Maclean's*, echoed the significance of Morenz's skating agility to his general reputation: "Morenz was a symbol of a time when the ice heroes were a rough-hewn lot. To the millworkers and tram drivers and off-duty cabbies who jammed the north end of the Forum and called themselves the Millionaires, he was a superhuman figure. Their battle cry, *Les Canadiens sont la!*, never reached such frenzy as when Morenz hurtled down centre, burst through the defence and crashed the puck past the goalkeeper."[5]

For most players, crashing and colliding with the opposition usually meant a failed attack. Not so with Morenz. His commitment to this style of play was reflected in his many nicknames, including Lightning Legs, the Canadien Comet, the Mitchell Meteor, the Stratford Speedball, the Stratford Bullet, and, most common, Stratford Streak, or simply Flash.[6]

This night against the Bruins, Hart's urging may have persuaded Morenz to try something extraordinary, something no one else in the league could even attempt. He had taught himself how to hurdle on the ice, to jump in the air when travelling forward on his skates. When American audiences saw it, they recalled the hallowed Hobey Baker, who did the same. As Morenz mastered the move, hockey writers grasped for newer monikers, such as the Hurdling Habitant and the Canadian Catapult.

Baz O'Meara of the *Star* described what he saw Morenz do against the Bruins, revealing how the superstar could still make an impression on a jaded veteran sportswriter:

> *The finest goal of the year, the most ornate of several seasons, and one of the most conspicuous scoring efforts of a starring career was supplied by Howie Morenz to put the Flying Frenchmen in the lead in the second period. Morenz whirled down centre and gathered momentum to bear down on [the Bruins' Lionel] Hitchman and [Eddie] Shore, who were playing a gates-ajar defence ready to put the pinches on if Howie shot as they apparently figured he would. As he reached them he shoved the puck ahead, and leaped through by a split second as they closed in to apply pressure. He landed flying, steadied himself, and drilled a shot at [goalie Tiny] Thompson, who gazed at him as though fascinated, and the light glared in token of surrender to a magnificent effort.*[7]

O'Meara described it as the "Moving Picture Goal," as if he was already re-experiencing it, over and over, in memory. Morenz had demonstrated his capacity to execute the kind of a play that "astonished even those who had become inured to greatness."[8]

Jumping forward (which may or may not have included a full rotation) was virtually unheard of in Morenz's time. A full-rotation hurdle might have been an easier way to manage than a static, unidirectional leap, but no one else was doing that in the league at his time, either. Half a century later, with several rule changes to open up the offensive game, and with coaches teaching young players how to jump in their hockey skates, coaches are still not training players to jump like Howie Morenz would jump.

The legend of this unique Morenz tactic was captured in words by the *Stratford Beacon-Herald*'s Milt Dunnell.[9] It served as the foundation of Roger Kahn's evocative account of Morenz's unique contribution to the game of hockey.[10] This idea of this being Morenz's most iconic play has resonated with other writers,[11] including *Bus Ride* novelist Don Gutteridge.[12] The impact on those who watched it, or who heard about it, remained so profound that when someone like Guy Lafleur did similar things two generations later (without the hurdle), the Morenz name was still invoked.[13]

As magical as it was in the moment against the Bruins, history shows that Morenz's dash-and-jump sequence was a physical gamble that did not always work. Aurèle Joliat remembered: "One night we were playing at the Forum and he went down on one of his fast rushes. These two Maroon defencemen, one of them was Dunc Munro, closed in and bolted their sticks together. Howie went up in the air about ten feet and landed on his head about fifteen feet away. Then he slid into the boards."[14]

More often he wouldn't even penetrate the barrier, but the magic of his game, and of the manoeuvre, was that he was willing to try. It was something that he would have practised so that it would be worth venturing as a tactic. That was the intimidating feature of the move: what he was willing to try worked often enough that opposing defencemen and goaltenders had to worry about it.

For the rest of the second period the game became a physical trial. The rush of adrenaline after the goal resulted in a penalty as Morenz tripped Eddie Shore. There was a brief exchange of goals near the six-minute mark of the third. Morenz began to bear down. The *Gazette*: "The Stratford Flash was in a fighting mood and he never gave up, always leading his team with courage and persistence even in the face of a tight hard-hitting Boston defence and following the discouraging equalizing goals scored by Boston in the first and third periods."[15]

When the game was over, ensconced on the rubbing table, Morenz was thinking less about the goal and told the *Gazette*, "When you've played Boston, you know you've been in a game."[16]

The Canadiens had won. He had done something unique and been remarkable. At the heart of it all was gratitude for what his skates allowed him to do.

Boston **2** at ***Canadiens* 3**

Morenz: 1 goal
2 penalties

Game 6	GP	G	A	Pts	PiM	HG	AG	HA	AA	GWG	GWA
Season Total:	6	8	2	10	13	5	3	1	1	-	1

CHAPTER 7

Tuesday, December 2, 1930

Canadiens vs. Quakers in Philadelphia

Morenz the Teammate: Playing with George Hainsworth

CECIL HART SPENT the first Monday in December promoting Tuesday night's game between the Canadiens and the Philadelphia Quakers to the newsmen of the *Philadelphia Daily News* and the *Philadelphia Inquirer*. This was the first time that Howie Morenz would be playing in Philadelphia.

Stan Baumgartner of the *Inquirer* described him as "the terror of the ice," saying he was "140 pounds of skating dynamite—a man whose artistry on the ice is bewildering, magnificent. Weaving in and out among the opposition like a snake, sinking his fangs at the goal in lightning-like bursts of speed, he paints a thrilling picture to the fans. And his shot for the goal is the most wicked in the league. That, ladies and gentlemen, is Howie Morenz, ice hockey's greatest star."[1]

The game was at the Arena, which opened on February 14, 1920, as the Philadelphia Ice Palace and Auditorium. The building's capacity for hockey was about 6,500, spread over two very intimate levels of seating: a horseshoe lower level and a full oval on the upper. Without pillars, the rink was considered serviceable for hockey as well as tennis, ice shows, boxing, wrestling, and even professional basketball, until the Philadelphia Spectrum was built in 1967.

Benny Leonard, the Quakers' new owner, had upgraded the lighting, added a scoreboard, and installed a public address system. The rink still had a few idiosyncrasies even for the NHL of the day. It had an unsuitably small ice surface, which *La Presse* described as "the most inconvenient way to play a game."[2] Another unique feature was the rink's iron railings at chest and shoulder level above the boards. The *Gazette* said the Canadiens found "the iron railings so dangerous to be checked against that they were rendered somewhat less effective than usual."[3]

Largely on the strength of Hart's advance promotion and Baumgartner's hyperbole, the largest audience of the year arrived to see the game. Neither the Canadiens nor the Quakers managed any substantial offence in the first period. The Quakers were a team with little offensive power, and early on couldn't seem to even penetrate past centre ice. The game shifted in character as the second period began. Chippy play led to the teams splitting ten penalties. There was some bare-knuckle sparring between Joliat and the Quakers' Cliff Barton. Hal Darragh engaged in some stickwork with Pit Lepine, which resulted in cuts (and two penalties) to Lepine. Morenz took note of the harm to his teammate and the player responsible.

For the whole of those first two periods, Montreal goalie George Hainsworth seemed detached from the game. Sometimes known as "the Shutout King," or "the old icicle,"[4] and at other times as "Cucumber George,"[5] he had built a reputation of being "as cool as a frigidaire"[6] in four years of NHL play. He appeared unflappable, even "almost bored"[7] by his job. It was a conscious posture that could impart confidence and calm to his teammates. Nothing too drastic could happen with him in goal.

The truth, however, was different. According to King Clancy, Hainsworth "used to die. He'd make a tough stop look easy, and you'd hear the ohs and ahs go up from the crowd. But just by looking at his face you could tell he was dyin'. There'd be little white lines around his mouth, and his eyes'd be this big."[8]

Beneath his calm exterior, Hainsworth was a studious and focused athlete—observing and remembering the tendencies of every forward in the league. Like Morenz, he would show up at the rink two hours before a game to prepare. Hainsworth was often emotional with the tension and effort required to perform at his best and was always desperate to win.

Now in his mid-thirties, Hainsworth had become the team's grown-up.[9] Much, but not all of that status would have been due to the occupational requirements and expectations of being a goaltender. Leo Dandurand instead shrugged him off as a "moody cuss."[10]

It would have been easy for Hainsworth to remain isolated from his teammates. He was of course a goalie. He liked to put a towel over his face in the dressing room during intermissions, supposedly to protect his eyesight. His difference in age and demeanour, compounded by his fundamental lack of French, amplified the distance between him and his teammates.

Since Hainsworth's arrival to the Canadiens in the fall of 1926, Howie Morenz had made specific efforts to protect Hainsworth from being overtaken by those temptations toward isolation. He was well placed to take on the role as they already had the common experience of junior hockey in southwestern Ontario, and now in the NHL would not leave him alone.

Morenz included Hainsworth as a member of his "Four Musketeers" for off-ice companionship, cards, and occasional extravagances at Hainsworth's expense. They discovered a mutual commitment to performance as both cried over their losses and learned to celebrate their wins. In time Hainsworth came to rely on Morenz to back him up in any crisis on the ice. They became partners. The *Gazette* called them "bosom pals."[11]

There was further reason for Morenz's cultivation of George Hainsworth as a friend. As someone committed to winning, Morenz respected the essential presence of a solid and confident goaltender. Morenz once told Charlie Conacher: "Chuck, give me one good defenseman and any goaltender in the league and I'll beat any team for twenty minutes."[12] With Marty Burke supporting him on defence, Hainsworth was the other foundation piece in Morenz's formula for success.

Hainsworth arrived in Philadelphia dissatisfied with his start to the season. He had played six games and the team lost half of them. He had allowed fourteen goals. Tonight, midway through the third period, the game remained scoreless. Then the Canadiens crowded a power play toward the front of the Quakers' net. Joliat finally opened the scoring, sneaking a puck past Joe Miller with Morenz providing a screen.

No longer on an equal footing with the champions, the Quakers needed to force some offence. For the first time in the game, George Hainsworth was called upon to play a central role. The Quakers sent four and then five men forward. In the midst of that congested Quaker pressure, Cliff Barton suddenly found himself unguarded in the middle of the Canadiens' zone with the puck on his stick. Hainsworth squared toward Barton.

A blur of red closed behind Barton. The *Gazette*'s report noted: "Just as he was about to shoot, however, a Flying Frenchman coming from behind lifted his stick and the puck went wild."[13] It was Morenz, obviously, who leapt into action and, in a flash, swept around a solitary defenceman and once again slipped the puck past Miller. His shot had been so quick, and accurate, Miller hadn't even flinched.[14]

Howie Morenz had not just killed a good chance for the Quakers to tie the game. His back-checking had protected Hainsworth from a more vulnerable moment—an intervention that helped to secure the fifty-fourth regular-season shutout of his goalie friend's NHL career. He had then taken the puck back the length of the ice to score the insurance goal that notched the Canadiens' first road victory of the season.

That Morenz goal at 19:07 of the third period still left unfinished business. Hal Darragh had cut Pit Lepine's face with a high stick in the second period. On the faceoff after the goal, Morenz ignored the puck and upended his opposing centre. It was probably Darragh, although the papers never said. They did observe how Morenz stood defiantly over his target before nodding to referees Bert Corbeau and Vic Wagner. They had to call the penalty, but there was no time for Morenz's absence to endanger the Canadiens' lead.

Morenz had once purposely put an opposing centre out of a game without anyone seeing an infraction.[15] This time, he had been willing to be more obvious. The crowd and the Philadelphia writers might have hated him for that, but he decided it was the right way to end his game. As Cecil Hart had promised in his promotional tour of Philadelphia's newsrooms, "He can do everything anyone else does and do it better."[16]

***Canadiens* 2** at Philadelphia Quakers **0**

Morenz: 1 goal,
1 minor penalty

Game 7	GP	G	A	Pts	PiM	HG	AG	HA	AA	GWG	GWA
Season Total:	7	9	2	11	15	5	4	1	1	-	1

CHAPTER 8

Thursday, December 4, 1930

Canadiens vs. Rangers in Montreal

Morenz: Greater than Any Rules

COLONEL JOHN STEVENS Hammond, part owner of New York's Madison Square Garden and president of the New York Rangers, was perturbed that his team had scored only seventeen goals in eight games. Being an artillery man, he understood that if you wanted to make things easier for shooters, you enlarged the target.[1] He arrived in Montreal for the game between the Rangers and Canadiens advocating the widening of the standard goal net from six to seven feet.

Hammond had support for his views. New York City sportswriter Paul Gallico had decreed that the limited scoring and limited ways of scoring, were a knock against the game.[2] Gallico thought that low scoring in hockey left fans cold and was stifling the professional game's growth in America. The league had been listening.

Rangers coach Lester Patrick was one of the most creative and fan-sensitive hockey executives in the world. His time with the Rangers had been a fairly constant struggle with Hammond for control of hockey operations. Tonight, Patrick wasn't talking about the size of the nets at all. In fact, at the end of the first period, with the score tied at two goals apiece, Patrick made a laughing dig toward his boss: "Nothing wrong with the rules. That shows how the game can be played."[3]

Gallico also complained that hockey was encumbered by a collection of arcane rules, exemplified in some of the first-period play: offsides, penalties for holding, charging, and tripping. Gallico thought the disruptions due to those "course of play" fouls made the game inaccessible to American audiences.

Patrick understood that neither the number of goals in a game nor the rules governing transgressions were truly important to the fans. Instead, it was the number of opportunities to score, and the kind of back-and-forth scoring that had happened in the first period, that created interest and excitement for paying customers.

After captain Bill Cook put the Rangers ahead early in the second period with his third goal of the evening, a series of penalties began to do precisely what Gallico resented. Three different Rangers defencemen were penalized a total of four times by attempting to restrain the Canadiens' attack. Joliat and Morenz, who themselves had been penalized in the first period, each got a second minor penalty in the second as well. Then Pit Lepine collided with Ivan Johnson. Lepine's stick drew blood.

Over the next several minutes, referee Bert Corbeau attempted to exert his authority. He called a minor penalty against Lepine for cutting Johnson, based on a rule the league had revoked the previous week. Lepine became indignant and argued the call. Corbeau then changed the minor to a five-minute major, and then a match penalty. Corbeau eventually tacked on a fifteen-dollar fine. Having run out of other consequences, both referees seemed uncertain about whether Lepine's match penalty should be served in the penalty box, on the players bench, or if he should leave the playing area entirely.

Lester Patrick had been goading Corbeau to take charge of the game while the Forum crowd worked itself up to its own state of high fury. As Corbeau dithered, the fans littered the ice with coins, papers, an overcoat, and even a single galosh. Still unsettled, Corbeau waved the teams back into play before the ice had even been cleaned. Yet another quirky ruling followed almost immediately, as referee Wagner called a Ranger goal back because of goaltender interference.

The players took control of the game after that. Both Joliat and Georges Mantha scored short-handed goals to give the Canadiens back their lead.

Ranger Frank Boucher scored early in the third to tie the game for the fourth time. Both teams then buckled down, aiming for a next-goal-wins victory.

Howie Morenz had success playing under a variety of rule systems. He played eastern NHL rules and Lester Patrick's western Pacific Coast Hockey Association rules. He played when there were only nine or ten players on a team. He played sixty-minute games before substitution became an opportunity and a strategy. He'd been a rover in seven-man hockey and then a centre in six-man hockey. In the 1920s and 1930s, he played centre the way centres would play in the freewheeling 1980s. Cec Hart sometimes used him as a winger, and sometimes on defence. As rules and styles and philosophies changed, Morenz adapted while continuing to play his own game.

What Patrick and Morenz both knew, and what Hammond and Gallico needed to learn, was that the game's rules were really only a platform to showcase athleticism. What Gallico couldn't see in Morenz, or in the game, was what fans, other writers, and players like King Clancy recognized instinctively.

When asked about Morenz's crowd appeal, Clancy explained: "He sold a hell of a lot of tickets at a time when hockey needed somebody to pull in the fans. If you saw Babe Ruth powder one over the fences, you didn't need to know the ass of your pants from first base to realize you have seen something special. It was the same with Morenz. You didn't need to know a hockey puck from your belly button to know that when you watched Morenz play, you had seen something special."[4]

It was why close calls at the goalmouth, just like Babe Ruth "striking out ferociously,"[5] could be equivalent, in a fan's eyes, to scoring a game-altering goal.

Instead of consciously playing within the rules and habits of the game, Morenz would push against their boundaries. Montreal author Andy O'Brien said, "He didn't follow the rules of the game. All he knew was that there was a puck and a net at the other end and God help you if you got in the way."[6]

Morenz had yet another quality that was essential for a professional player in a league that evaluated teams by wins and losses. Earl Seibert, a Black Hawks defenceman, added, "When Howie decided the Canadiens needed a goal he went and got it, and there was little the best defence could do about it. He was a terror to all of us."[7]

That very idea stirred Morenz as soon as the Rangers tied the game 4-4 midway through the third period. He saw Georges Mantha tear down the left wing with the puck. Morenz raced to the front of John Ross Roach's net to create a scrum. Mantha's perfect pass to him ended up in the net for a Canadien lead with just seven minutes remaining in the game.

The Rangers would not quit. They put the puck in the Canadiens' net again, only to have that goal called back on an offside. Lester Patrick launched himself back to the top of his team bench again with vigorous complaints about the officiating. The Rangers continued to cause high anxiety for the home team and the paying customers through the final minutes, but regulation time expired with Canadiens still ahead.

The Canadiens had stayed within the rules to win their third game in a row. According to the *Gazette*, and despite the rules, the game had provided "thrills aplenty."[8]

NY Rangers **4** at ***Canadiens*** **5**

Morenz: 1 goal
2 penalties

Game 8	GP	G	A	Pts	PiM	HG	AG	HA	AA	GWG	GWA
Season Total:	8	10	2	12	19	6	4	1	1	1	1

CHAPTER 9

Sunday, December 7, 1930

Canadiens vs. Americans in New York

The Glamour: Morenz in New York

HOWIE MORENZ STOOD on the ice at Madison Square Garden waiting for the start of the Sunday night game against the New York Americans. With a short back rocker turn on his skates, and a sweeping rotation of his shoulders, he could take in the whole auditorium. Once again, another record crowd had turned out to see the Canadiens play.

Each season's first appearance at the Garden refreshed the memory of his first visit here on December 15, 1925. "Much water will flow under the Brooklyn Bridge before New York witnesses a sporting carnival with so much fuss and ostentation as that which attended the Garden's gala opening and the introduction of pro hockey in Gotham," wrote the *New York Times*.[1]

Rangers founder Tex Rickard had imagined the crowds that Morenz could bring into his new Madison Square Garden. Having seen him play at the Mount Royal Arena in Montreal, Rickard did three things: added an ice plant to the Garden construction plans, added a professional NHL team as an eighteen-date tenant on the Garden's calendar, and secured a promise that Morenz would baptize the rink.

Morenz had played in that first game. The Canadiens were serenaded onto the ice by the Governor General's Royal Foot Guard Band. The Americans were paraded in by the band from the United States Military Academy at West Point. The new Prince of Wales Trophy awaited a winner.

The arena was draped in bunting and American and British flags. Vendors walked between the rows of seats selling apples, oranges, and souvenir hockey sticks. There were fancy figure-skating shows between periods. There were seventeen thousand spectators in the Garden as well as a local radio audience.

It had also been warm. Cooper Smeaton refereed, and later remembered how "it was so hot that night everybody nearly passed out. Howie Morenz of the Canadiens was so warm he'd lie on the wet cement between shifts just to keep cool."[2] Leo Dandurand felt so much heat beneath his coonskin coat that his tuxedo and boiled shirt became both unbearable and unwearable.[3]

Morenz scored a goal that night, on a rebound from a shot by Joliat; the final goal in a 3-1 victory. The crowd gave the then-twenty-three-year-old a standing ovation, and he still remained a darling of the city's fans. The first night's celebration had moved on to a supper dance at the Biltmore, and Texas Guinan's nightclub after that. It was one of the most memorable nights of his young bachelor life.

That opening night in December 1925 confirmed Rickard's conclusion that when he had seen Morenz play hockey, he had "seed [sic] nothing like it."[4] Rickard gushed about the crowd. With that opening performance, Morenz had established himself as a headliner. He could even draw a crowd to the Garden when playing injured.[5] Within the year of that original appearance, Rickard had arranged to have an additional NHL team, Tex's Rangers, also playing in the building. That meant that Morenz would be scheduled to draw an audience to Rickard's Garden a minimum of eight nights a season, not counting playoffs.

Among the New York press it was not uncommon for the *New York Times* to use a picture of him to alert its readers when he was scheduled to appear—as if he were a star of the theatre. The paper would consistently also cover off-ice events in Morenz's life, in and out of the hockey season, just like it would for other leading celebrities. This season the *Times* would celebrate Morenz with a profile feature and a photo on the eve of the Stanley Cup finals, long after both local teams had been bounced out of playoff contention.[6]

Tonight's first New York game of the 1930–31 season started slowly. According to the *Gazette*, "the ice was slow—less than 24 hours before the

Garden had hosted its semi-annual six-day bicycle race, making it difficult for even Morenz to attain a good speed."[7] The Canadiens' attack was still fierce. Within the first ten minutes, Morenz had taken a penalty for handling the puck, and Aurèle Joliat had given the Canadiens a lead with a short-handed goal.

The crowd might have been deflated by the ease of Joliat's scoring play, but Morenz had the crowd on its feet once again when he returned to the ice. Each rush, each pass, each deke, each shot he made played out on the knife-edge between success and failure. There was the risk of losing the puck, the chance of making a spectacular play, all of it underwritten by the guarantee that he would venture to amaze. The *Montreal Star* described him that night as being in tip-top shape, thrilling the spectators with "spectacular runs and flashing attacks that constituted a continuous threat to the American goal line."[8]

The Canadiens' dominance became more apparent during the second period. They kept the game in the Americans' end for almost fifteen minutes. Morenz pushed the Americans back on their heels but was closely watched—though not by the referees, who turned a blind eye to the star being held, cross-checked, and repeatedly tripped or thrown to the boards. The crowd watched it all with good humour, and as Morenz continued to slip or fall, one spectator shouted, "You are going to get rheumatism if you don't stay up."[9]

That kind of admiring attitude toward Morenz distinguished New York from other cities on the circuit—except perhaps Boston. The New Yorkers knew that the Canadiens with Morenz were likely to win anyway, which perhaps allowed fans to watch with a more detached appreciation.[10]

Morenz eventually did draw the Americans into a string of penalties. During the third power play, his efforts paid off. Bill Brydge pulled Morenz down in the act of shooting. On the power play that followed, Morenz set up Wil Larochelle for the goal that gave Canadiens a 2-0 advantage. The Americans began to play somewhat better after that, helped by some penalties to the Canadiens. Just before the end of the period, Vernon Ayres scored his first ever goal of a very short NHL career to make the score 2-1.

Morenz continued to exercise control over the pace of the game. The *Montreal Star* noticed that "his best performance came in the third period, a few minutes after the play started. Taking the puck at [Roy] Worters' left, less than ten feet away from the net, he raced with it all the way down the arena, around his own net and to within fifteen feet of the Americans' goal; his shot was blocked by Worters, but it brought the whole crowd to its feet cheering. And his skating alone would have been sufficient to keep the spectators interested."[11]

The teams traded goals in the third, allowing for some brief uncertainty near the close, but the Canadiens ultimately prevailed.

Morenz loved New York because it always gave him the kind of unquestioning recognition he craved. Each visit to the Big Apple, even five years on, reminded him and his admirers of that heady time in the mid-1920s when the Garden had opened. Without even scoring, but rather by putting on an exhibition of skating and shooting, and passing for the second Canadien goal, this visit had once more burnished his reputation as the world's premier hockey superstar and elite hockey entertainer.

***Canadiens* 3** at NY Americans **2**

Morenz: 1 assist
1 penalty

Game 9	GP	G	A	Pts	PiM	HG	AG	HA	AA	GWG	GWA
Season Total:	9	10	3	13	21	6	4	1	2	1	1

CHAPTER 10

Tuesday, December 9, 1930

Canadiens vs. Maple Leafs in Montreal

Franchise Players: Morenz vs. Clancy

THE CANADIENS DID not arrive back in Montreal from their Sunday night game in New York until Tuesday morning. The Toronto Maple Leafs arrived early Tuesday afternoon. The Leafs had bobbed up to first place in the NHL's Canadian Division, having lost only once in their first nine games, and having started the season with five straight shutouts.

However, in the past week the Leafs lost two of their best young forwards to injury, and the goaltender for those five successive shutouts was not able to play, either.

Conn Smythe paid less money to fewer players than many teams in the league, even in good times. Smythe did add two replacement forwards to his roster (who would not play), and young Benny Grant was tabbed to play goal. Despite these emergency additions, Smythe was still five players short of the permissible league maximum of fifteen. His Leafs would be relying heavily upon their veteran defenceman, Francis Michael "King" Clancy, to anchor their game.

By purchasing Clancy from the Ottawa Senators in October, Smythe had secured the centrepiece of his franchise development plan. Howie Morenz described Clancy as the best "all-round" player in the league.[1] Smythe's deeper purpose in pursuing Clancy was to give his hockey team character.

Clancy, Smythe said, was "colourful" and had "lots of guts."[2] Younger players would be asked to emulate not only Clancy's approach to the game, but also his respectful attitude to Smythe. In that regard, journalist Kelly McParland would later observe that the Clancy purchase "was among the most important Smythe ever made."[3]

While Howie Morenz had celebrated his birthday on September 21, Conn Smythe's horse, Rare Jewel, had unexpectedly won the Coronation Stakes at the Woodbine Racetrack in Toronto. Smythe's horse had paid off so wildly that the Leafs were able to buy Clancy for $35,000 plus two players said to be worth $15,000. An all-cash offer of $40,000 from the Maroons for Clancy had been turned down.

The market suggested that Morenz was worth more. The Rangers had offered $60,000, and the Maroons $75,000, for him in 1925. Saskatoon had made an offer of $25,000 in 1927. When he led the league in goals, assists, and points in 1928, the New York Americans and Detroit both offered $50,000. The Bruins had proposed $50,000 plus Lionel Hitchman as recently as 1929.[4] Dandurand had demurred on all offers, famously responding that Morenz was "beyond price."[5]

Anticipation of this Morenz–Clancy confrontation was thick among the mid-week Forum crowd, which overflowed the north end an hour before game time. Unlike the fans, Morenz and the Canadiens did not seem to be particularly engaged. They were slow off the start. It was only when Leaf defenceman Red Horner jolted Morenz hard into the boards that the game really started. Morenz banged Horner back in retaliation and drew the first penalty of the game.

Clancy consciously took a different approach to the game than Morenz. He had neither the physique nor the durability of the Canadien, who was two inches taller and ten pounds heavier. When they first met on the ice, Morenz had gone by Clancy and his defence partner to score. Clancy wrote in his memoir that he threatened to kill him if he did it again: "The next time he came down it was in much the same way, but he paid more attention to me than to Boucher. He put the puck between my legs and, as he flashed by threw a crosscheck at me that grazed my neck."[6]

Clancy was less physically aggressive than Morenz, preferring to play defence with his stick as a provocateur. Tonight, due to the Leafs' reduced manpower, Clancy was particularly careful to avoid any risk of any kind of attention from the officials. The first period was scoreless.

Clancy carried the Toronto offence through the second period. He appeared to play as much in his own teammates' heads as he did in those of his opponents. The Leafs would surge ahead with him on the ice, and then lull into a defensive shell whenever he rested. It was for that very reason that the *Toronto Star*'s Charlie Querrie considered Clancy more valuable to the Leafs than Shore was to the Bruins and Morenz to the Canadiens—his leadership amid the action.[7]

A vivid demonstration of that came halfway through the second period. The Leafs rushed up the ice and took a shot on Hainsworth from a wide angle. Hainsworth made the save, but lost his balance. Clancy "was in with a bound" to slap the rebound into the net.[8] It had been a typical Clancy goal, dashing forward suddenly, apparently out of position, but opportunistic, ready to do what his team needed done.

Signs of restlessness appeared in the crowd as Clancy and his teammates held that 1-0 lead into the third period. There was a big fight among the crowd in the north end. On the ice, Morenz became more physical, banging his way impatiently through his opponents. A high stick from Morenz left Andy Blair with a cut on his cheek but no penalty was called.

The Canadiens' faster skating eventually led to a Montreal power play and a tying goal by Pit Lepine. The Canadiens continued to surge. For a time, Leaf goalie Benny Grant stood his ground against the seventeen third-period shots hurled at him by the Canadiens. His play may have been the best of his career. However, with each passing minute, the Leafs around Grant were becoming more ragged. After their Harvey Jackson collapsed of exhaustion, each subsequent play exhibited the Canadiens' superior manpower.

Leaf co-coach Art Duncan turned again to Clancy to calm the game and preserve the tie. Clancy nullified one headlong rush by Morenz with about five minutes remaining. Leaving Morenz prostrate against the south-end boards behind the Toronto net, Clancy chose to lead a rush going back the other way.

Morenz hoisted himself to his feet, dug the forward points of his blades into the ice, and began to chase. What happened next, according to the

Montreal Star "was the high point of the game, one of those lone sorties which set his game apart from his fellows."[9]

For the second time this season—first against Weiland in Boston—Morenz overtook the Leaf rush while deep in his opponent's end. In less than a couple of seconds he stole the puck and turned back towards the Toronto goal. Clancy, Blair, and Horner seemed stunned into immobility. Flying in on Grant, Morenz remained entirely in command: "The streaking centre star hesitated for a split second as he had Grant hypnotized, and then burned one to the far corner," wrote the *Gazette*. Grant, "seemingly mesmerized by the tricolor flash, never moved an inch."[10]

Some fans noticed something else about the goal—Morenz's shot. The *Montreal Star* wrote that the puck "actually seemed to curve" as it flew by the goalie's leg.[11] This too, for those who noticed, brought the crowd to its feet. Morenz had that flair to create many layers of "spectacular" in his performances: a late goal to win, performed as a solo, with a unique flourish.[12]

Clancy had led his teammates away from their task of preserving the tie game. He had taken himself out of his role at the club. He had not only left his own end undefended but had not protected the puck from his most capable adversary. The spectacular and athletic Morenz finish had been a visible and irrefutable demonstration of why contemporaries—players and fans and owners alike—valued Morenz so highly in comparison to near peers such as Clancy.

Toronto **1** at ***Canadiens* 2**

Morenz: 1 goal
1 penalty

Game 10	GP	G	A	Pts	PiM	HG	AG	HA	AA	GWG	GWA
Season Total:	10	11	3	14	23	7	4	1	2	2	1

CHAPTER 11

Thursday, December 11, 1930

Canadiens vs. Senators in Ottawa

The "Singing Skates" of Morenz's Game

HOWIE MORENZ USUALLY brought his ukulele with him on road trips. Anyone within earshot would hear tunes such as "If I Had a Girl Like You,"[1] or the new radio hit in Montreal, Leo LeSieur's "Ah! le hockey!" His love of music paired with what his sister described as a good singing voice. Others were less generous. Morenz was self-aware enough to appreciate that by favouring hockey over piano lessons, he was not as good a musician as he might have been. Even if his own strumming and picking were entirely recreational, music enveloped his game.

The big red barn called the Ottawa Auditorium opened on December 1, 1923, just in time for Morenz's arrival in the National Hockey League. It had been the scene of his first NHL goal and the location, the following spring, of the first Stanley Cup victory for him and his "singing skates."[2]

He arrived tonight singing and whistling, knowing that he often played well here and expecting to do so again. When he emerged onto the ice for warm-up, a cohort of university students stood, cheered, and began to sing the team's *cri de guerre*:[3]

Halte là, halte là, halte là
Les Canadiens, les Canadiens
Halte là, halte là, halte là

Les Canadiens sont là
Les Canadiens (bis) les Canadiens sont là.

The song traced its roots to the "mountain men" of the Pyrenees[4] and had developed deep cultural roots in Quebec. Applied to the Canadiens, the song had found a new anthemic purpose.

Morenz had been getting "baking treatment" with hot towels for a sore back,[5] so Cec Hart didn't send him over the boards until there were fewer than five minutes remaining in the opening period. The Senators already led 2-1. Morenz burst onto the ice with impatience, immediately taking a tripping penalty. He returned two minutes later, even more determined. One Canadien shot bounced off the net, allowing Georges Mantha another. His second try deflected by Senator goalie Alec Connell. Mantha managed a third attempt, again unsuccessfully. Morenz found the rebound and slid it past Connell.

With just forty seconds left in the period, his goal brought forth a long and thunderous standing ovation from the crowd.

There was no other arena in the National Hockey League—except for the Forum—where music was as connected with hockey as at the Ottawa Aud. These two arenas with the longest and strongest Stanley Cup traditions housed fans who literally sang the praises of their players. As Morenz made his way to the dressing room, he heard "La Fanfare du Hull" playing through the intermission.[6]

Midway through the second period, as the home team took a 3-2 lead, Ottawa fans were prompted to sing "Hail! Hail!," sung to a tune borrowed from Gilbert and Sullivan musical *The Pirates of Penzance*.[7] The home crowd's singing, and the Senators' lead, held until the end of the period. While the regimental band reappeared to play primarily French-Canadian tunes through the second intermission, the Aud's rush enders serenaded their Senators with another chorus of "Hail! Hail!" to start the third.[8] That prompted the Senators to extend their advantage to 4-2.

Inexplicably, the Senators chose to play defensively from that moment on. The Canadiens sensed the change and took quick advantage. Marty Burke stormed up the ice with Morenz in the role of decoy, passed to Gagnon, and then buried the return pass to make it 4-3.

Cecil Hart chose to play five forwards inside the Senators' blueline looking to tie the score. Pit Lepine and Joliat and Gus Rivers were up front. Morenz was on defence, just inside the Senators' blueline. This formation hemmed in the Senators for several frantic minutes. Morenz drifted through the offensive zone and away from his defensive position. He was engaged along the boards behind Ottawa's net when suddenly a Senator had the puck outside the blueline, skating at full speed—away from all of the Canadiens and toward Hainsworth. Morenz gave immediate chase.

To fully appreciate what happened next, one needs to have a contemporary vision of what was meant by talk of Morenz's "singing skates." A few years earlier fans at the Forum had begun to sing a song that translates as:

Morenz is so fast
That they call him the fastest
Of the 'Les Canadiens' club
To get his point across,
He always finds a corner[9]

This season another folk ditty was coming into use among the Forum's Millionaires:

Howie, Howie Morenz
Is not an aeroplane
But probably as fast
As a big car[10]

The skating that inspired this kind of music started when he was seven, which would have been the winter of 1909 into 1910, on the Thames River in Mitchell, Ontario. He learned to skate without boards or other enclosures. He told the *Gazette* that though his brothers taught him the arts of stick-handling and shooting, when it came to skating, "I always had them beaten before they started."[11]

NHL referee Bobby Hewitson had the privilege of observing Morenz early on, with the Stratford Juniors: "Even then Morenz was a whiz, but he got better as he went along. When he played for the Canadiens, speed was his game. He moved down centre ice giving a little hop every once in a while, as he would literally skip over the opposing players' sticks."[12]

His stroke style was in part a product of the hours spent navigating the rippled and ridged, imperfect and bumpy ice found on rivers, on lakes, as well as on the ice in community arenas. His contemporaries understood his speed advantage as being his ability to accelerate from the point of launch. Bobby Hewitson caught the brevity of it: "Three little steps and a hop and Howie was wide open. You couldn't catch him."[13]

Bob "Swede" McCulley, who tried out for the Canadiens in 1923 with Morenz, remembered how "you could *hear* him. When he circled behind the net you could hear him, just like a horse's hooves on the ice. He'd cut huge grooves in it and the ice would fly in chunks."[14]

Once Morenz was moving, Trent Frayne explained how his whole body became involved: "The Morenz skating style was as spectacular as his speed. His flying arms and bouncing stride gave him a unique whirlwind flair."[15]

The most common metaphors used about his skating were of flight, or wind, a "rushing gust of wind," or just a blur,[16] even if his speed compared with modern play might have been merely impressive rather than superlative.[17] Even at his athletic peak, during his Hart Trophy MVP years, Morenz was sometimes bested in pure speed races. Yet head-to-head speed races around a rink did not really reflect game situations. Carrying the puck, even for the best, makes a player a step or two slower. Jack Adams added that specific qualifier to his praise of Morenz: "He is the fastest player *with the puck*."[18]

The velocity he could generate on skates constantly stymied his opponents. "It has to do with the shattering impact of pace," explained Ken Dryden. "Simply, it becomes harder to play. Offense, defence, team skills, individual skills; with less time for each, each must be done more quickly . . . And if we don't find enough time, if the game moves too fast for its patterns and skills, it loses its coordination and breaks down. It becomes over-matched, overwhelmed by speed."[19]

Opponents and teammates also knew that whatever speed Morenz showed, he also seemed to always have another gear. The *Globe*: "To be the all-time great, speed was but one asset which he combined with a great scoring eye and shot and an uncanny ability to call on reserve powers and give just a little more than the other fellows."[20]

He had done this spectacularly against Boston in the third period of the Cup-clinching game at the Forum last spring. After missing on a shot from twenty-five feet out, the puck boomeranged back off the boards to the waiting stick of Eddie Shore, who was close to his own blue line. Shore started from there, moving at his own top speed toward the Canadiens' end of the ice. As witnessed by Conn Smythe, Morenz then "followed up his shot with a long leap, and then he was circling behind the net. He seemed to be going faster than ever." The Leafs owner witnessed Morenz "simply burst out past the end of that net, a flying fury on skates. Those sturdy legs were pumping like pistons; his head was down and I've never seen any hockey player travel like he did then. He went in terrific bounds, his skates seldom seemed to touch the ice." Eddie Shore had a long head start with no one tailing him just past centre ice when Morenz "nabbed the puck off Eddie's stick," said Smythe, identifying that play as "the most amazingly 'impossible' play I've seen in all my years in hockey."[21]

The writer Andy O'Brien, kid stickboy at the Forum at the time, remembered the same play, but thought that Shore had reached the Canadiens' blue line by the time Morenz caught him.[22]

Morenz's skating was as much of a defensive asset as an offensive one. Writing in the *Stratford Beacon-Herald*, "Chick" Appel said, "He was undoubtedly the top two-way player of all time, in that he possessed such blinding speed and could be left out of the play and still wheel and overtake the attacking unit before it reached his team's defensive area . . . It was his dashing, breakneck speed, his reckless end-to-end rushing and his ability to overtake rival puckcarriers that made him the darling of Montreal."[23]

The Senator who had darted away with the puck in the second period was Alec Smith. The *Ottawa Journal* described how Smith "broke through and there wasn't a soul between he and Hainsworth until Morenz streaked down and poked the puck from him when he was about to shoot. It saved a sure goal."[24]

In Ottawa's Aud, with a sore back, Morenz had done it again—for the third time this season. The whole house erupted as loud and as long as if he had scored. After the game, he acknowledged both the triumph and the burden of chasing down Smith's breakaway. He told reporters: "It was the hardest skating I ever did."[25]

However, the Canadiens were still behind. According to the *Ottawa Journal*, during a late penalty to Smith, and little time left, there was a "merry scramble in front of the Ottawa net with every man for Canadiens buzzing around. Morenz finally sent a sizzling low shot and before Connell could clear it, Joliat was on the puck like a wolf and whipped it in."[26]

Boisterous bilingual singing from the stands carried the game into the overtime. The combination of melody, volume, tempo, and lyric became a mixture of plea, exhortation, adulation, prayer, and finally an incantation of faith.

Morenz heard all that as the overtime began. He was no longer substituting. He had already done enough to make himself the game's star, but found the puck on a pass from Burke when the Canadiens were short-handed. The *Montreal Star* caught the moment: "He hummed along like a greyhound, his body bent over his stick as he flew in on Connell. The latter feinted, and Morenz met his move with a side shift, and whipped the puck behind the Ottawa goalie."[27] He rounded the end boards in a moment of private ecstatic celebration, his stick victoriously raised in the air.

A swarm of teammates feted him. There were still more than six minutes of overtime left to play, but his goal proved to be the clincher. The fans remained on their feet, shouting, applauding, and continuing to sing. Half a century on, composer John Roby would pen lines in tribute to this precise kind of finale:

> *People dug deep to see the Stratford Streak even when a buck was hard to find,*
> *They'd lay down a dollar so they could scream and holler, when Howie raced*
> *across the blue line,*
> *It was worth twice the price to see the Fire on Ice slamming in a winning goal*
> *And nine times on ten it was Howie Morenz,*
> *The kid who played with heart and soul.*[28]

The last image of him on the ice that night, raising his stick in the air in victory, suggests that Morenz might have been savouring more than the goal. He would have been experiencing his own physical music, the surges of adrenaline and waves of endorphins that fueled his love for the game.

***Canadiens* 5** at Ottawa **4**

Morenz: 2 goals
1 assist
1 penalty

Game 11	GP	G	A	Pts	PiM	HG	AG	HA	AA	GWG	GWA
Season Total:	11	13	4	17	25	7	6	1	3	3	1

CHAPTER 12

Saturday, December 13, 1930

Canadiens vs. Americans in Montreal

Physical Realities: Howie Morenz and Nick Wasnie

TWO NIGHTS AFTER his dominant performance in Ottawa, Howie Morenz was once again going to be a substitute. Although he had complained of a sore back after the game in Boston and needed baking treatment after the Toronto game, coach Cecil Hart was not resting him because of some injury. Hart felt that despite his moments of magnificence in Ottawa, Morenz had sometimes appeared "uninterested" in the game. Hart was concerned that Howie was playing himself into physical exhaustion, and that it was time for the team to rely more on others.[1]

The game Morenz learned on the frozen Thames River was the "no substitution" game. When you played, you played the whole game. That was the true test of every player's fitness and endurance. He applied that same concept to the organized indoor game with seven players and no subs. It had still been the expectation in the six-man game when he arrived at the NHL level in the fall of 1923.

Morenz's body and mind remained geared to play that kind of sixty-minute game. He believed that superior endurance remained his competitive edge. He could persevere when others felt physically worn out. The foundation of his game was his ability to use his body to unnerve, hurt, and overcome his opponents in all facets of the game.

Morenz stood five foot nine, which was above the league average.[2] With cheeks already somewhat jowly in his late twenties, he looked misleadingly heavy. On hearing that Morenz weighed 165 pounds, Charlie Conacher remarked that "all his weight was in his face."[3] Aurèle Joliat described the uniqueness of his friend's physical presentation with characteristic hyperbole: "What resources there were in that strong body, in that pair of prodigious legs that took him on the ice from one end of Canada to the other."[4]

Journalist Elmer Ferguson described him in more comprehensive terms, hinting that it was not so much his physical durability but rather a unique mental fortitude that transformed him into "a restless, pacing, tense tiger, yearning for the kill, as he slashed into his battle, whether the fight was big or small."[5]

Ferguson thought Morenz did not pace the demands made on his body. Every moment he sat on the bench, he was simmering: "He frets when idle, and when he is going into a hockey game, it is like a finely tuned thoroughbred going to the barrier, keyed up to the highest pitch of nervous efficiency, straining and fretting for the start," wrote Ferguson. "Odd that an athlete who has played hockey before a million or so people in his major-league career should be so high-strung. But likely that's what makes him a great athlete."

Even on the ice his body seemed incapable of calm, with his knees visibly knocking during the playing of the national anthem. Retaining the youthful conceit that he was physically indestructible, he never calculated how to conserve energy or to allocate energy in portions. Marty Burke saw the same thing, from a different perspective: "When Howie Morenz wasn't on the ice for forty-five minutes in a game, he was mad at the world."[6]

Hockey scientist Lloyd Percival identified Morenz, and his meso medial body type, as the superior type for centremen into the 1970s. Jack Adams agreed, observing in 1928 that Morenz's height and weight made him "almost the perfect player." Percival went further, seeing the same aggressive psychological attitude seen by Ferguson as being an inherent feature of the meso medial type.[7]

Morenz always spent his body's resources profligately. His philosophy was to always be ready to play, regardless of the state of his body, and would often play hurt. As a youth, he once played with a broken, swelling toe. Another time he played with a broken, splinted finger. Both times he scored pivotal goals.

George Owen described the battering Morenz received every game. "The reckless way Morenz rushed," said Owen, "you knew he was going to get flattened half a dozen times a game when he reached the defence. And he was, regularly. He simply went all out. But he had that 'rubber ball' flexibility. He'd bounce right up."[8]

Neither injury nor exhaustion counted as reasons not to play. He had played since his youth with the anticipation that *un cartilage déplace* in his right knee would eventually force his retirement. Butch Kelterborn saw him play as a midget when that knee "was as big as your grandfather's stovepipe hat."[9] Howie's father remembered him cussing about the leg that he had to drag along through most of another junior season. After games it would swell to the point that it became difficult to put on his pants.

He played most of the Cup playoffs in his rookie NHL season with a badly bruised hip suffered in the first game against Vancouver. Just last season he had forced Cecil Hart's hand in Ottawa when he dressed for a game knowing that he had a bad ankle. Ineffective early, he finally prevailed on Hart to let him play with scant minutes remaining and the Senators in control 4-2. His play that night turned the tide as he assisted on one goal, then scored to tie the game, and finally scored a classic winner in overtime.

Chick Appel in Stratford described him as "a human projectile. Never sparing himself, he drove headlong into any and all defences. Battered and bruised by heavy bodychecks handed out by experts . . . Morenz arose time and again to renew devastating charges on enemy nets."[10]

Leslie Roberts of *Maclean's* recalled how hockey heads had been predicting Morenz's physical demise since his arrival in the league: "They would remark, 'This can't go on for long. Nobody can keep up that pace. He'll either crack his skull or burn out his bearings!' But he didn't. He kept on going. He went faster, not slower. Every year he hit new heights."[11]

The game came first. The condition of his physical body was always secondary. He also took satisfaction from the knowledge that any batterings he received consistently wrecked the same havoc upon the bodies of his opponents. Even Eddie Shore and King Clancy suffered when they caught a piece of him.

Coach Hart's concerns lingered. He believed that Howie's indifference to his body's condition, and Hart's own habit to rely upon Morenz to win games, was physically overloading his star.

Against the Americans, Morenz's game began late in the first period on a Canadien power play. As in Ottawa, his impatience with arriving late to the ice led to a quick penalty. Later he propelled himself into the Americans' net in an over-eager attempt to score.

Through the late minutes of the first period and then into the second, Morenz was reduced to a more individual game. Disconnected from the first line, and receiving reduced ice time, meant that he only made about half a dozen of his famous rushes. After the Americans scored a goal about halfway through the game, Hart began to give right winger Nick Wasnie a more regular turn.

Where Morenz was often compared to a thoroughbred racehorse, Wasnie reminded spectators of a draft horse. He was two years younger and slightly larger than Morenz. He could achieve by physicality what Morenz managed through speed and delight. Out of training camp, Wasnie had been expected to play on the first line, creating room for Morenz and Joliat. Johnny Gagnon had seized that place instead and pushed the Canadiens' offensive style in a loftier direction.

Unlikely to win any flat races, Wasnie's physical type was still essential to the success of any NHL team. The Winnipegger was strong like a Manitoba farmer, large enough to be abrasive, durable, often brave, and imposing. There appeared to be no Morenzian recklessness to his play. He was a solid, defensive-minded forward who could explode with occasional and focused force.

A few minutes after the Americans' goal, Wasnie bulled his own way toward the front of the Americans' net and tied the game with a "violent back-hand swat" of the puck with his stick.[12] That sharp thrash was one of his unique talents, contributing (in the view of some) to his "invention" of the slapshot.[13] Goaltender John Ross Roach of the Rangers believed that Nick Wasnie had the hardest shot in hockey.

Wasnie's role as a utility forward with some offensive capacity gave him limited visibility among the Flying Frenchmen. His occasional, episodic opportunities to play in short bursts filled a need for the team and provided him with a lengthy professional hockey career.

Nevertheless, like Morenz, Nick Wasnie shared the same indifference to the game's ravages upon his body. Wasnie played his whole career in professional hockey with an undisclosed, and probably undiagnosed, cardiomyopathy.[14]

His ability to play the game at its highest level at all was a physiological marvel.

Morenz began to play differently after Wasnie's tying goal. Both the *Star* and the *Gazette* noted his speed, and some desperation, in his efforts to break the tie. Those half-dozen of his famous rushes still made him, rather than Wasnie the goal-scorer, the highlight of an otherwise dull game. The game finished as a draw.

The *Star*'s Baz O'Meara thought the fans were starting to expect "a little too much of Morenz."[15] In fact, the fans' expectations of both of them—as athletes and entertainers—seemed a little too much. In Wasnie's case the physical demands were unknown, and in Morenz's case he simply didn't care.

NY Americans **1** at ***Canadiens* 1**

Morenz: 1 penalty

Game 12	GP	G	A	Pts	PiM	HG	AG	HA	AA	GWG	GWA
Season Total:	12	13	4	17	27	7	6	1	3	3	1

CHAPTER 13

Thursday, December 18, 1930

Canadiens vs. Black Hawks in Montreal

Strategies for Defending Against Morenz

AS THE CANADIENS hit the ice for their last home game before Christmas, Howie Morenz was again expecting to play well. His physical irritations had dissipated. He was back in his starting role.

An excellent chance came early, as he slipped around the Chicago defence for a battle of wits with Charlie Gardiner. The *Gazette*: "The curly-haired Chicago netminder let Howie have the whole side of the net. Morenz tried to fool him and drilled a low shot to the inside corner, but Chuck crossed him up and moving with the flip of Howie's wrist picked the drive off with his glove, barely inches from the ice. Chuck took a gambler's chance to outwit the deadliest sniper in hockey."[1]

Morenz was familiar with the challenge, saying: "When we met the Hawks, we were lucky to win by 2 to 1, or 1 to 0 scores. The reason was Gardiner. We considered him 75 percent of the team. When I was able to get one single shot past Chuck in a game, I felt that I had had a big night."[2]

Tonight, Hawks manager Bill Tobin had directed coach Dick Irvin to devote two players to contain Morenz. After that first dash, his game became claustrophobic. A pair of Hawks "clung to him like leeches," said the *Gazette*, and "did little else all evening."[3] Cecil Hart tried to double-shift Morenz. Tobin and Irvin adjusted by assigning a second pair of checkers to him.

The Hawks' defensive strategy came with an offensive cost. Their forwards rarely made it into the Canadien end. The *Gazette*: "The only time that the Chicagoans made a real attempt to score was when they gained a break with the Canadien front rank caught down the ice."[4]

Even with the crowded double coverage in the middle of the ice, Morenz was able to establish the pace and location of the game. Early in the second period, he and Gagnon created a rush that ended with the whole Hawks team piled in front of their net. He had another run toward the Chicago goal with Nick Wasnie almost parallel, but his pass missed. Another chance was upended by a trip from Tommy Cook.

The next time Morenz broke away from his double coverage he was tripped again, this time by Helge Bostrom. If two pairs of shadowing Hawks weren't able to stop the star Canadien without taking penalties, Tobin and Irvin were close to the end of ideas. The Hawks had begun to experiment with rotating their forward lines and defence pairings at regular, timed intervals in order to always have freshest, and most situationally appropriate players on the ice—an idea adopted from Lester Patrick's successfully strategy of changing lines against Morenz and the Canadiens in the Cup Finals of 1925. The Hawks now even platooned some players to save them from having to play every game, which promised to keep them fresher still.

Handling Morenz's speed was of course a distinct challenge. Detroit's Herbie Lewis remembered how being forced to focus on Morenz freed up the other Canadiens: "Three little steps and a hop and Howie was wide open. You couldn't catch him. It meant that everybody had to centre on Howie and leave Art Gagné, his right winger and Aurèle Joliat, his left winger, wide open for passes."[5]

If defenders were only watching or waiting to see what Morenz might do, they would be too late to do anything. "The only way you could stop him was through team play," said Frank Nighbor, who played against Morenz as a Senator and Maple Leaf. "When Howie wound up and came at us, [my wingmen] drove him into the centre. If he could make it between the boards and either of them, he'd do it, but it was tough."[6]

Nighbor's Senator teammate, Frank Finnigan, confirmed the strategy: "With Morenz I always had to be a couple of strides ahead of him, and I'd go up, and I'd try to run with him, because if I started with him, then I was soon thirty feet behind!"[7]

The Nighbor strategy grew partly from the rarity of forward passing when Morenz arrived in the NHL, and partly from the barrier style of defensive alignments during the 1920s. Nighbor's strategy was also helped by the nature of North American rink design, where narrow ice surfaces made it easier to force play into the middle of the ice.

Morenz's response was to impose the physical cost of any collision upon the defenders. That offensive approach reflected the same attitude as his contemporaries in other professional contact sports: Red "Galloping Ghost" Grange on the American football gridiron, and Ty Cobb on baseball's basepaths. While his opponents knew what was coming and could brace themselves, they knew that stopping him would hurt, and any success on their part would be fleeting.

King Clancy recalled that response: "Morenz had skated right up to me and suddenly cut loose with a long snap-shot at the net. Then he had followed through at top speed. He hadn't even bothered to try to shift around me. He had merely skated straight into me, and over me!"[8]

Clancy was also the only player to ever discover an effective way to disable Morenz without being penalized: "I got close enough to reach him. I tapped him on the side of the knee with my stick and he dropped so fast I fell over him." Morenz marvelled at his own reaction: "It was just like someone hit me with a mallet on the side of the knee." Clancy tried the tactic on others but was never able to repeat it.[9]

The rest of the league came to a common, inevitable conclusion about how to play defence against Morenz. "Opponents realized the only way to handle Howie was to knock him down," wrote Bill Brandt. "As a result, he took a terrific beating in almost every game."[10]

Journalist Frank Graham said that the New York Americans, under the guidance of Shorty Green, were the chief proponents of this strategy:

> *"Every time he gets the puck, knock him down," Green cried to his men. And it was one of those nights when they were successful against the Habitant centre star who usually skated rings around his opponents. He was knocked to the ice*

a dozen times, butted and shoved and manhandled. When the final bell sounded with the Americans ahead 1-0, the weary Morenz stopped at the Amerk bench. "If there's any son of a bitch who hasn't had a shot at me, you've missed your chance," Morenz said. "I'm going home."[11]

In the third period, Cecil Hart moved Morenz away from the Hawks' double coverage by having him play from the defence. The Hawks continued to tie him up, but when one of his shadows, Vic Ripley, was kicked out of the game, Vic Desjardins was assigned double shifts against Morenz. Tommy Cook, another of his shadows, was then drawn into his second penalty of the night by Morenz. Two of the four Hawks assigned to cover the Canadien were now out of the game.

The power play that followed ran Desjardins ragged. He stuck beside Morenz, step for step, by grab and drag, leaving the rest of the Canadiens to his Hawks teammates. The game remained scoreless, but Desjardins's exertions were costly. With about three minutes to go, he left the ice and collapsed unconscious in the Hawks dressing room.

In the Toronto game ten days earlier, it had been Harvey Jackson collapsing. Now it was Desjardins' turn. Both men had been overused. Both times that overuse resulted from exertions required to contain Morenz.

After two early but unsuccessful chances of their own in the overtime, the Hawks reverted to six-man defence. Morenz created the Canadiens' best chance to score, but the ice was bad, time ran out, and the hopes of victory for either club vanished like mist.

It had become apparent to the whole arena that Charlie Gardiner was really the most important component of Chicago's defensive system. Containing Morenz consumed their whole game. The price of holding Morenz scoreless had been four players, exhausting at least one of them, while losing others to penalties. If that was the cost of not losing, what hope could the Hawks have of actually winning?

The Canadiens were troubled, too. Howie Morenz and his team had shown Charlie Gardiner the best they could offer. In two games, requiring 130 minutes of hockey, they hadn't scored once.

Chicago **0** at ***Canadiens*** **0**

Morenz: Nothing

Game 13	GP	G	A	Pts	PiM	HG	AG	HA	AA	GWG	GWA
Season Total:	13	13	4	17	27	7	6	1	3	3	1

CHAPTER 14

Tuesday, December 23, 1930

Canadiens vs. Rangers in New York

The Dance in Morenz's Game

MANHATTAN DID ITS best to distract Howie Morenz in dozens of ways. In 1930, new skyscrapers were still rising magnificently above the city. They stepped forward like show people: tall and able, exuding drama and flair, demanding attention day after day. The impressions they created endured for decades.

Every time he walked out the doors of New York's Grand Central Station, Morenz was reminded of his first sight of Ruby Keeler in 1925: tap-dancing at the Biltmore Hotel after he had opened the Garden. That year, Keeler, a Nova Scotian, was just sixteen. She looked as young as the schoolgirls he had known in Stratford, as well as the one he attempted to claim as a prize after an exhibition game in Tavistock.

The two young Canadians both enjoyed singing and playing the ukulele. Keeler was just as athletic as he was. They might have made a match, a date at least, because professional hockey players were regarded as sexually exotic entertainment for the city's most important women.

By December 1930, Keeler was only a distracting memory of what might have been. It was her dancing he remembered most, whether he was at the community street dances when he was home in the summers, or when he toyed with the idea of opening a dance pavilion on the main road near Stratford as a retirement project.

Part of Keeler's bewitching charm had been how her own profile reflected his own New York experience. Like him, she was a prodigy: her New York

City performance skills had been featured on the nightclub/speakeasy circuit since she was thirteen. Keeler had also emerged under the tutelage of a benefactor with Montreal connections: Morenz's own acquaintance, Texas Guinan of Le Cabaret Frolic in the Plateau.

This night, the New York Rangers employed a dance-like pattern to their play from the start of the game at the Garden. Bill Cook and his brother Bun, with Frank Boucher at centre, began to waltz across the Canadiens' blueline, turning away from and then swirling around Montreal's defence. Soon enough a series of sharp, anticipative, and intricate passes gave Bill Cook the opportunity to score the game's first goal. The Rangers, playing with clock-like precision, made it look like the Canadiens had not even been on the ice.

For Frank Boucher and the Cook brothers, the ice surface of the Garden was their stage, the place where they performed movements choreographed on their hotel room floor. Along with their boss, Lester Patrick, they believed a hockey player, at his highest, was an artist on skates. The Cooks and Boucher often appeared to be more interested in *how* the game could be played, *how* the dance could be performed, than simply how to ensure that the puck ended up in the net.

The Rangers continued to whirl out of their own zone like a flight of birds catching an updraft of wind. They swept across centre ice like birds of prey, hovered momentarily at the Canadiens' blue line, round-eyed, unblinking and alert, analytical and ruthless, before swooping in toward the Canadiens' goal. Bill Cook scored again, with ease, just before the first intermission.

The second period began with the Rangers having a goal called back, though soon enough they put the puck in the Canadiens' net again. With the home team leading 3-0, disdain for the Canadiens' unresponsive play filled the Garden. The visitors seemed entirely out of sorts. They lacked precision, stumbled, even fell as they tried to anticipate the moves of the Rangers, who continued to be sublime.

Cecil Hart substituted freely for Morenz in the first period. The *Montreal Star* mused that "it is probable that he watched the game more from the stands" than participated in it after that.[1] There was one mid-game moment when Morenz single-handedly took the puck out from behind the home net, dodged the Rangers' defence and scored a goal.[2]

Unlike the waltzing style of the Cooks and Boucher, Morenz's play was most often remembered as this kind of sudden, improvised brilliance. Even as jaded a columnist as Jim Coleman would turn wistful: "Did you ever see fire dancing on ice?" he wrote. "Did you ever see Pavlova or Nijinsky? No, I realize that you know nothing of these things so there's no point in attempting to describe Howie Morenz to you."[3]

Like Ruby Keeler, Morenz's best solo performances fascinated, fading everyone else on the ice into a faceless background. Those performances became what dancers refer to as their "duet with space," and what became indelible in audience memory.

The idea of hockey being a contest of highly choreographed dance sequences, disrupted by solo improvisations, had not yet fully formed in Morenz's time. But fans, writers, and even hockey executives were already observing and documenting the connection.

The skating of the best players was already described as balletic. Recognition of the ability to dance as a foundational hockey skill would become more accepted through the work of men like Eddie Shore and Lloyd Percival. By the time of the 1972 Summit Series, it had become commonplace to describe the skills of the best Russian hockey players in terms of dancers.

Tonight, Morenz's brief performative turn as the centre of New York's attention provided little help to the Canadiens. For most the game his mind seemed to be elsewhere. He took a couple of unnecessary and counterproductive penalties in the third period. Later, Bill Cook mimicked Morenz's own style by making his own solo dash up the ice, scoring his third of the night against the "flat-footed" Canadiens.[4]

Bill's less appreciated brother Bun was able to score the game's final goal just twelve seconds before the end, on a break where Morenz might normally have been expected to run him down.

By the close of that night's performances, Bill Cook had been elaborate. The *Gazette* reviewed Morenz as having been "both brilliant and bad at various times."[5]

Contemporary hockey observers differed about which of them, Cook or Morenz, was better. Over their parallel careers the answer would be more a matter of artistic taste than objective assessment. Morenz, like Keeler, demonstrated the more naked, visceral, and spontaneous approach to the dance of the game. Cook was more suited to a sophisticated, cultured, and organized style as a member of a choreographed ensemble. The fans loved both.

***Canadiens* 1** at NY Rangers **5**

Morenz: 1 goal
2 penalties

Game 14	GP	G	A	Pts	PiM	HG	AG	HA	AA	GWG	GWA
Season Total:	14	14	4	18	31	7	7	1	3	3	1

CHAPTER 15

Saturday, December 27, 1930

Canadiens vs. Senators in Montreal

Georges Mantha and the Christmas Gift of Brothers for Howie Morenz

CHRISTMAS FOR THE Canadiens that season unfurled in many forms over the course of twelve days between December 18 and 30, 1930. There were gifts from the team and cards from celebrities. Morenz and George Hainsworth spent consecutive days with their wives and sons, while Sylvio Mantha enjoyed his first Christmas with his wife, Irene.

The other Canadien Mantha, Georges Mantha, was expecting to spend time with his intended, Claire Deslauriers, but also took time to attend to his other love in the city. He was turning an empty corner lot in the community of St-Henri into an outdoor rink. It was the kind of patch on which he had learned to skate. The city's outdoor parks and rinks were where he felt most alive. He would eventually fashion a whole post-NHL career in the city's public recreation.

Georges spent the entirety of his organized amateur career as a defenceman. Upon becoming a Canadien, he was converted to a forward by Cecil Hart. Now in his first full season, he was described by the *Gazette* as "a beautiful skater, packing into his stride a speed that equals if it does not surpass that of Howie Morenz himself."[1]

Tonight, in his eighty-ninth NHL game, less than a half-hour walk from those outdoor ice surfaces in St-Henri, Georges would make his first NHL start, on the wing with Howie Morenz against the Ottawa Senators at the Forum.

Georges and captain Sylvio Mantha consistently declared their relationship as brothers. Their nicknames were *pere* for Sylvio and *Ti-Georges*, the little brother. However, the documented record is less straightforward. Census data, birth records, and personal accounts contain inconsistencies and even contradictions that cast doubt on the Manthas' real filial relationship.[2]

The bond between Georges and Sylvio remained a certainty. They negotiated their contracts together, protected each other on the ice, and often claimed a greater joy in each other's success than their own. Whether they were biological brothers or not, they were family on ice.

Games played with your brothers meant that you were looking out for each other, looking after each other, and celebrating each other. It was an ethos later echoed by Guy Lafleur when talking about his days as a Canadien: "All the guys on that team, we formed a family, and the family we were playing for was maybe more important than the family we had at home."[3]

After the Canadiens and Senators traded early goals, Georges scored the Canadiens' go-ahead goal at 16:22 of the first period. He added another in the opening minutes of the second, then assisted on the Johnny Gagnon goal that eventually gave the Canadiens a 6-3 lead.

After his experience of two off-games in a row, Howie Morenz was fully rested and began distributing some gifts of his own. He assisted on Georges' second goal and another by Armand Mondou moments later.

When Georges forced Joe Lamb of the Senators to take a penalty, Morenz kindled some excitement with a full-length rush down the ice. The *Ottawa Citizen* described how Morenz circled around the defence, and then "fifteen feet out, he let go a terrific backhander, and it hooked into the far side of the net, just inside the post."[4] Scoring that kind of end-to-end, unassisted goal was perhaps the most appropriate gift that Howie Morenz could have offered to his fans on a post-Christmas Saturday night, but he had added the magic of showing that he was still able to take the goaltender—and the expectant crowd—*par surprise* with a backhander.

The wide-open game concluded with an 8-5 victory for the Canadiens. It was a true team effort. In this largest explosion of the season, the Canadiens' offence was spread among six different players, of whom four had multi-point nights. That ethos of fraternal teamwork allowed all of them to dominate the Senators.

Morenz's years with the Canadiens provided his only real opportunity to evoke the kind of fraternal experience enjoyed daily by the Manthas. His oldest brother, Wilfred, who was seventeen when Howie started to skate, had moved to the United States before Howie had really started to learn the game. His nearer brother, Ezra, had died when Howie was only thirteen. He had seen brotherly relationships on the ice and in the dressing room before, with Aurèle Joliat and his brother, Rene, in 1924, and Pit Lepine with his brother Hec in 1925.

Even though a player like Morenz couldn't quite call forth a blood relationship with any of his teammates, the fraternal bond became just as real as it was for the Manthas. When asked about his relationship to Howie Morenz, Aurèle Joliat once told *L'Illustration Nouvelle*, "I considered him a member of my family."[5] Johnny Gagnon also eventually discovered, based on this season's association, that he had come to feel the same way about Morenz.[6]

It wasn't so important in the dressing room at the Forum what birth certificates or baptismal certificates or census records said. What was important was how Morenz and his teammates related to each other. They understood their commitment to victory as fundamentally fraternal—being able from moment to moment to sense each other's strengths and vulnerabilities without the need for words, trusting instead and always in their common willingness to celebrate the family instead of any one individual. As they had done this night.

Ottawa **5** at ***Canadiens*** **8**

Morenz: 1 goal
2 assists

Game 15	GP	G	A	Pts	PiM	HG	AG	HA	AA	GWG	GWA
Season Total:	15	15	6	21	31	8	7	3	3	3	1

CHAPTER 16

Tuesday, December 30, 1930

Canadiens vs. Maroons in Montreal

Howie Morenz and the "Big" Goal

HOWIE MORENZ LAY on the trainer's table deep in the Canadiens' dressing room, wincing with every breath he tried to take, his ears still alert to the rumble of the feet and shouts of the crowd. He supposed that the game was close to the end of the second period by now, and he hadn't heard the kind of thunder that would have signalled a goal. It had been 1-0 for the Maroons when he had been helped off the ice.

The Maroons' rookie Jack "Pop" McVicar had caught Morenz hard about halfway through the second period. He was not ready. As he spun off McVicar, he collided with Jimmy Ward before landing on the ice. After lying there for a time, he was helped up, guided to the bench, and supported to the dressing room on the shoulder of trainer Jim McKenna. The fans had not seen him since.

Doctor Sir Henry Gray appeared at the dressing room door. He and Dr. John Corrigan stood over Morenz's prostrate body on one side of the training table, trainers Eddie Dufour and McKenna on the other. Morenz wheezed out a demand that these four men somehow get him back into the game.

This last game of 1930 had begun brightly. Morenz had led three early rushes. Dave Kerr, the young, Allan Cup-winning goaltender in the Maroons' net, had stopped him each time. After Hooley Smith gave the Maroons their lead, Morenz was determined to equalize for the Canadiens. He fed Pit

Lepine for a perfect chance early in the second period, but Kerr foiled that too. It had been on his next rush when "Pop" McVicar hit him in full flight, and, in the words of *La Presse*, "demolished" him.[1]

After examination, there were no obvious broken bones, although breathing caused pain. Any kind of wrapping to protect the ribs would restrict breathing to mere gasps. He would have scarcely enough air to propel a single dash up the ice. But he insisted.

He tugged his sweater over a wrapping bandage with a grimace, had his skates tightened by Eddie Dufour, and tottered back out to the bench. There were still a few minutes left in the second period when he returned to action. His shifts were short, and the *Gazette* thought that "it took him some time to regain his accustomed speed."[2] Even into the third period, he continued to have trouble playing as he wanted. He was too slow and fumbling easy chances.

The Maroons clung to their 1-0 advantage into the final five minutes. Several in the crowd remembered the clogged streets and sidewalks and stairwells that had preceded the game. They thought it wise to beat the rush and headed toward the exits with a few minutes to go.

The Canadiens continued to search for an opportunity. By habit, they continued to look toward Morenz, in apparent disregard of his physical limitations. On the Maroons' side of the puck, there was a clear appreciation of what was coming. Maroon defenceman Lionel Conacher explained: "Morenz was great in those 1-0 games. His record will show that. You could knock him down, but you knew he'd get up and that on the next rush he probably would beat you."[3]

The beat writers knew Morenz's history of personally deciding the outcome of close games. Bert Perry of the *Globe* described how it had started during last year's playoffs with his winners against the Hawks and Bruins: "When Canadiens are a goal down or are on even terms with their opponents and require a goal or two to get a lead, usually Morenz leaps into one of his thrilling solo rushes and lands the puck in the desired spot. In at least four games this season he has provided the winning counter."[4]

The difference tonight was that Morenz was clearly playing hurt. Getting up and down the ice was difficult. Then, as the clock ticked down, his game actually appeared to brighten.

Cecil Hart decided to put five forwards on the ice and instructed four of them to play up on the attack. Morenz was among them. Lepine and the

Maroons' Bill Roche went off for scragging, opening just a little more room. The Maroon defence flung a loose puck the length of the ice. Aurèle Joliat collected it and carried the puck back across the Maroons' blueline. It was still expected Morenz to be the one who would create the scoring chance, because Joliat actually passed *backwards* to Morenz at that point.

The *Montreal Star* said that Morenz "took it gingerly, side-stepped the Maroon defence, and went in slowly varying his accustomed pace as he stickhandled instead of rushing pell mell into the goal."[5] *La Presse* picked up the narrative at a pace that reflected what had happened on the ice: "Like a chess player who calculates his moves, the Canadiens' centre slowly made his way through the Montreal defence. Slowly, slowly, he approached the Montreal net."[6]

The play developed so slowly that Morenz seemed to be floating toward the goaltender. Kerr and his defencemen waited impatiently, expecting to respond to Morenz's characteristic sharp and sudden release.

Kerr's anticipation overcame his patience. He dropped to his knees as the Maroons' defence corps finally moved within reach of Morenz. Kerr realized immediately that the shot hadn't come as expected. The *Montreal Star* applauded: "It was a brainy play as Morenz was almost surrounded by nudging Maroons when he made the counter."[7]

Some described this last Morenz goal of 1930 as one of the most brilliant of his career. Morenz himself acknowledged at least its uniqueness: it was the first time in his life he had taken such a long time to shoot.[8]

Despite his aching ribs, Morenz had more to do than score that goal. He lined up for the faceoff and shoved the puck toward Jack McVicar off the draw. Whether it was he or McVicar who chased after the puck was not immediately clear to the *Montreal Star*. The paper reported that the two players "kindled a minor feud during proceedings. An early bump by McVicar affected [the Canadiens'] hero somewhat early in the play, but the defenceman was jarred by Howie near the end so things were even."[9]

Just as McVicar was flattened, he managed to pass the puck to his defence partner, Jimmy Ward. Morenz couldn't catch up to the puck, but he got within reach of Ward, and yanked him down in front of both referees. His tripping penalty would carry through into the overtime.

Dave Kerr and George Hainsworth remained impregnable. Howie had been injured early, returned to the game to score the crucial goal, and then avenge his injury. It was the kind of thing he had done in Philadelphia, and a warning to the Maroons of his answer if any of them dared to hurt him again. He had concluded the game as a draw.

***Canadiens* 1** at Maroons **1**

Morenz: 1 goal
1 penalty

Game 16	GP	G	A	Pts	PiM	HG	AG	HA	AA	GWG	GWA
Season Total:	16	16	6	22	33	9	7	3	3	3	1

CHAPTER 17

Saturday, January 3, 1931

Canadiens vs. Maple Leafs in Toronto

The Mitchell Meteor Playing in Foreign Territory: Toronto's Arena Gardens

ONE OF THE remarkable cultural features of Howie Morenz's career was how the unilingual anglophone from southwestern Ontario transformed into such a *Montréalais* during his time with the Canadiens. In large part that was due to his experience playing in Toronto as a member of the Canadiens. Each trip to Toronto was like travelling to a foreign country.

Although the local Toronto players and press acknowledged his status as a leading player in the league and a leading draw at their box office, both abetted fan behaviour that put the safety of Morenz, his teammates, and league officials at risk. The result was an emotional rift between Morenz and Toronto.

The Arena Gardens, sometimes referred to as the Victoria Arena Gardens, or just the Mutual Street Arena, was built in 1912, with an official capacity of about eight thousand. By game time on Saturday evening, Arena management estimated they had allowed more than nine thousand into the building—perhaps the largest crowd that ever packed itself into the Gardens.[1]

Morenz first played here in March 1920 during an OHA semifinal as a midget, before his Memorial Cup appearances. Many of the others playing tonight had also been on this ice as boys and young men before turning professional. Stanley Cups had been won here. Homegrown players like Morenz were expected to prove their worth here.

With such a large crowd the building became claustrophobic. Young Toronto novelist Morley Callaghan noticed how the clamour and commotion of a crowd at the Arena would send "the skin on his back tingling."[2] Players had to negotiate a game in three full dimensions: up and down the ice, as well as what might be descending from above.

Morenz took note of where his father and sisters were sitting and swung into place for the opening faceoff. The *Gazette* described what followed the puck-drop as: "sixty minutes of the most hectic hockey seen in the local National Hockey League campaign for some weeks."[3]

The Leafs rebuffed an initial push by Morenz and Joliat. Leafs Andy Blair and Joe Primeau took turns staying even with Morenz. Close checking distracted Aurèle Joliat, while Johnny Gagnon soon found himself on his knees gasping for breath—a butt-end to the stomach had put him out of the game early, apparently on orders from Conn Smythe.[4]

An early long shot from just inside the Canadiens' blueline bounced off the unpredictable end boards of the Arena, fooling Bert McCaffrey and allowing Harvey Jackson to surprise George Hainsworth for the first goal. The Canadiens tied it but then quickly fell behind again. The game was on.

Jackson's besting of both McCaffrey and Hainsworth on the opening goal turned both Ontarians wearing the Canadiens' colours into *diables rouge*. Lou Marsh of the *Toronto Star* referred to their teammates, responding in an effort to tie the score, as "Red Streaks" who "swirled around the Leafs' kraal . . . like Malays running amok."[5]

The Toronto media's colonial and imperial military references were more consciously employed to prick at the prejudices of every paying customer.[6] Not only were those in the Canadien sweaters different, they were inferior. Not only were they athletic opponents, they were supposedly cultural opponents as well.

Cultural and racist attitudes were not unique to Toronto. Arthur Langlois decried their exposure earlier in the week in Montreal, when Howie Morenz scored his late equalizer for the French-Canadian club against the Anglo Maroons. The English portion of the crowd had "let themselves be carried away by a bellicose spirit," said *Le Petit Journal*.[7] Morenz felt that same kind of animosity when on the ice in Toronto. He worried about how his own family in their seats.

A collision between Nick Wasnie and Lorne Chabot became a fight involving Charlie Conacher. Red Horner slammed Sylvio Mantha against the ice "like a manhole cover dropped off a roof," wrote Lou Marsh in the *Toronto Star*.[8] When Horner was penalized for tripping, the crowd's antipathy overflowed to the point where a chair was tossed onto the ice.

Whatever the fans in New York and Boston might yell, whatever newspapers and programs and pennies they might throw, Morenz was challenged differently in Toronto. The Leaf players became willing agents of the crowds' excesses.

He remained a constant target. The task of controlling him that had been shared by Andy Blair and Joe Primeau in the first two periods became the responsibility of the Toronto defencemen, and occasionally Charlie Conacher, in the third period. Morenz managed six rink-length rushes nonetheless. As the pursuit of an equalizer made the Canadiens' more frantic in their play, Red Horner intervened again when he and Morenz were chasing the puck in the third period.

"Horner nicked Howie over the forehead heavily enough to draw a bit of blood," reported the *Montreal Star*. "He was given a penalty and protested it was an accident."[9] This was in character: whenever penalized, Horner would claim that it was an "accident," a perfunctory retort regularly echoed by Conn Smythe on Horner's behalf.[10]

Morley Callaghan observed this tolerance for this kind of physical mischief whenever Morenz was in Toronto. An observation he made early in Morenz's career remained apt in early 1931: "Did that guy out there stop the punishment they were handing out to Morenz in the first period? . . . For the love of Mike, sure they're handing him punishment, making him like it. I hope they kill the bastard."[11]

Meanwhile, the *Montreal Star* wrote off Horner's stickwork as "the fair-headed boy" doing "kiddish things.[12]

With a seeping wound across his forehead and his face marred by dried blood, Morenz soldiered on with increasing frustration. After two successive shots from close range were stopped, Morenz was so angry he broke his stick on the ice in anger. Shortly after that, he also took an unnecessary tripping penalty, provoking more hoots of derision from the Toronto crowd.

When the game was over and the Canadiens were finally ready to leave the Arena, the chair-thrower, cocky from the Leafs' success, stood by the door, ready to wish them all a good evening. Morenz was remembering all the other faces in the crowd who, season after season, paid to see him be hurt, and to fail. He had no kinship with them. By joining the Canadiens, he had become a foreigner.

***Canadiens* 1** at Toronto **2**

Morenz: 1 penalty

Game 17	GP	G	A	Pts	PiM	HG	AG	HA	AA	GWG	GWA
Season Total:	17	16	6	22	35	9	7	3	3	3	1

CHAPTER 18

Tuesday, January 6, 1931

Canadiens vs. Falcons in Montreal

The Funny Guys: Howie Morenz and Jean Pusie

HOWIE MORENZ'S ROUTINE for welcoming rookies to the NHL included a smile and a cryptic jest: "I just want you to tell you boys that my sister's brother is the greatest hockey player that ever lived."[1]

He might also murmur a caution: "You know, you're a hero today, but tomorrow you never know what you will be. Wear the hat that fits you."[2]

Both parts of that welcome were a gentle way to remind newcomers that modesty was expected at the NHL level. Even if a player actually believed he was the greatest, as Morenz did, the only appropriate way to say so was through this kind of oblique, light-hearted jest.

Jean-Baptiste Pusie appeared at the Canadiens' camp in October proclaiming to coach Hart that "Pusie would be the greatest."[3] Later that season, he regaled Roger "Broadway" Jenkins with stories of his prowess as a member of the Canadiens, without having figured out who Jenkins was. Jenkins listened patiently and then responded: "I'm Roger Jenkins. I play on the bench too—for Chicago."[4]

Pusie had seen some on-ice action late against the Senators on December 27, but had not played in the Canadiens' draw with the Maroons, nor on the road trip to Toronto. The longer he sat on the bench without playing, the more he felt his ignored greatness wasting away. Tonight, Pusie would be offered his opportunity against the Detroit Falcons. He flattered himself that he had been called up because he had scored a few breakaway goals in the International League. Instead, Leo Dandurand and Cecil Hart were thinking he might be useful as a defenceman.

The game summary shows that within sixty-five seconds of Joliat's opening goal, Herbie Lewis of the Falcons tied the score on a defensive failure by the Canadiens—who it was that failed was a fact kindly unreported by journalists. There had also been a slapstick tumble by Hainsworth as the puck dribbled across the goal line. It was the kind of goal that "a child would have pushed aside," claimed *La Presse*.[5]

Howie Morenz grinned at Hainsworth's miscue. He understood how greatness in hockey could be humbled in an instant by embarrassing physical mishaps. It happened to every player eventually.

Pusie could only see the first Falcon goal as the kind of mistake he could not afford to make. When Morenz scanned the faces of his teammates during the first intermission, he noticed the hunched shoulders of the Canadiens' anxious young tryout, who was staring holes into the floor. Morenz was aware that the young Pusie was the son of Dominique Pusie, sergeant of detectives of the Montreal Police. Morenz might have tried to relax the rookie by regaling him with the story of how he and Sprague Cleghorn had thrown lit firecrackers underneath city police cars, for fun, during their Stanley Cup summer of 1924. Oh, how the police constables scrambled then!

Morenz could banter and joke between periods because of his stellar hockey résumé. As a rookie of limited skills, Pusie possessed no store of accomplishment, nor any reserves of modesty, to relax with even a momentary laugh. He was tighter than the laces on his skates.

When the second period began, George Hay's backhand shot caused Hainsworth to implode in another slapstick collapse, allowing the Falcons to take the lead. After another ninety seconds, the Falcons doubled their lead while the Canadiens scrambled.

Georges Mantha brought the Canadiens within a goal, while Howie Morenz attempted every kind of trick to get the teams back on even terms—once "jumping through the defence,"[6] but hitting the goal post.

There had been a time when Morenz thought like Pusie. When he started to believe that he was wonderful, being unsuccessful sometimes caused him to lose his temper. Lou Marsh—the Toronto sportswriter and referee—intervened to reorient Morenz's attitude. Morenz continued to struggle with his emotions but became better at accepting that he was playing a game. He would not always be in control. Sometimes the game's quirks would embarrass him. He had to be able to laugh at himself and accept failure brought by misfortune.

As the Canadiens' defence continued to be shredded and the score mounted, Pusie's dream of playing the hero as a full-time member of the Canadiens was being shattered into smaller and smaller pieces.

His hubris about his own hockey skills, and resentment at adversity, put him in a psychological cage. Instead of seeing the humour of his own failings and attempting to get better, Pusie chose to make fun of the game itself and those connected to it. He treated teammates, goaltenders, opponents, officials, and even the fans, with condescending disrespect. His need for adulation overtook his life both at the rink and away from the game as well. He sought out ways to abuse the vulnerable, including children and ex-girlfriends.

McGill University's resident humourist Stephen Leacock could have provided some gentle advice. Leacock built much of his humour on the truism that humans of all ranks and stations were helpless against the chance jests of misfortune. His moral message was that it was best to treat others kindly, without malice or ridicule.

Leacock would have understood why Pusie's attitude was so different from that of Morenz. The writer grumbled about the vacuity of pursuing champion status in any kind of athletic endeavour. He thought the restless generation of the 1920s was "so spoilt with the idea of a World War that we won't be content with anything less." Leacock understood how the temptation of greatness and fame could create deluded, distorted, unbalanced, and dangerous human beings. Better, he thought, to set one's sights on the more modest goal of being known "as the second-best checker player in York County, Ontario."[7]

The score mounted from 3-2, to 4-2, and then 5-2 in fewer than eight minutes of the third period.

With less than ten minutes left, a deflated sigh passed through the Forum crowd. At the far end of the Canadiens' bench, Pusie's head snapped up. He had missed yet another surprising save by Falcon goalie Clarence Dolson against Morenz. What he saw next intrigued him even more. The *Gazette* reported how the great Howie Morenz then "got so exasperated finally in watching Dolson kick out tagged markers to the corners that he repeatedly banged his stick on the ice—something rare for the poker-faced Howie."[8]

A little later, three Falcons had an undefended breakaway against Hainsworth and scored to close out their 6-2 laugher against the Cup champions. Those two events provided Pusie with ideas to vent his own inner rage—and milk it for laughs—in years to come.

Tonight, Pusie could at least believe, in a way, that his debut had made him the equal of Howie Morenz. Each of them left the game with no goals, no assists, and no points. Not even a penalty between them. Pusie's record after four NHL games was the same, equating to an average of, well, nothing. If a hockey career was measurable only by those statistics, it might look like he had never played at all.[9]

Detroit **6** at ***Canadiens* 2**

Morenz: Nothing

Game 18	GP	G	A	Pts	PiM	HG	AG	HA	AA	GWG	GWA
Season Total:	18	16	6	22	35	9	7	3	3	3	1

CHAPTER 19

Thursday, January 8, 1931.

Canadiens vs. Americans in New York

Howie Morenz and the Freak Goal

THE THURSDAY NIGHT New York crowd of ten thousand included a cluster of the city's fashionable high-hat-and-tails crowd. The Americans were becoming a top-drawer New York attraction. They had won six and lost only once in their last nine games. With their star-spangled uniforms, the Americans seemed buoyed by the attention, poised to reclaim some of their social cachet in the biggest sports entertainment market in North America.

The Canadiens fell behind early, but Howie Morenz led an entertaining response, prompting loud roars of appreciation from the crowd. "His speed and skating delighted the audience," reported the *Montreal Star*. "He tricked and fooled the Americans' forward and defence lines almost at will, he penetrated within the net area frequently, but he missed all his shots at the net."[1]

Then, with about half a minute left in the opening period, Pit Lepine tried a backhand flip-shot toward the top corner of the Americans' net. Goalie Roy Worters swung at the puck with his stick and fanned on it completely. The teams went to their dressing rooms for the first intermission tied at one.

New York coach Eddie Gerard warned the newsmen before the game that: "Each goal represents a mistake. When a game ends 6-4 that means there were ten mistakes. I'd rather see my boys win 1-0."[2]

Morenz roamed the Madison Square Garden ice through an otherwise dull and monotone second period, disrupting the Americans' rushes while searching for opportunities to score. Roy Worters stood impregnable in his way. In this sixth season of his twelve-year career, Worters was enjoying his busiest and most effective campaign as a professional goaltender. His six shutouts in his first seventeen games counted as one of the best ratios of his career—and was best in the league to that point in the season. He was at his athletic peak, facing one of his greatest adversaries.

For nearly forty minutes of their athletic contest, Worters and Morenz cancelled each other out. The whole of that second period might have disappeared and been forgotten, except for what happened at its end.

Georges Mantha crossed the Americans' blueline with the puck and flung a rising shot in the direction of the Americans' goal. Worters saw it all the way. Like a shortstop snagging a rising but lazy line drive, he reached out with his mitt and snagged the puck easily. Morenz and the rest of the crowd watched the puck settle quietly into the goalie's glove. The *Gazette* described how, with every eye in the Garden on him, "Worters handled it easily and then—much to the amazement of the house—tossed the puck nonchalantly over his shoulder. It landed squarely in the mesh."[3]

"A deadly silence fell on the Garden, not a sound being heard for a time when Worters, saving Georges Mantha's vicious shot at the net, flopped on the ice and remained there temporarily, with both teams lining up in their own home territory," wrote the *Montreal Star*. "It was a tie game and would have ended thus. But the gods that rule hockeydom ruled otherwise and went so far as to make Worters score for his opposites."[4]

For Morenz, the mistake was foreseeable: "Worters is much more impetuous and nervous and, I don't know if you've noticed, but he has a special talent for making any stop look hard."[5]

Worters's unforced error would be remembered for decades, but Morenz doubted it was an actual error. He and others recalled more of Eddie Gerard's pre-game remarks about how goals were scored in the NHL: "It means a defence man was lured out of place. One of the wings missed his man *or the goalie was not alert*."[6]

Morenz recalled that Worters whiffed on the Lepine goal at the end of the first period. He now wondered whether both goals had actually been conscious misplays. Worters had understood since his arrival in the Big Apple that Bill Dwyer's hockey club didn't take the game very seriously. The goalie's attitude and perspective were: "Join the Americans and laugh yourself to death."[7]

If Worters hadn't actually been compromised by gamblers, his play on both goals would have represented a rank kind of carelessness. His lack of concern was obvious to the paying customers and to the *Montreal Star*: "Nobody would believe the goal was scored until the light flashed up and the loudspeaker in the arena gave Georges Mantha credit for the goal. A brief riot broke out, shouts signifying pity for the Americans and booing for the 'Flying Frenchmen' rocking the gallery to the boxes."[8]

Too many New Yorkers were already familiar with this kind of odour. Stories promoting the integrity of NHL games always seemed to emanate from Madison Square Garden. There was a recurring need to reassure the public that the games they paid to see were honest.

From Morenz's perspective, not taking the game seriously was just as bad as fixing an outcome. If the professional game was not a truly competitive athletic contest, its foundation was threatened. If the paid performers did not take the physical contest seriously, the games became meaningless. Worters's casual attitude challenged Morenz's sense of himself and his purpose for playing.

Morenz engineered two open breaks against Worters in the third period. He missed both times. On a third chance he put a shot less than two inches over the crossbar. It was as if he could have scored but, because of his suspicions, refused to let Worters off the hook for giving away that second-period goal. Even though his misses in the third period left him pointless in three games, it made a more important statement.

He was not alone. Worters' own teammates played the third period as if they too felt betrayed and demoralized. They were sluggish, with the *Gazette* noting their "amazing reluctance to go after the tying counter in the closing minutes of the final session."[9] The *Montreal Star* described how ten thousand New Yorkers responded: "The crowd left the Garden quietly, apparently undecided who deserved their sympathy. They drew a middle path and refrained from any demonstrations when the smoke of the battle had cleared away."[10]

Worters never played as well after that. He only recorded two more shutouts over the next twenty-five games, giving him a total of only eight over forty-four games: the second-poorest season ratio of his career. The Americans failed to qualify for the playoffs that year—by the single point they would have gained by a draw that night against the Canadiens.

But the hockey gods are a mischievous bunch: Just weeks after that awful game, those gods would reward Worters—the man who threw a playoff-eliminating goal into his own net—with his first and only Vezina Trophy award recognizing the best goaltender in the NHL.

***Canadiens* 2** at NY Americans **1**

Morenz: Nothing

Game 19	GP	G	A	Pts	PiM	HG	AG	HA	AA	GWG	GWA
Season Total:	19	16	6	22	35	9	7	3	3	3	1

CHAPTER 20

Saturday, January 10, 1931

Canadiens vs. Maple Leafs in Montreal

Howie Morenz and the Flying Game

ON FRIDAY LEO Dandurand let it be known that he was on his way to Providence, Rhode Island, to look at players. Cec Hart would join him there after the Canadiens' game against the Leafs on Saturday night. While Howie Morenz never had a passing thought that his own place was in jeopardy, he was aware of the current of anxiety running through the team.

Morenz believed that the players in the room could demonstrate that they were still *l'équipe*—the Cup team of less than half a season ago. He remained convinced that the men needed to win again were already in Montreal. Saturday night would have to be about showing off his own teammates, opening up opportunities for his wingers, inspiring them all to show that they still belonged here.

From the moment the Canadiens broke from the faceoff, Morenz put the puck on Johnny Gagnon's stick for the opening goal. The crowd's eruption electrified the Forum and flowed through the hearts of the Canadiens like liquor.

From then on, the Canadiens' pace mesmerized the Leafs. The Canadiens swept out of their own zone like a summer storm stirring up across the surface of a becalmed lake. Whether one was on the ice with them, or with the fans in standing room on the upper concourse, everyone could see the

Canadiens gathering themselves on offence. They surged across the ice with all the sudden, simultaneous, co-ordinated and instinctive turns of barn swallows. Other teams might call themselves Falcons or Hawks, but when Montreal swept across the ice in this formation, they were the birds of prey.

This was Morenz's favourite game. It was no longer just his solo speed. His teammates accelerated themselves to join him in full flight. Together they were exuberant and confident, with the *Gazette* gushing that "their color, dash and blinding speed left the Leafs and fans alike breathless."[1]

It was not just their pace. In the mid-1960s, Marshall McLuhan identified hockey's inherent edifying quality as being "the *pattern* of a game that gives it relevance to our inner lives . . . not who is playing nor the outcome."[2]

That pattern was seen by the crowd and felt by the players. With each new play the Canadiens' pace quickened, as if they were chasing the closing light of a late winter afternoon on an icy lake. The pattern liberated them from any concern about scoring, or winning, or the fear of losing. Nothing was relevant except the warm satisfaction of being part of imaginative moments when the simple fact of playing allowed them to know that they were unbeatable. The *Gazette* figured they were "shaking off of the mental and physical slump that had enveloped them in varying degrees for about a month."[3] Morenz led them there, allowing them all to believe that they could play at his level.

Morenz and the Canadiens became as assured and unstoppable as the birds evoked by their play. Instead of tiring as the game went on, their power continued to grow. They followed their first-period goal with two more in the second, and three more in the third. The home team was moving too fast for the Leafs' defenders to cope. Toronto disintegrated.

One Leafs' play in the third period struck one *Globe* reporter: "With five men strung across the width of the rink like a line of soldiers, they carried the puck from behind their own blue line right to the Montreal end without a Canadien player getting a stick on it."[4]

It was a competing McLuhan pattern, but of an entirely different character than that of the Canadiens. The Leafs' temporary mechanical and militaristic order contrasted sharply with the joy evident in the Canadiens' game of speed and flight.

King Clancy observed how his defence partner, Hap Day, had become a regular target of the Canadiens. He shouldered the task of attaching himself to Morenz, but the more that the Leafs paid attention to one star Canadien, the rest of the Montrealers "took full advantage of the situation," reported the *Globe*.[5]

This game demonstrated something else that readers of box scores might otherwise have missed. Morenz's talents required teammates who had the skills to not only play with him, and at his speed, but also the ability to capitalize on the opportunities he created.

On some nights, his ability to distract opponents from other capable scorers was as important as his ability to lay off a pass—as on Gagnon's first goal. One of his midget teammates remembered, "He was always fighting. I never saw Morenz quit. He was so far ahead of the rest of us fellows on that midget team the year I played with him that we didn't have any licence to be in the same rink. But Morenz always was ready to help a fellow nick a goal. If you were up there with him, he'd slip you a pass often when he could have scored himself."[6]

He did that for the rest of his career.

When people worried about Bobby Hull being too much of a solo performer, the response was that Hull was so fast that he often left his wingers behind. A generation or more after that, Mark Messier would say the same about Wayne Gretzky.[7] Tonight at the Forum, Morenz's teammates kept up with him.

King Clancy was rueful but honest: "When Canadiens go like that, nobody can beat them."[8]

As the last seconds ticked off the clock, the Forum crowd's cheers rose in praise.

Morenz remained a little in awe at how the Canadiens' natural game, his own innate game, could so thoroughly dominate some of the best professional players in the world. He wondered how this group in the dressing room could ever be any better. He believed they deserved to remain together.

The thousands leaving the Forum were pondering something else. They understood that the defining qualities of Morenz's best play had become the defining qualities of the team's best play. He had infused the team with his own character and made his style the team's enduring touchstone: the desire to succeed, with both flourish and elan, at airborne speed. The *Stratford Beacon-Herald* said, "He was probably the greatest reason why Montreal Canadiens came to be known as the Fabulous Frenchmen, and why he was rated as the greatest of them all."[9]

Having shown them what was possible, generations of fans and players couldn't be content with the Canadiens playing any other way.

Toronto **1** at ***Canadiens* 6**

Morenz: 1 assist

Game 20	GP	G	A	Pts	PiM	HG	AG	HA	AA	GWG	GWA
Season Total:	20	16	7	23	35	9	7	4	3	3	1

CHAPTER 21

Tuesday, January 13, 1931

Canadiens vs. Quakers in Philadelphia

Ethnicity: Benny Leonard and Howie Morenz

PHILADELPHIA QUAKERS' OWNER Benny Leonard didn't miss any of the racial insinuations tossed in the direction of the Canadiens by Stan Baumgartner of the *Philadelphia Inquirer*: "A FRENCH hockey team, founded by an Irishman, managed by a Jew whose best player is a German . . . and one of the best was Aurèle Joliat, a Swiss."[1] His reference to Morenz as "German" was not a slur, but rather a conscious promotional effort to catch the interest of Pennsylvania's large ethnic German population.

Classifying athletes by their religion, ethnic background, or immigration status was commonplace in the Morenz era. The presumption was that "racial" difference always equated with "racial tension." Elmer Ferguson of the *Montreal Herald* was frank in his twist of that idea: "You wouldn't know there are any racial divisions on the team, that its units are French-Canadian, a Welshman, two German-Canadians, a Belgian-Canadian, Irish-Canadians and Scotch-Canadians. They're a harmonious whole, a great organization, one for all and all for one."[2]

Leonard's own career as a professional fighter had grown out of that same kind of environment. He ultimately embraced the social ostracism he'd been served as a "ghetto" Jew, and eventually flaunted it by promoting the development of the Maccabean Games. The strife and resentments of that social atmosphere taught him that any athletic antagonism could be properly and firmly resolved by a timely left hook.

Leonard applied that perspective to his struggling Quakers as well. His own athletic success relied upon physical violence, and so he hoped a similar tool kit could build a path to respect for his team. When he first introduced them to Philadelphia, he promised to make them winners—even if corporal punishment was needed to do it.[3] "I tell my hockey players they have the other club on the run and all they need do is keep them at stick's length the rest of the game. Maybe I give one or two a little jab to prove my point, but I don't swing hard on them."[4]

He was also willing to join his players in the penalty box from time to time, because, in his words, "I thought if there was going to be any more fighting around, I would not mind having a hand in it."[5]

Anticipating Fred Shero's "Broad Street Bullies" of the 1970s Philadelphia Flyers, Leonard wanted his team to approach their work with a little fury, maybe even some anger. On Christmas Day in Boston, the Quakers' exercise of violence had created a melee that required Boston police to step out on the ice—twice—to enforce a pause in the hostilities.[6]

For this game, Leonard continued to advocate violence as a way to subdue opponents. By promoting the foreign make-up of the Canadiens (in contrast with Morenz's German ancestry), the media provided a veneer of justification for his team's tactics of belligerence.

Predictably, the Quakers began the match with aggression. Allan Shields scored a surprising opening goal and then took Morenz down in front of the Philadelphia net. When Morenz got up, he had a five-inch gash above his right eye. Shields received a major penalty for tripping, but Morenz had to leave the game for stitches. The Quakers then turned on Johnny Gagnon, who got into a stick-swinging duel with "Peaches" Lyons.

The Canadiens refused to be goaded. When Morenz returned with stitches, Philadelphia's D'Arcy Coulson tried to impose some further physical duress, but Morenz shrugged him off. The Quakers continued their efforts to provoke. The Canadiens were accused of sneaky retaliation. The referees left everyone alone so long as no one was actually prevented from playing.

As a younger player, Morenz was provoked by most kinds of interference and would retaliate. With guidance from referee Lou Marsh as a junior, and then

Sprague Cleghorn in his first years with the Canadiens, he learned that it was better to play through abuse than to retaliate. His willingness to tolerate hard provocation had become widely known around the league. Wally Kilrea, sitting on the bench for the Quakers, knew why.

Wally was the little brother of Hec Kilrea. Hec had been a rookie with the Senators in 1925 when he knocked Morenz out cold with a stick to the head. Morenz was unconscious long enough that he had to be carried off the ice. There are several versions of the story, but the essence is that when he regained consciousness, he quickly became aware that there was a move afoot to suspend the rookie for his egregious violence against a league headliner. Morenz, then only a sophomore player, calmed everyone around him by insisting that Kilrea's rash act had been an "accident."[7]

By sloughing off such grievous and flagrant behaviour as accidental, or as part of the game, Morenz was able to diminish any sense of accomplishment in his tormentor's mind. Violence had never intimidated him. While he resented its interference with his play, inflicting and absorbing blows with his opponents became a routine part of the game's physical challenge for him. Trent Frayne recalled that "Morenz, with his comparatively small frame, never backed up from the big men. He loved the violent exchanges, the speed and the competition of the game and the roars of the fiery partisans."[8]

Like Benny Leonard in his prime, Morenz was not going to let a hard blow and the loss of some blood distract him from the task at hand. From time to time he even claimed he had sworn off fighting entirely. However, even with the maturity of his seven full seasons in the league, opponents remained aware that interfering with Morenz still risked an immediate violent reaction.

Of course, the calculated violence, often after a game had been decided, was an entirely separate matter. Morenz remained willing to inflict hard endings on opponents, as he had inflicted on Hal Darragh in Philadelphia, and Jack McVicar in Montreal, earlier this season.

Late in the second period, Morenz created his first successful scoring opportunity out of a Quaker rush. Those watching the game were unsure just where he acquired the puck, but everyone saw where it ended up except for Philadelphia goalie Jackie Forbes. His unassisted goal came with less than five minutes remaining in the middle period. From the start of the third it was clear that the Quakers' effort to manhandle the Canadiens over the first forty minutes had exhausted Philadelphia instead.

Before the Quakers could manage even a single third-period shot on Hainsworth, the Canadiens put themselves another goal up. The Canadiens played the remainder of the game in complete control of the home team. Morenz had ignored Allan Shields entirely after the early slash to his head. That disregard freed him to not only create the whole of the Canadiens' offence, but do it so deftly that few fans in attendance remembered Shields's involvement in the game at all.

The conscious choice by Morenz to reject the kind of belligerence encouraged by Leonard was all the more remarkable given his own background. When he first arrived in Montreal, his ethnic background had been promoted as Swiss. It was a charade that continued to be given currency a half-century later.[9]

There may have been some peculiar anxiety in Montreal because the ethnic composition of the Canadiens had always been an important part of the club's creation story. And because the Great War was still a fresh memory, hiding German ancestry was also viewed as a smart box-office play.

But Morenz himself had neither doubts nor reluctance about his roots. He self-identified his "race" as "German" in U.S. immigration documents.[10] His hometown of Mitchell was proud to proclaim his German extraction.

Some writers attempted to make an issue of Morenz's ethnic background in an effort to flesh out his character. As late as 1973, Trent Frayne was still elaborating on Howie's "European" connections and supposed "recent immigrant" status, writing: "Morenz's parents emigrated from Germany prior to World War I and settled amid a wide swatch of German immigrants around Stratford and Kitchener (a town whose name was changed from Berlin during the war)."[11]

The 1911 census and birth records do not back up Frayne's "immigrant" claim, nor do any vital statistics documents. The *Globe* (not the Canadiens) had made it clear in an April 1931 report that Morenz had been "a Canadian for three generations back."[12]

Even if his German heritage had been an issue on the ice, and there is no suggestion that it was from his playing opponents, Morenz never chose to fight past it. Taunting words meant nothing to him. He only chose violence when an opponent drew blood—and even then only when, or if, it suited him.

***Canadiens* 2** at Philadelphia Quakers **1**

Morenz: 1 goal, 1 assist

Game 21	GP	G	A	Pts	PiM	HG	AG	HA	AA	GWG	GWA
Season Total:	21	17	8	25	35	9	8	4	4	3	2

CHAPTER 22

January 15, 1931

Canadiens vs. Maroons in Montreal

Trades and Discards: Bert McCaffrey and Howie Morenz

SINCE HIS ARRIVAL in 1923, Howie Morenz had watched the opportunity to wear the Canadiens' sweater being given and then taken away from many players. It happened to his mentor, Sprague Cleghorn. This week it was happening to Bert McCaffrey, his near neighbour from Listowel, Ontario.

Morenz had an affection for "Mac." Even though he was at least thirty years old when he first pulled on a Canadien sweater, Mac's instincts made him precisely the kind of mature, defensive substitute the team needed. He played in important games at three different levels of hockey and never seemed to get anxious. There was regret and uncertainty in the Canadiens room because of his departure. None of them knew what the change would do to the team.

McCaffrey did not take part in any of the debates about the reasons: fitness, usefulness, or efforts to "Frenchify" the line-up. He adopted a co-operative and respectful attitude to the impending transition. The *Gazette*: "When McCaffrey was informed of the trade, tears came to the veteran's eyes, and he stuttered that he had never played with a club with which it was so pleasant and so gratifying to be."[1]

He had arrived with that same attitude two Christmases before. He was a scoring ace as an amateur and turned professional with the Toronto St.

Pats in October 1924. Conn Smythe sent Mac to Pittsburgh just before Christmas 1927, where he transformed himself into a defenceman. When he was plucked from the last-place Pirates by the Canadiens, he seized the opportunity to play for the Stanley Cup. It had been the one serious team prize available in hockey that he had not won. He responded with impressive defensive play and a championship dignity that he had learned as an Olympic hockey champion. He had even scored the opening goal for the Canadiens in 1930's Cup-clinching game.

Mac didn't want to leave. He was demoted to the Providence Reds after clearing waivers. That allowed him to remain "in touch," keeping alive the possibility he could be called back to the Canadiens if needed.[2] But he understood he probably wouldn't be back.

Whether or not he returned, McCaffrey knew that having Howie Morenz as a teammate would remain the most spectacular and inspiring experience of his hockey career. His one last chance to play with his Cup teammates came in this "midwinter madness" game against the Maroons on Thursday night.

There were two special Morenz moments to mark Mac's farewell. The *Montreal Herald* identified the first as Morenz's "assist" on the Canadiens' 2-0 goal:

> *Snaring a puck in the Canadien end . . . he whipped around behind the nets, speeded up his sturdy legs, and set sail. [Nels] Stewart made a lunge for him as he swung out from behind the cage, but Morenz, quick as a cat, side-stepped nimbly and swept on. Near the line, [Hooley] Smith, one of the game's greatest hook-checkers laid in wait. As Morenz neared him, Smith too lunged, stick extended, but Morenz, with a dazzling swing, sheered off to the side and Smith fell flat from his own effort.*[3]

Morenz fell too but kept the puck and picked himself up:

> *As the crowd roared its applause for this dazzling bit of play, Morenz kept going. He raced over the blue line into the Montreal end and deftly passed to Joliat, who was completely uncovered as the defence centred on Morenz. Joliat flashed in, and looking up like a sure goal-getter, whipped a blazing drive, but [goalie Dave] Kerr blocked it. Then, from the other wing, in pounded Larochelle, picked up the loose puck before the Maroon defence could reach it and popped it home.*[4]

The second Morenz moment in the game was even more electrifying. It was Howie's unassisted goal early in the third to extend the lead to 3-0. *La Presse*: "Howie swept across the rink like a cyclone, leaving Montreal's colour-bearers far behind. Seeing Howie coming, Kerr prepared for a tremendous shot, but Morenz took him completely by surprise by simply sliding the puck along the ice. Kerr, who had planned a high, quick shot, was taken completely by surprise and realised too late what had happened."[5]

The celebratory howls of the Forum crowd might have tempted Bert McCaffrey to think, enviously, that the "Streak" was so central to who the Canadiens were that, unlike himself, Morenz could never be traded from this team.

Before he arrived to play for the Canadiens, McCaffrey had already learned the question to ask about a trade: was it an opportunity to do something greater? He had already been moved twice. He understood that management could discard him at any moment. When Toronto dispatched him to Pittsburgh, he resolved to make himself into the player that Pittsburgh needed him to be. After he had earned his promotion to the Canadiens, he had done the same.

He committed himself psychologically and physically to squeezing as many seasons out of his aging body as he could. He surprised the Canadiens with his summer training and the level of fitness he brought to training camp the previous October. He knew he'd done everything he could to earn a spot on the team. But his place there ultimately depended on the owners.

Although Morenz watched it happen so often to others over his first seven years in the league, he still did not truly appreciate the journeyman player's experience of struggling up the ladder of professional opportunity, and the battle to remain at the top against successive waves of younger and more aggressive young men. To that point in his career, his own hockey journey had been an uninterrupted upward trajectory of success and adulation.

Morenz believed that if he was ever to be the subject of such an unthinkable transaction, his service to hockey would entitle him to be part of the decision-making. If the time ever did come when he couldn't play for the Canadiens, he would probably choose to stop playing altogether.[6]

The game wound down with a comfortable 4-1 cushion over the Maroons.

McCaffrey came to terms with the fact that he was leaving the Canadiens. There were gifts, last moments on the ice and then in the dressing room with his teammates. Mac looked around the room, utterly content with his fate, knowing if the Canadiens asked him back, he wouldn't hesitate to try again.

Morenz: 1 goal
1 assist

Game 22	GP	G	A	Pts	PiM	HG	AG	HA	AA	GWG	GWA
Season Total:	22	18	9	27	35	10	8	5	4	3	3

CHAPTER 23

Saturday, January 17, 1931

Canadiens vs. Maple Leafs in Toronto

The Challenge of Maple Leaf Alley

BOTH THE *GLOBE* and the *Toronto Star* had big hockey stories. One of them was about how for the third straight Saturday night Howie Morenz, "the Famous One," and his Canadiens would be playing against the Leafs.

The other hockey story was bigger news. Boosted by twenty-five thousand ticket requests for this game alone, the Maple Leaf Hockey Club's board of directors decided to move forward with the building of a new arena—hopefully in time for the opening of the next NHL season in November 1931.

The Leafs surprised the Canadiens from the opening, and within four minutes "Ace" Bailey split the Montreal defence and scored. Two minutes later Bailey scored again.

These successive blows ignited Morenz, wrote the *Toronto Star*: "Then Howie Morenz, the Canadiens mid-ice fireball, galvanized into action and for a while he went around like his shorts were full of rocket tubes. He went around the Leaf defence so fast that [Hap] Day got tired trying to follow him so the next time the Montrealer came down he met him with a check that lifted Leo Dandurand's star ten feet into the air and deposited him twenty feet away on his back with a jar that must have loosened his fillings."[1]

That elaborate open-air flight and crash landing hurt Morenz's whole core. What the fans saw as a spectacular cartwheel of uncontrollable flight ended abruptly with a landing that shook every muscle and bone and joint in his body. The pain arrived in an instant and remained for hours. Morenz wasn't able to participate in the power play that followed. Furthermore, both he and Joliat "were harried by encircling sticks every time they went swinging through the defence," wrote the *Montreal Star*. "Many a sly jab was handed out and Morenz in particular was tripped several times."[2] The remainder of the game became a test of wills expressed almost entirely by physical means. One encounter with Red Horner provoked Morenz into a penalty.

Conn Smythe looked on with interest. He believed that hockey success required the physical intimidation of opponents. That idea of being able to win "in the alley" was not original to Smythe—the very same observation was made by Dandurand years earlier: "Down in their hearts, [players] should feel that they can beat the opposition in the alley as well as on the ice. I don't want hockey hoodlums, but I do want he-man hockey talent that can meet any and all situations."[3]

Morenz was as much a disciple of that creed as both Smythe and Dandurand—but not as an exclusive tactical approach to the game. He had other, more exquisite, performance tools.

When he returned to the ice, he launched himself into the air to avoid Horner, going over top of him. The defenceman still made contact. Morenz crash-landed for a second time. Horner did not get a penalty, the referees having determined that Morenz had already leapt in the air by the time the Leaf's check landed. Again, Morenz took his time getting back up.

During the first intermission, the team owners—Smythe on one side and Dandurand with Joe Cattarinich on the other—faced off within a whirlpool of interested fans. Their argument was all about Morenz: whether the Leafs were trashing the league's premier star and ticket-seller with unnecessary violence. The Leafs didn't change course in the second period, now with Charlie Conacher taking the lead.

Morenz managed to put the puck into the Toronto net, but the goal was called back on an offside. He was visibly sulking. "When he finally did come out of his peeve," wrote the *Toronto Star*, "his temper was not a bit improved when Conacher came from nowhere to nip the puck off his stick just as he was going to burn the fuzz off Chabot's pads."[4]

Morenz's game revived when Wasnie's goal made the score 2-1, but Clancy made sure to get in his way. Just as the fans were anticipating the second intermission, there was an outbreak of stick swinging between Conacher and Morenz. Conacher's jabs landed on top of Morenz's stitches from the Shields-inflicted slash injury in Philadelphia.

Morenz was livid. As he and Conacher and Jackson jostled for space in the penalty box, he unloaded: "I didn't see you do much battling or playing in that last game in Montreal. When you show that stuff away from home, I'll listen to your fight stories."[5] He continued to blast Conacher after the game, comparing his behaviour unfavourably to that of Clancy: "King never makes any cheap threats. He just keeps on going. He gives everything he has, but he won't resort to loud talk to try and intimidate anyone."[6]

The Leafs rededicated themselves to close checking in the third period. Morenz was barely able to reach his typical speed. In fact, by that point in the game, Morenz had become physically ineffective.

Harvey Jackson extended the Leafs' lead on a power play. With five minutes left, coach Hart pulled Morenz off the ice.

Smythe spared not a thought for the real consequences of conducting a hit-by-hit destruction of the league's greatest drawing card. Since at least the Horner hit at the end of the first period, Morenz had been playing with a chipped rib. It may have even happened at the time of the earlier toss by Day.[7] Despite the pain, Morenz had felt compelled to keep playing.

His disdain toward Conacher provided the critical insight. Morenz needed to demonstrate his defiance of any attempt at physical or psychological intimidation, even if it caused physical torment to himself. As for that physical torment, his ability to play in the club's next game was doubtful.

***Canadiens* 1** at Toronto **3**

Morenz: 2 penalties

Game 23	GP	G	A	Pts	PiM	HG	AG	HA	AA	GWG	GWA
Season Total:	23	18	9	27	39	10	8	5	4	3	3

CHAPTER 24

Tuesday, January 20, 1931.

Canadiens vs. Rangers in New York

Gus Rivers, Howie Morenz, and the Business of Identity

THE "CHIP IN the ribs" from Saturday night in Toronto meant that Howie Morenz would not be accompanying the team to New York. The *Montreal Star* reported that the injury would take "several days to knit" and Morenz was "strapped up under doctors' orders and, though able to be about, it is felt that a few days' layoff is essential."[1]

It was the first time in nearly two years he would not be part of the team. Morenz had played in ninety-six consecutive games—perhaps an even hundred, counting exhibitions—since January 24, 1929. Since his arrival as a rookie in December 1923, he had only missed eight of the Canadiens' 289 regular-season games and none of their twenty-seven playoff games.

Morenz hadn't spent any time worrying about who caused the injury or when. In the absence of any perceived intent to injure, Morenz refused to blame anyone. A psychology of blame was inconsistent with his sense of play, of risk, and personal daring. It was also consistent with a refusal to acknowledge vulnerability or weakness created by an opponent.

The missed trip to New York afforded Morenz a chance to ponder what life would be like when he could no longer play hockey for a living. It was not a pleasant meditation. He once grimly expressed it to Aurèle Joliat in blunt terms: "After I can't play this game anymore, I want to die."[2]

He had cultivated his identity as a hockey player since his early teens. It was who he was. It was how the public knew him. To contemplate the end of that identity carried him into a place of empty, blank anxiety.

The annual Montreal Motor Show was on all week at Delormier Stadium, and at select car dealerships along Ste-Catherine Street West. Morenz had grown up with a young man's fascination for cars, helped perhaps by the fact that the Stratford Midgets' manager, Roy Brothers, operated a car dealership in Stratford. The show provided a tempting distraction from his injury.

The centrepiece of the 1931 edition of the show was undoubtedly a seven-seater Cadillac V-16, the kind of vehicle fit for captains of industry, entertainers, and the elite level of American professional athletes.[3] As a machinist apprentice in the railway shops at Stratford, Morenz needed only a moment's glance to appreciate the fine engineering of the vehicle. The V-16 would put someone back $11,000, about an entire season's hockey salary, or a few seasons if you weren't Howie Morenz.

Morenz was not the only Canadien interested in cars. Bert McCaffrey sold them in Toronto for off-season income. Armand Mondou was about to purchase the fanciest vehicle of any of his teammates. Gus Rivers, the forward sub who joined the Canadiens a year ago, had a more sophisticated appreciation of automobiles than any of them, working off-season as a mechanic in his family's garage back in Winnipeg.

The Morenz family's entrepreneurial history was unremarkable. His father, William, tried to support a family of eight by selling fine china in the middle of farming country. That wasn't viable. William spent the rest of his working life employed by other people: first as a clerk in a Mitchell dry goods store, and then with the railway at the Stratford shops.

Despite his father's discouraging experience, Morenz's first seven years in Montreal gave him some entrepreneurial confidence. His career happily coincided with a time when advertisers began to link products to "successful" people.[4]

His name, and sometimes his photo, were used to sell everything from clothing to corn syrup, cigars to skates. The *Herald* reported that he made more money from advertising "than he could have made in fifty years as a first-class mechanic."[5] He had also done real sales work in Montreal, selling home heating wood, coal, coke, and fuel oil for Munro Coal Co. Ltd., and Dominion Fuel Oils Limited. Unlike his print ad work, in-person selling took real time, repeated effort, and the skill of being able to close a sale instead of just talking hockey with potential customers.

The game Morenz was missing against the Rangers went into overtime tied at 2. George Hainsworth, who had a thriving electrical and radio business in Kitchener, Ontario, was playing an outstanding game, stopping a barrage of Ranger shots. A new hero emerged in the overtime: Gus Rivers. "A young rookie, sparse in weight, years and experience, stepped into the shoes of the great Howie Morenz here tonight," wrote the *Gazette*. When overtime was called, "it was then that Canadiens missed the searing long rushes of Morenz most. It was then, also, that young Rivers turned the trick that Morenz so often has turned to break up ties."[6]

The young car mechanic from Winnipeg was not quite a rookie. He had been with the Canadiens since January 25, 1930, and had even scored an important playoff overtime goal against the Rangers on the way to last spring's Stanley Cup.

Rivers had been a puzzling secret and curious addition to the Canadiens. Signed as a light defenceman, he was converted into a spare winger and an occasional centre. The question of what special talent he brought to the Canadiens, and what to do with him, persisted throughout his NHL career. He eventually spent most of his game time at the NHL level on the bench.[7]

The Canadiens passed him off in the early months of 1930 to media as Gustave Desrivieres, Des Rivieres, Jules Rivers, and at least once in Boston as "Riversieres." It was a conscious strategy, even though Rivers was as English as George Hainsworth.[8]

Tonight, with Morenz missing, he had been given a rare opportunity to perform. Hart's reason for doing so was simple: what Gus Rivers did best in hockey, according to the *Montreal Herald*, was emulate Howie Morenz: "The decisive goal came with scarcely more than three minutes to go when Gus Rivers, reserve centre, took the puck alone and worked his way through the entire Rangers outfit to smack it in from under Roach's nose."[9]

Rivers's first goal of the 1930–31 season, and the first since last spring's playoffs, had been straight out of the Morenz playbook in style and impact—while Howie Morenz was still home in Montreal, wondering what to do with himself.

***Canadiens* 3** at NY Rangers **2**

Morenz: Did not play

Game 24	GP	G	A	Pts	PiM	HG	AG	HA	AA	GWG	GWA
Season Total:	23	18	9	27	39	10	8	5	4	3	3

CHAPTER 25

Thursday, January 22, 1931

Canadiens vs. Senators in Ottawa

Albert Leduc, Howie Morenz, and Community Identity

When the first-place Canadiens travelled to Ottawa for their "exhibition" against the last-place Senators, Howie Morenz was once again absent for medical reasons. Teammate Albert Leduc, motivated by murmurs about his lacklustre play against New York, initiated the play on Wil Larochelle's opening goal, scored the Canadiens' second, and then assisted on Johnny Gagnon's goal to seal the Canadiens' 3-0 victory. Those were his first points in nearly a month.

Leduc dominated the game in other ways, too. In the first period he was penalized for a rough check on Hec Kilrea. Later, as the lone defenceman back when Kilrea and Frank Finnigan got a two-on-one break, he successfully disrupted that too. He played a stellar, well-rounded game.

Although capable of nights such as this, Leduc was better known for other qualities, and particularly his laboured skating style. The *Globe* claimed it had given him his "Battleship" name: "His steaming rush down the ice is sometimes the pièce de résistance of an otherwise dull game. His legs working like pistons, Albert dashes down and swerves at no defence . . . he dives headlong into the opposition when he reaches it."[1] It was how he had scored the 2-0 goal early in the third period.

Leduc came to the rink every day feeling like a Stanley Cup champion. He was at his athletic peak and taking a regular turn with the Canadiens. He remained immensely grateful for what had begun when he was just a teenager and earned fifteen dollars to play an exhibition game with Art Ross and the Montreal Wanderers.

He counted as career blessings both his first NHL goal in his first NHL game and the fact that both had happened the night Madison Square Garden opened. He cherished memories of needing stitches after suffering cuts from legendary veterans like Bert Corbeau; playing goal once for two minutes against the Black Hawks, during which he allowed the goal that both lost the game and left him with a lifetime goals-against average of thirty. He even counted as blessings the opportunity to play with former opponents when they came to the Canadiens, and with others when he was eventually traded.

Leduc had a knack for getting along well with everyone. In fist-swinging contests with Bill Phillips of the Maroons and Busher Jackson of the Leafs he would soon have both of them laughing as they took their punches. This season he had also promoted himself fully as "Affable Albert,"[2] making a point of hugging and kissing his teammates when they did well. When he hugged Howie Morenz, Leduc would sometimes kiss him twice.

It was his ability to share a sense of joy with others that made him an effective bridge between the English and French players on the Canadiens—particularly within Morenz's inner circle of Musketeers. That social facility also became the foundation of his off-ice life. He became the first of many former Canadiens to work as a brewery representative for the Molson empire, and used his name and personality to boost his own beverage products and several hockey businesses—including the sticks he manufactured and sold, emblazoned with the "Battleship" name.

Leduc's example should have provided Morenz with a clear demonstration of how to use a successful playing career with the Canadiens to foster a lucrative and parallel off-ice career. Both had access to the willing ears and support of Louis Letourneau, the former Canadiens' owner and established Montreal businessman. Both had community connections: Leduc with the Knights of Columbus,[3] Morenz with the Kiwanis and Masons.

One might have thought that Morenz would also have understood, as "Battleship" Leduc did, the marketability of a well-known name. Back at the Montreal Auto Show, New Brunswick Ford dealer Kenneth C. Irving was deeply seduced by that General Motors' V-16 Cadillac, and soon put it to work as a calling card. "He drove it about the Maritimes, and wherever he stopped, people gathered to feast their eyes on it," wrote biographer Doug How. "In later years he'd regret selling it, but while he had it that Cadillac provided him with much more than luxury transportation . . . 'He got more advertising out of that car! It got people talking about him.'"[4]

Howie Morenz already had that kind of public persona, even without the prop of an expensive and luxurious vehicle. Yet his fundamental difficulty in making the transition from player to businessman was that he never understood what Albert Leduc always knew: his greatest economic opportunities would follow directly from who he had been during his hockey career.

Complicating his transition from player to business was a problem of fundamental proportions. The magic name of "Morenz" was not actually magical at all. It was difficult for the French mouth and ear. When he had first been signed by the Canadiens in 1923, it was reported that the new rookie sensation from Ontario was Howard *Morentze,* or *Morentz,* or even *Morenze.* The French press did not even refer to him by the affectionate "Howie" until January 1924.[5]

The bungling of his name by the French press lasted for over two years—longer than they had maintained the charade of "Desrivieres" for Gus Rivers. For those two years the Canadiens' management never corrected the French press on Morenz's behalf. The Francophone reporters never checked with their English colleagues, nor their friend Howie, about how to properly spell his name. It had only been when the Canadiens had opened Madison Square Garden in New York in mid-December 1925 that the French press saw how "Morenz" was spelled in New York and adopted that spelling.[6]

Morenz was never tempted toward an ownership interest with the Canadiens. It was an opportunity that had lured Dunc Munro to the Maroons, and which Lionel Hitchman and Eddie Shore were already arranging with the Boston Bruins. Others spoke about him becoming a general manager—perhaps in Chicago, perhaps as part of a prospective Canadiens ownership group. But he never voiced such an interest. Nor did he imagine buying his own team, as Eddie Shore, Armand Mondou, and even Albert Leduc would do.

He only real identification with hockey was on the ice, as a player.

***Canadiens* 3** at Ottawa **0**

Morenz: Did not play

Game 25	GP	G	A	Pts	PiM	HG	AG	HA	AA	GWG	GWA
Season Total:	23	18	9	27	39	10	8	5	4	3	3

CHAPTER 26

Saturday, January 24, 1931

Canadiens vs. Americans in Montreal

Return of the King

RUMOURS ABOUT THE significance of Morenz's injury worried fans of the Canadiens for a week, but on the third game day after his injury, they spotted him at the Forum, leading his teammates onto the ice for warm-up.

Morenz did not start the game. By the time he took his first shift, Johnny Gagnon had already given the Canadiens a lead. When his skates did hit the ice, all twelve thousand spectators rose to pay him homage. Hart had planned to cautiously reintroduce Morenz to regular play, but Morenz insisted on more. He wanted to make up for lost time.

Quebec was a heavily Catholic province in depth and breadth. For the Canadiens' fans, Howie Morenz's return completed a comforting Christian sequence. There was the rhythm of his injury, his absence, and then return, all of which replicated their familiar, sacred narrative. The ability to suffer a disabling injury, and then to return whole, also hinted at a god-like indestructability and immortality.

The *Montreal Star* though reported what the crowd could not see. Beneath the uniform Morenz "was all trussed up with tape, and his injured rib is not yet ready."[1]

It was 3-1 for the Canadiens early in the third period when Marty Burke carried a rush into the Americans' zone. He passed to Morenz and the puck was in the net for the Canadiens' fourth goal. Morenz's fluid technique providing an apparent inevitable goal gave the impression of being little more than a practiced ritual.

Descriptions of Howie Morenz as the "blow torch" of the Canadiens' offence,[2] and the rest of the Canadiens' offence as *le feu roulant*,[3] were not coincidental. This was a time when the fans and writers understood that "fire" signified a Christian apostolic experience. Having fire was a holy gift. Iconographic religious imagery depicted the gift of the spirit as a flame alighting on the heads of saints. Wil Larochelle opted for exactly that same imagery in thinking about his teammate: "In leadership and for dynamic play, Howie had no peer and it was his fire that raised the whole team to the heights of hockey accomplishment."[4]

By the 1930–31 season, Morenz had become the club's, and the league's, most accomplished, capable, and inspiring player. He had become the personification of the Canadiens' success for nearly a decade. Fans had learned to look to him to ignite their fervour. As his presence on the ice made the Canadiens' winning become more predictable, liturgical expectations associated with him solidified. The gathering of the faithful, acknowledgement of his presence with the reverence of cheers and applause, moments of worship as he led the attacks, sometimes prayer if the Canadiens faltered or fell behind, followed by an uplifting release of joy and celebration with a goal, and then victory.

Morenz was the first to permit fans to imagine hockey as a religious experience,[5] as some still do. No one in Montreal then dared to think or speak of Morenz as a mere mortal either. Indeed, long after Morenz's playing days were over, even Rocket Richard's biographer continued to refer to Morenz as being a player on a different level. As much as Richard became a political figure, Morenz was "the immortal."[6] That place occupied by Morenz in the culture of the Canadiens remains unique in the history of the club.

Morenz could not have created his exalted place as the Canadiens' hockey high priest, or immortal, on his own. As a somnolent attendee at Evangeline Grace Lutheran Church in Mitchell, he would not have seemed a likely candidate to fulfil any religious imagination—but in Montreal he had. His fans and his teammates invented that role for him. The ease with which fans could attribute a messianic status to him became the seed for the phenomenon that fans who followed the Canadiens were engaging in an "implicit religion" around the team, rather than simply watching a group of paid professional hockey players. That too has remained unique in the history of both the NHL and other North American professional sports teams.

Leo Dandurand was quite aware of this and acknowledged how the whole team drew on the hearts of fans (and even uncommitted spectators) in a way that was like religious faith. He too equated the values demonstrated by sport, and his Canadiens, with those of the Christian faith. He drew the connection between antiquity's association of sport and religion to the Canadiens' demonstration of the values of courage, endurance, esprit de corps or teamwork, self-discipline, justice, and fair play. As the Greek poet Pindar expressed it:

> *The race of men is one thing, that of the gods is another . . .*
> *But nevertheless — we can become something like the gods,*
> *through excellence — excellence of mind or of body*[7]

With barely a minute left in the game, the Canadiens led 5-1. Morenz took a pass from Joliat and scored the game's final goal. The shot appeared to hit an Americans' stick before going in the net.

It was a triumphant return: athletically, statistically, even metaphysically. *La Presse* was moved to conclude its game report with a reverence often reserved for the Christ himself: "The worth of the Habs at this stage of the season indicates that it will be difficult to bring them down from their throne of glory."[8]

Morenz became aware through Monday's newspaper reports that he had been credited with the final goal against the Americans. He contacted the NHL office and asked for a change to be made to the official record. It had been Joliat's stick that deflected the final shot into the net.[9] Morenz proved himself again to be a good man, and perhaps even a saint, on his return.

NY Americans **1** at ***Canadiens*** **6**

Morenz: 1 goal
1 assist

Game 26	GP	G	A	Pts	PiM	HG	AG	HA	AA	GWG	GWA
Season Total:	24	19	10	29	39	11	8	6	4	3	3

CHAPTER 27

Thursday, January 29, 1931

Canadiens vs. Quakers in Montreal

The Morenz Bloodlines and Le Gros Lesieur

SATURDAY NIGHT AT the Forum began with a musical presentation by the thirty-piece Royal Montreal Regiment marching band, but the more notable pre-game event was Howie Morenz Jr.'s first official involvement in an NHL game. The *Gazette* described how the young fellow "stood at attention during the playing of the national anthem, unconcerned at the eleven thousand spectators eyeing him. He threw the puck between the sticks of his father and [the Quakers' Hib] Milks."[1]

Howie Jr. wasn't quite four years old, but had been a Montreal celebrity since the age of one, and had already become a regular in the Forum stands and in the Canadiens' dressing room.[2]

There were nascent hopes that he would follow in his father's hockey footsteps. With the indulgent permission of his mother, Mary, the younger Howie was claimed the previous spring by Roy Brothers' London Tecumsehs of the International League.[3] Howie Sr. would soon alert an assembly of young boys that: "I have a son, and I will be tickled to death if he becomes a hockey player, and I hope he will be a good one."[4]

Howie Sr. sometimes also mused publicly about wanting to "play major league hockey until Howie, Jr., would be old enough to take over his dad's No. 7 on the Flying Frenchmen."[5]

These kinds of generational dreams fed the imaginations of fans, newsmen, and family alike. The Canadiens themselves had not been immune. The club could have delayed Howie Jr.'s ceremonial fourth birthday appearance until his actual birthday: a scheduled Thursday night visit by the Detroit Falcons on February 26. But in January 1931, everyone in Montreal was already too impatient for that.

Quaker goalie Petch Cude was, like Howie Jr., appearing on Forum ice for the first time ever. Just past the four-minute mark the Canadiens led 2-0 and were never threatened after.

Although still hampered by his sore ribs, Morenz was making a difference in the game by his mere presence on the ice. But the Quakers were keeping such a close watch on him that he was unable to get a shot on goal. Instead, his teammates carried the game, and the *Montreal Star* noted he was "an accessory to a lot of plays, and helped along in the scheme of entertainment by reeling off startling rushes ever so often that indicated he was still at top form."[6]

The one time Morenz almost scored, Quaker goalie Cude made "a magnificent dive across the ice to grab the puck with his hand," reported *La Presse*, "while on the club bench, manager Cooper Smeaton and all his companions were trembling with joy at having seen him steal a sure point from the most dangerous scorer in the NHL."[7]

Although every one of the thousands in the Forum had willed Morenz to score, he had not. Hopes and expectations alone weren't enough to create success.

In addition to Howie Jr., Howie and Mary Morenz had two younger children—Donald and Marlene—but Howie Sr.'s closest relationship was always with his eldest son. He kept a particularly watchful eye on the boy's skating and hockey play as he grew up. "He plays center, too," he told the *Detroit Free Press*. "He's got the same hump and does everything just like I skate. I thought at first he was just imitating me, but I watched him and he just skates that way naturally."[8]

Morenz's own hockey bloodlines were impossibly shallow. His father, William, was already in his mid-forties when Howie took up the game.[9] There is no hint that William ever even tried to skate or to play the game. Howie's hockey career had really been an adventure of his own.

It was a stunning leap when Morenz graduated from intermediate hockey to the NHL on his first try. His successful rookie Stanley Cup campaign and eight years of NHL success had been remarkable. But he had no concept of how hard a struggle it was for even moderately skilled players to reach the big time.[10] For his son to become a "pretty good" hockey player would never satisfy the expectations of those who had been lifted by the experience of having seen the father. Nor would "pretty good" satisfy Howie Sr.'s dream—or anyone else's—that his son would take his father's place on the Canadiens.

As he matured, Howie Morenz Jr. understood the burden of those impossible expectations and recognized what his father could not: "I'm afraid I would have to disagree with those who say athletic talents are hereditary. I doubt very much that hockey came more easily to me than it did to other kids I knew. I had to learn the hard way the same as they did."[11]

That should have been clear to Howie Sr. that night against the Quakers. As the Canadiens continued to dominate through the third period, leading 4-1, there was a surprise from their new defenceman, Art Lesieur.

Morenz drew the Quaker defence to the fringes of the ice surface, when the 200-pound, big-bodied Lesieur found himself with a sudden breakaway opportunity. He churned down the ice as quickly as he could, swung at the puck in front of him, made contact with it, and tumbled headlong into the net—along with the puck. It was a scoring play that was a combination of ineptness and accomplishment rarely seen at the NHL level.

The Canadiens first noticed Lesieur three years before, in 1928, when he was playing with the Providence Reds. They called him up then, creating "a mild bombshell" in professional hockey circles. According to the Associated Press, "Lesieur's experience borders closely to a Horatio Alger tale. He himself was hard to be convinced that he was wanted by Les Canadiens, for in hockey circles Lesieur is only a sand lotter."[12]

He was American: a child of the French-Canadian diaspora, born in Fall River, Massachusetts, which at that time was the third largest French-Canadian city in North America. He had only started playing hockey in the mid-1920s, but attracted attention almost immediately because of his size.

Lesieur played seventeen uneventful games for the Canadiens in 1928 before being loaned to the new Chicago Black Hawks. Lesieur returned to the Providence Reds for another year before failing to make the Canadiens out of camp in October 1930. He returned to Providence until being called up on January 14, 1931.

This most recent return to the NHL had been rocky. Lesieur received a major for fighting in the first period of his first game at Toronto. Another tripping penalty tonight against the Quakers gave him a total of ten penalty minutes in his first five games back.[13] The goal that had been a surprise as he fell over would be his only goal of this season.

In statistical terms, Art Lesieur put together a rather inconsequential NHL career. He had just enough ability to earn the chance to play with the Canadiens for only a few weeks when he was twenty-three years old. Having secured that chance, Lesieur had to keep earning the right to remain with the club. With neither bloodlines nor realized potential, his NHL career was always insecure, existing on borrowed time. Without the ability to reliably fill a particular team need, Art Lesieur never got to stay.

Howie Morenz's grandson Danny Geoffrion, who played 111 NHL games (thirty-two with the Canadiens), and great-grandson Blake Geoffrion, who played fifty-five NHL games (thirteen with the Canadiens) understood both realities of professional hockey's expectations. Whether created by the hype of a family name or the desires of fans or the simple dreams of fathers, qualifying to play at the highest level was more than many could manage. Staying with the top players was even harder. Danny Geoffrion explained what his grandfather should have already known: "It's tough getting there, but it's tougher staying there. I know, because I didn't get to stay."[14]

Quaker goalie Cude and his teammates drew a positive about their own play during their 7-1 shellacking by the Canadiens. *La Presse* reported how they consoled themselves: "Despite their defeat, Cooper Smeaton's men left the ice feeling very pleased with themselves, because not only had they put up a good fight against the world champions, but they had also managed to prevent the great Howie Morenz from scoring."[15]

The Quakers weren't counting Howie Morenz's two assists, which would have been enough on their own to give the Canadiens their victory. Nor did they note the fact that they had suffered their most lopsided loss to the

Canadiens this season. They continued, in defeat, to permit him to define their game.

So it was for the Canadiens' fans as well. Having lived in the presence of Howie Sr.'s greatness, there was never going to be enough imaginative space left for someone of the same name to follow.

Philadelphia **1** at ***Canadiens* 7**

Morenz: 2 assists*

*although not shown in the newspaper summaries, the official National Hockey League records accorded assists to Morenz on both Gagnon goals

Game 27	GP	G	A	Pts	PiM	HG	AG	HA	AA	GWG	GWA
Season Total:	25	19	12	31	39	11	8	8	4	3	3

CHAPTER 28

Sunday, February 1, 1931

Canadiens vs. Black Hawks in Chicago

"Black Cat" Gagnon and the Morenz School of Jazz

A SENSE OF "JAZZ" is essential for understanding how the Montreal Canadiens played hockey in 1931. Mark Gridley, author of *Jazz Styles*, says the genre is unique "for two very special aspects: a) its provocative rhythms and b) its insistence that performers create their parts as they play them. Each jazz performance represents a new and original creation. Hearing live jazz is exciting not only for the way it makes us feel but also for the realization that we are following the musical thinking of the musicians at the very moment they are inventing their music. They are taking us along with them."[1]

Howie Morenz nourished his own affection for jazz often at Texas Guinan's Cabaret Frolic in Montreal's Plateau district. His Canadiens played the same game of flow and imagination that he heard there. It was a playing style that became a little more obvious in the spiritual birthplace of the "Chicago school" of jazz.

With the concurrent arrivals of Bix Beiderbecke and Louis Armstrong to Chicago in the 1920s, the beating heart of jazz changed from a style featuring group improvisation to one that highlighted unique solo performances. That musical idea was perfectly timed for Howie Morenz's arrival in the NHL. As jazz solo performances showcased improvisation atop their ensembles, Morenz began to employ creativity and imagination in his own solo performances. That was why "Black Cat" Johnny Gagnon was poised to become his perfect winger.

In this Chicago game, it took only thirty seconds for Gagnon to score the first goal of the evening, after Morenz swept the puck into the Canadiens' end after the faceoff, and passed to Gagnon, who rushed the Black Hawks' end.[2]

Originally pencilled in as a third-line player with Armand Mondou and Gus Rivers, Johnny Gagnon wasn't really liberated to play his own style until he was moved to the top line. Even then, he had needed time to become accustomed to the rhythms of Morenz and Joliat.

Morenz and Joliat had been sharing the puck between themselves and with right-winger Bill Boucher since 1923. Lou Marsh remembered, "Those three whipped the old pill back and forth like infielders warming up."[3]

Gagnon struggled at first getting up to their speed and blamed that on Morenz. "At first I had a little trouble playing with Howie," he said. "He wasn't too good as a playmaker, so I'd play more with Aurèle. He always used to get the puck and pass it to me, and then I'd pass it to him."[4]

When Gagnon became acclimatized to his linemates' pace, his game transformed. He had his first two-goal game at the Forum on January 10, and then four more goals in the next three.

Gagnon was then recognized as the best of the league's first-year men, but wasn't doing it alone. Even though he could point to how his opening goal had been recorded as unassisted, the entire play had taken shape as an improvised bar of music. It was the pass from Morenz and the soaring arcs made by both Morenz and Joliat toward the farther side of the ice, which caused the Chicago defence to shade away from Gagnon. That opened the whole other side of the ice for Gagnon to bang his initial shot off the back boards and then collect the puck for his shot past Charlie Gardiner.

The Hawks controlled the remainder of the first period with rugged offensive play, which tended to make Gagnon—one of the smallest players in the league—invisible. Morenz remained in the forefront of the defensive action. His superior ability to navigate the abrasive aspects of the NHL game became evident to *the Chicago Daily Tribune*, when "the flashy Morenz fell in a collision and as he dropped to the ice his stick caught Gottselig, the Hawk wing man, between the eyes. Blood gushed from the tall boy's nose and he tried to leave the floor under his own power, but collapsed and had to be carried."[5] No penalty was called on the play. It was the kind of thing that Morenz could shrug off, but the small and often injured Gagnon could not.

The best demonstrations of the Chicago school of jazz happened when soloists learned how to, in the words of Bix Beiderbecke, "play around the lead."

To "play around the lead" meant that a performer would rarely offer one note when an arpeggio would be more exciting, or when adding grace notes during the progression of a melody could elevate the musical experience. Beiderbecke could decorate recognizable tunes by adding embellishments so elaborate and perfect that the originals became rather plain and uninteresting. That was how he made his playing unique, his originality compelling, and his spontaneous performances timeless.

Howie Morenz possessed that same facility and power. He could respond to each new opportunity with a performance that was personal, original, and unapologetically exuberant. The sportswriters noticed how his performances were often a matter of mood and attitude. On his best nights he could give himself the same imaginative permissions he had enjoyed while learning his fresh-air, open-ice hockey skills on the Thames River in Mitchell. That same kind of outdoor environment had produced Johnny Gagnon.

As the season progressed, the two were learning how to jointly elaborate on that style. They were learning how to reflect off each other. That relationship reappeared early in the second period, when Morenz again spurted to the Chicago end with the puck and passed it to Gagnon, who scored again.

That goal launched the Canadiens on a torrid sequence of offensive chances led by Morenz, but the Hawks cut the lead to one, then tied the game with less than a minute remaining in the period.

In the third, the Canadiens were unable to establish an advantage until Johnny Gagnon jumped on a different kind of opportunity, taking a cue from Morenz by carrying the puck from the Canadiens' blue line and charging past Chicago's defence. He took a shot from the corner, blocked by Gardiner, but then Gagnon whipped behind the nets and sent a pass to Pit Lepine, who scored.

It was a goal that Gagnon created with a sudden and superior expression of his own abilities and then completed through a teammate.

As the Hawks pressed to pull even, the *Gazette* recorded how Morenz played his own solo turn for the final goal of the night: "Howie Morenz put his final stamp on things by breaking away from the milling Hawk pack to round a lone defenceman and then whip the puck behind Chuck Gardiner."[6] The Chicago school of jazz expected its best players to show initiative, to be loose, and even a little bit wild, in testing the limits of their skills, as Morenz had just done.

Beiderbecke and Armstrong had laid down a challenge for a generation of section musicians, the same way that Morenz did for his contemporaries. Did they have enough imagination and creativity to produce their own solo, to complement another's flourishes, or would they remain mere background ensemble players, faceless and interchangeable from team to team?

Morenz was fully aware of the symbiosis between himself and his linemates. Gagnon's offensive inventiveness was so perfectly matched with his own that the two seemed to be more alter egos than linemates. Both, in their best performances, could share and play around the lead with each other.

For Beiderbecke, Morenz, and Gagnon, playing at the top of their game came with high tension. They were expected to be consistently and brilliantly creative. As early as 1928, Beiderbecke could sense the limits of what he could endure. Getting back from a tour that included a gig with the Whiteman Band at Toronto's Massey Hall, he told an old sweetheart: "I don't know where I'm going from here." "It was almost as though he longed to be just a young boy again," wrote Beiderbecke's biographer. "He kept saying he'd reached the top and there was no other height to reach, therefore the only direction was down, and that he was afraid sometimes. It wasn't said despairingly, I believe. Just matter of fact."[7]

The cornetist's impending fall represented a warning for both Morenz and Gagnon.

Gagnon's NHL and subsequent senior hockey career would implode due to a lethal combination of temper tantrums and arrogance. He eventually recognized that he really had been at his best when playing with Morenz, when they had had the chance to feed off each other, and to tease their own ideas out of their shared opportunities.

In 1975, Gagnon watched the Soviet Wings team touring the American Hockey League, and what he saw on the ice reminded him of how he and Howie Morenz used to play: "You watch. These Russians don't just throw it in. They skate. They hop when they skate. They stop on a dime. They know all the moves. The Russians play the game the way we used to play it."[8]

***Canadiens* 4** at Chicago **2**

Morenz: 1 goal
1 assist

Game 28	GP	G	A	Pts	PiM	HG	AG	HA	AA	GWG	GWA
Season Total:	26	20	13	33	39	11	9	8	5	3	3

CHAPTER 29

Tuesday, February 3, 1931

Canadiens vs. Maple Leafs in Montreal

Howie Morenz Becomes "the Nonpareil"

The Canadiens and Maple Leafs were on the same train that left Toronto's Union Station on Monday afternoon. Conn Smythe and some of the Leafs took advantage of that proximity to taunt, even threaten, the Canadiens about their Tuesday night game at the Forum. If any writer was going to reveal the Leafs' transgressions to the public, it was going to be Baz O'Meara of the *Montreal Star*.

O'Meara came to Montreal in 1929 from Ottawa as the gentleman sportswriter, always ready to expound on matters of sportsmanship. He expected sportsmen to reflect society's better values. To him, the Leafs' behaviour on the train was not "fair play" and had to be exposed.[1] He saw the same antagonism as the game began.

After taking the first penalty of the game, Morenz initiated a late power play goal by Larochelle, even as Hap Day was slashing him, resulting in another Leaf penalty. It then took Morenz just thirty-three seconds until he struck again and landed a heavy shot into the net, giving the Canadiens a 2-0 lead at the first intermission.

Although O'Meara continued to write for the *Star* into the 1960s, his podium of morality already seemed a bit antiquated. The fashionable sportswriting in 1920s newspapers was about defining greatness for a mass audience. That required poetry rather than strict reportage. As Jim

Murray put it succinctly decades later: "Contests are merely contests without dramatization. It is sports writing which defines the quest, spins the myth, and makes us care."[2]

That role was most often performed in Montreal by two writers. In English it was sometime-NHL publicist and *Montreal Herald* columnist Elmer W. Ferguson. In French it was Charles Mayer, whose work appeared in both *Le Petit Journal* and *La Patrie*. Both shrugged at objectivity. Both cultivated and bragged about their personal friendships with Morenz. Both would inject their own personal experiences into their stories about him. Both traded on their relationship with him for personal advantage. Morenz reciprocated by providing substance for all their hype.

Montreal's English sports writing fraternity in 1931 also featured a group of young men at the *Gazette*. Duncan Macdonald, Mark T. McNeil, and L.S.B. Shapiro reported on the Canadiens in a rotation as if hockey was a purely athletic event. They were more gameswriters than sportswriters. They saw their primary role as explaining what had happened for readers who had not seen the game. While *Gazette* reports often lacked any hint of romance, morality, or even emotion, they did provide a useful objective distance, particularly in a city where the Maroons and Canadiens were regular combatants.

Toronto coach Art Duncan could be heard shouting at his team about Morenz, "Take him out!"[3] The roughhousing that ensued stoked fury within the hometown crowd. When the period ended, the Leafs were waving their sticks and inviting the paying customers to come within range. Conn Smythe sought out the press to taunt them with threats about "what the Leafs would do to the Canadiens in the return game in Toronto."[4]

Albert Laberge of *La Presse* heard the snarl in Smythe's voice and turned away in disgust. Laberge was an aesthete. He had been with *La Presse* since 1900. He wrote a novel, *La Scouine*, that the Roman Catholic Church had denounced as an *ignoble pornographie*. Even though he preferred to write poetry, he had no trouble adjusting his voice to the sports page.

His perspective was unique. Just about to turn sixty, Laberge was much older than the rest of the sportswriting fraternity. He was already thinking about retirement. He was never beholden to a National Hockey League that was only in the midst of its fourteenth season. He had no desire to be chummy with the players. He had reached the stage of his career when he felt utterly free to choose his own words to express his own judgments. He had moved beyond coverage and analysis into interpretation.

Occasionally, like tonight, he could encapsulate the main features of a game with a pungency that rendered specifics superfluous. *La Presse*: "They tried to demolish each other with terrible body checks, to decapitate each other by continually holding the stick up to the face, to damage each other's ribs by administering dangerous six-inch blows, and to send each other sprawling on the ice with fangs in the legs. Time and time again, the general battle came close to breaking out, and even today it is hard to understand why there were no fights on the ice."[5]

Laberge recounted Smythe's grandstanding as if it was more important than the game—which he believed it was—and wrote in deeper hues than the *Gazette*'s report of a "battle of words" with "spirited conversation."[6] Laberge was blunt, reporting Conn Smythe's challenge that when the Canadiens came to the next Toronto game, "it would probably be prudent to bring a whole regiment of soldiers and police with them to protect them, because the fight would be terrible."[7]

While the *Star*, like the *Gazette*, talked in euphemisms about "verbal exuberance" and "belligerency" as the game's "window dressing,"[8] Laberge identified Smythe's bellicosity as the true harm.

For Laberge, the game had become a demonstration of how Conn Smythe felt free to abuse, denigrate, and enrage *les Canadiens* in general, including those who played for the hockey team. Laberge derided Smythe for his attack on "*les portes-couleurs du Canada*," and rebuked him for his effect on the game:

> *There was also a battle of words worthy of the most heated politicians . . . even the referees were hurled abusive epithets by the players. Opponents shouted at each other with expressions worthy of the most illustrious coachmen of yesteryear. Morenz, Leduc, Burke and Larochelle exhausted all the verbs of the first conjugation to satisfy the wishes of Horner, Conacher and Jackson of the visitors. Toronto manager Conn Smythe himself gave the referees a veritable harangue, treating them with expressions that are forbidden to be reproduced in newspapers. Some spectators also forgot themselves and we heard some ladies in evening gowns and some gentlemen in tuxedos, people usually colder than the ice, forget their code of etiquette and indulge in some truly astonishing violence of language.*[9]

In Laberge's view, Smythe's degradation of the game's atmosphere justified the Canadiens' self-defence.

More disturbing to Laberge were Smythe's comments about police and armed force. Those words resonated with an audience easily inflamed by references to culture and class warfare on a national stage, just as Laberge had described in his own novel. For him, the on-ice Canadiens were allegorical warriors on behalf of an oppressed and disrespected community of French-Canadians within Canada. He encouraged his readers to recognize how Smythe's gaucheries transformed hockey games into arenas of social and nationalistic conflict.

Although Clancy managed a goal in the third period, the Leafs' earlier intimidation efforts bankrupted them of energy, neutralizing any offensive threat they might have posed. Meanwhile, Morenz led his team to victory with a goal and an assist.

Laberge cared little for mindless enthusiasm about professional athletics, but he recognized something different in Morenz. He was seeing an athlete at the zenith of his power. Instead of gushing forth with well-worn clichés about the Mitchell Meteor, Stratford Streak, or even "*l'homme éclair*,"[10] Laberge described him as the "*prodigeux*" and "*l'incomparable*," and how "the Canadiens' famous centre really doesn't have a rival in the NHL. He was more wonderful than ever."[11] By February 23, Laberge wrote how Howie Morenz had proved himself to be "*le Nonpareil*."[12]

For Laberge, Howie Morenz was the player who defied and overcame the brutish attacks and arrogance of those who opposed the Canadiens—none more reprehensible than Smythe's Leafs. It was also important to Laberge that the Ontario-born Morenz adopted a leading role as champion of an oppressed people in a different province. Morenz was not merely a remarkable visitor—he convinced Laberge that he was one of "*des Canadiens anglaise qui combattent pour nous*" (the English-Canadians who fight for us).[13]

Charles Mayer would soon use the phrase "*nulle autre pareille*" (like no other) to describe Morenz.[14] Some English media also started using superlatives, including "peerless." However, Laberge's own pithy assessment of Morenz's significance in Quebec was never acknowledged or adopted in the English literature of the game. At the time it was enough that the Québécois, and the Montrealais, knew what Laberge was talking about.

Toronto **1** at ***Canadiens* 2**

Morenz: 1 goal
1 assist
2 penalties

Game 29	GP	G	A	Pts	PiM	HG	AG	HA	AA	GWG	GWA
Season Total:	27	21	14	35	43	12	9	9	5	4	3

CHAPTER 30

Thursday, February 5, 1931

Canadiens vs. Maroons in Montreal

Pit Lepine: The Morenz Substitute

IT WAS SAID that Leo Dandurand could out-dress Beau Brummell. Who else could have carried off a "natty ensemble of chocolate blue and green" at the Canadiens' October golf tournament?[1] Not to be outdone, coach Cecil Hart was considered, based on his ties alone, to be "one of the best dressers" among Montreal sportsmen.[2]

Howie Morenz tried to compete. He boasted a large wardrobe, changing often throughout the day even when not playing. He developed a taste for three-piece suits, with spats and boots for footwear. He always wore a tie except when playing golf in whites. He had even been featured in a Montreal tailor's newspaper advertising, with his own "look."

Sartorial excellence was important to the Canadiens. Generations later, American sportswriter Dave Anderson acknowledged that same reputation for elegance by reference to the sweater alone: "They appear to be skating in Pierre Cardin velvet blazers. Not that there aren't some muscles under the velvet. And a few elbows."[3]

Each of the current players had the funds and proximity to Montreal tailors to indulge themselves. Each of them had been given a new tailored suit as a Christmas bonus. The teammates from last spring had the same commemorative Stanley Cup tie pin and cufflinks to wear as accessories.

If there was competition among the young men of the Canadiens in terms of fashion, and even with Dandurand's own pretensions, centre Alfred

"Pit" Lepine was *le Beau Brummell des Canadiens*.[4] This status was based as much on *how* he wore his clothes as *what* he wore. According to many, he looked like a movie star on and off the ice. He had presence.

Lepine was in his sixth season as the Canadiens' substitute centre, playing when Howie Morenz needed a rest, when the Canadiens were killing penalties, and even more when Morenz was injured. Occasionally they played together—when the Canadiens needed an extra push and Morenz was put on a wing or defence.

Early in a raucous first period against the Maroons, Lepine saw Dave Trottier and Morenz collide. As the two parted, blood spurted from Morenz's mouth. He spat some onto the ice and some more into a towel, but it kept flowing. Trottier's stick had sliced right though his lower lip. He needed stitches.

Trottier's sudden bloodying of Morenz had permanent consequences. The resulting scar became his "distinguishing mark" on U.S. Customs entry forms.[5] Al Parsley of the *Montreal Herald* claimed to see the same scar light up as a sign of the player's stress and anger.[6] This particular injury would also confirm Lepine's edge over Morenz in movie-star good looks.

Lepine scored the first goal of the game early in the second period, with a shot from beyond the defence. It was a repeat of the kind of goal he had made against Philadelphia a week before. Last season he scored five goals in a single game and assisted on the sixth against the Senators at the Forum, the brightest individual moment of his career.

Lepine's more familiar role related to other parts of the game. He possessed the most felicitous defensive stick skills in the NHL. Aided by his height and reach, he evolved Frank Nighbor's mere poke into a hook or sweep. Lepine became known as both "the rapier," as well as *l'artiste de "poke-check."*[7]

The Maroons got their equalizer while the Canadiens were two men short soon after Lepine's opening goal. The Canadiens got the lead back on a rink-length rush by Albert Leduc. Then Howie Morenz scored one of his famous goals.

Blinding the fans to everything else that had happened to that point, and with just seconds remaining in the period, a stitched and offended Morenz went from end to end while catching four Maroons up the ice. The crowd rose to its feet, bellowing as he propelled himself forward, faster and faster as time was expiring. He arrived at the front of the goal and shot the puck without fanfare into the net.

Every part of that goal exhibited a kind of dashing finesse: shrugging off the injury, taking advantage of the moment, creating his own opportunity, and netting the puck with just six seconds remaining. It was the kind of glamorous Morenzian moment that so easily and thoroughly eclipsed Pit Lepine's own labours.

Cecil Hart relied heavily on Lepine to protect the Canadiens' 3-1 lead into the third period. The Maroons clawed their way back, scoring one, and then adding the tying goal with about two-and-a-half minutes to go. They continued to press, forcing a faceoff in front of the Canadiens' net.

Pit Lepine would ordinarily have been given responsibility for this faceoff. Morenz stepped in against Nels Stewart instead. The *Montreal Star*:

> *Stewart, his usually indifferent attitude vanished, his shoulders hunched as he bent down to make the draw, faced the high-strung poker visaged Morenz. Their sticks locked for an instant and Stewart sent the disc behind to [Babe] Siebert, who crashed a shot as his stick reached the speeding puck and Stewart batted in the rebound.*[8]

Morenz had not only failed to control the faceoff, but had not blocked Stewart from the rebound. Because of his two flubs, the Maroons secured an unlikely and precious lead with just ninety-one seconds remaining in the game.

Hart decided that both Morenz and Lepine would finish the game together. Morenz rose to the challenge and charged down the ice with the puck. Bearing down on the Maroons' net, his countenance was stern and tense. "He was pinned to the left rail near the nets, twisted away from his cover, and sent a pass skidding out to Lepine," reported the *Star*.[9] Lepine's stick met Morenz's pass and the puck was in the net, in time to avoid a loss. The game finished in a draw.

It was often said that Lepine could have been a starter with several other teams. There were offers that Leo Dandurand rebuffed. However, the truth about Lepine was that, for a big man, he seemed unfortunately fragile. He suffered several broken bones over the course of his career. While Morenz played defiantly through injuries, as he had tonight, Lepine often seemed limited by them, contributing to his delicate reputation.

Morenz's years of reckless energy in the starting centre's position also created expectations for others filling that spot. Lepine's sophisticated defensive skills were, despite tonight's tying goal against the Maroons, rarely as useful for meeting the frantic and desperate demands of offensive emergencies.

Lepine also seemed less willing than Morenz to assert himself, to seize the moment, and to act like the boss. Joliat felt Lepine "was not violent enough."[10] He was perhaps too sportsmanlike a competitor, and too supportive of and deferential to others. He never seemed comfortable dominating opponents. Even when he coached, he didn't share Morenz's idea that victory was always imperative.

Perhaps Lepine was accustomed to living in a shadow. He was the younger brother on every hockey team he played for—even the Canadiens. Growing up in a Quebec that had not yet experienced its Quiet Revolution, he may have also accepted that as a French-Canadian his appropriate place would have been behind Morenz the *anglais*, or even behind all of the Canadiens' previous great Franco-Ontarian stars (Lalonde, Laviolette, and Joliat). Lepine may have accepted, or never questioned, that he could not inherit the torch that Morenz and others held so high.

***Canadiens* 4** at Maroons **4**

Morenz: 1 goal
1 penalty

Game 30	GP	G	A	Pts	PiM	HG	AG	HA	AA	GWG	GWA
Season Total:	28	22	14	36	45	13	9	9	5	4	3

(Top Left) sixteen-year-old Howie Morenz at the Stanley Barracks in Toronto—a one day career with the Royal Canadian Dragoons. (Top right) fourteen years old, Rover with the 1917 champion. Mitchell Juveniles. (Bottom) eighteen years old with the Memorial Cup finalist Stratford Midgets in 1921.

(Top left) with wife Mary; (top right) with Howie Jr. in what he claimed was his favourite picture.

The Canadiens of 1930–1931.

With wife Mary and daughter Marlene.

A selection of promotional photos.

(Top left) a disappointing golf day at Lachine's Forest Hills Golf Course; (top right) the St Catherine's Street entrance to the Montreal Forum; (bottom) in action against the Rangers.

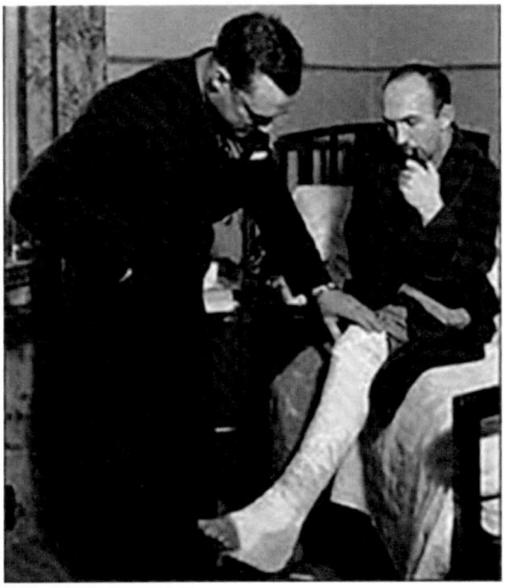

DETAILS COMPLETS DE LA PARTIE TORONTO-CANADIENS
PAR L'ENVOYE SPECIAL DU "PETIT JOURNAL" (Voir page 21)

Température : BEAU et FROID — 40 PAGES — ★★★EDITION FINALE

MEMBRE de l' A.B.C.

LE PETIT JOURNAL

Au Service du Public

Tirage : Plus de 85,000 copies

Vol. V — No 20—Bureaux: 1242 rue St-Denis. — MONTREAL, DIMANCHE, 1er MARS 1931 — Tél. HARBOUR 7166 — Prix : 5 CENTS

UNE FEMME ACCUSEE DE MEURTRE

Howie Morenz se rend à l'hôpital et comble de joie un de ses petits admirateurs qui eut les deux jambes broyées par un train

When Howie Morenz visited child amputee Yves Gabias in hospital at the end of February 1931, he initiated a tradition among the Canadiens, and hockey players generally, of bringing hope to the dispirited (bottom). The media were also eager to document his own hospital stays.

Approximately 15,000 people attended Howie's funeral at the Montreal Forum. Conservative estimates proposed that another 25,000 lined the streets to the cemetery.

Longtime teammate Aurèle Joliat contemplates Morenz's vacant chair.

This sculpture of Morenz in flight, imagined and realized by Marc-Andre J. Fortier, is installed outside the Canadiens' current home, the Bell Centre, in Montreal, Quebec, Canada.

The Stanley Cup as constructed in 1930—1931

CHAPTER 31

Saturday, February 7, 1931

Canadiens vs. Bruins in Montreal

Armand Mondou's Best Days with Howie Morenz

HOWIE MORENZ SPENT his Friday evening before a Saturday match-up against the Bruins doing one of his favourite things: answering questions about hockey from several hundred youth at the Trenholme Park Athletic Association.[1] By Saturday morning he was in the lobby of the Mount Royal Hotel with some of the Bruins, chewing on the end of a cigar and gabbing. Then he headed toward the Windsor Hotel, where a Boston artist by the name of Pastoret was showing a sketch of him—presumably without the stitches that remained in his lip.

His walk between the Mount Royal and the Windsor became an excursion. Never a reclusive athlete, he was generous in dispensing smiles and waves to anyone who recognized him. He stopped to chat with friends, acquaintances, and any strangers he encountered on the way. Even when he didn't have a game, he would sometimes go downtown just to shake hands with people and to bathe in his popularity. Those moments were as happy as any he lived.

Morenz may never have seen Pastoret's drawing, but he certainly would have seen his image drawn by Ernest LeMesurier in the souvenir *Canadiens en Caricature* booklet put on sale at the Forum that evening.[2] It made him look about twenty years old. Eight seasons of NHL hockey, the passage of time, and the escapades of youth had apparently not yet filled out his cheeks nor thinned his hair. The smile was slight, but still obvious and assured.

Having the social cachet to attract the unsolicited interest of artists was a testament to the cresting of his cultural celebrity. He was a model of youth, athleticism, and success, which was how artists rendered his image. That kind of representational image had appeared on Morenz hockey cards as early as 1923, and in several sets that followed.

Representations of Morenz on paper as youthful, vital, powerful, and unscarred were conscious constructions. In charcoal, paint, or ink, those idealized depictions preserved aspirational athletic values that might easily have been undermined by photographic reality.

It was the youthful Howie Morenz the fans wanted to imagine and remember, and it was this youthful Howie Morenz that became embedded in the public mind.

Because of a fighting suspension to Gagnon, Morenz was going to play on the second line against the Bruins, with Gus Rivers on his right and Armand Mondou on his left. Mondou was in his third year with the Canadiens.

A centreman until the moment of his arrival at the NHL, Mondou had shrugged at his change to left wing. Life couldn't get much better than to be paid to play hockey behind Aurèle Joliat, on a team led by Howie Morenz. The only thing better would be a night like tonight—when he would get the chance to actually play *with* Howie Morenz.

Mondou was, with Morenz, among the fastest skaters on the club. As soon as they were over the boards against the Bruins, Morenz called on him for some of that speed as he carried the puck into the Boston zone. Eddie Shore forced Morenz wide as Mondou raced for the front of the net. Morenz flung a back-hand shot toward goalie Tiny Thompson. It rebounded toward Mondou, who placed it in the net after only six minutes of play.

The visiting press thought Morenz had passed to Mondou, but the "rebound" was the more accurate call.[3] Although Mondou had made a name for himself with the Providence Reds as "*le Morenz de la Canado-Americaine,*"[4] his scoring at the NHL level was sporadic. With 199 regular season goals already to his credit, Morenz would not likely have purposely passed to Mondou—even when forced to his backhand.

It was a thrill for Mondou to be set up by Morenz to score a goal. Being a member of the Canadiens was already quite enough to provide his life with meaning. As he became accustomed to how his teammates lived the NHL life, he also learned how to be as famous.

He frequented Montreal's nightclubs after games. He joined Morenz in indulging in gambling, alcohol, and other "more elemental" hobbies available in Montreal.[5] Both Ernest LeMesurier and *La Presse* cartoonists often depicted Mondou with *les enthousiastes féminines*.[6] Montreal's press devoted many column inches to the seriousness of those female relationships and his persistent bachelorhood.

Mondou's emulation of his teammates didn't stop at indulging his appetite for female company. He chased wider attention. He dressed like Lepine. He drove one of the rarest cars in the country: a Jordan sedan. He also devoted himself year-round to his role as a local sports celebrity. Many community sports days in and around Montreal could count on an appearance by Mondou.[7]

Having watched Morenz up close, Mondou understood that his best life had to include youth, energy, and success—with the greatest of the three being youth. He succeeded. Around the time of Mondou's retirement at age 33, journalist Ralph Adams said that he "looks about twenty-four."[8]

After Mondou's opening goal in this game, the Bruins quickly scored two in response. Morenz, Mondou, and Rivers threw themselves into the effort to equalize. The Canadiens were unable to find the net again, and by the third period the "Flying Frenchmen" had become "the flagging Frenchmen."[9] George Owen ended Morenz's night with a hard high stick that wasn't penalized.

The game's conclusion was as dissatisfying as most static drawings of Morenz have proven to be. So many representations of him feature a disconcerting stillness, rather than the swiftness that fans adored. The most familiar painting of this nature hung for years in the Ste-Catherine Street lobby of the Forum. It depicted Morenz leaning slightly forward, in his full livery as a Canadien, stick in hand, apparently waiting for a puck. He is looking forward intently, but he is also posed, motionless, and alone.

His eyes are highlighted in many images. In the Forum portrait, they look straight ahead. Artists often tried to make his eyes appear to engage the viewer directly, but even that kind of imagined connection is distracting. The eyes cannot overcome the too-real absence of flight. By having him flexed in a faceoff crouch, the portrait has not even a sense of imminent explosiveness.

Two dimensions of pen ink or paint most often failed to evoke Morenz's dynamism. Sculpture too has often missed the mark in capturing Morenz's essence. A frieze of his face, or the full, forward-leaning figures cast from time to time suffer from the fact that the artwork still leaves him alone, without teammates, without opponents, and without a contest.[10]

There are only two known exceptions to the depiction of Howie Morenz as permanently young. One featured Howie Jr. as a teenager; the equal billing of the younger Howie in the drawing required an older-looking father.[11]

The second was being completed for the end of the coming playoffs. Artist M. Hugh Delaserre was already creating an imaginative painting of an aged Morenz, twenty years in the future but still playing hockey at the beginning of the 1950s.[12] The implicit message of that work was that so long as Howie Morenz could continue to play hockey, he would be young enough. Armand Mondou was present at the unveiling of that painting and understood it immediately.

Mondou made an effort to channel the essence of Morenz, reaching for homage and equivalence, without pretending to become a replacement. Through emulation, Mondou was the one who created an active, living representation of how it was the game that kept life vital, swift, and young.

Boston **2** at ***Canadiens*** **1**

Morenz: 1 assist

Game 31	GP	G	A	Pts	PiM	HG	AG	HA	AA	GWG	GWA
Season Total:	29	22	15	37	45	13	9	10	5	4	3

CHAPTER 32

Sunday, February 15, 1931

Canadiens vs. Americans in New York

Telling the Howie Morenz Story

IT WAS AN indirect way to get to New York City. With a week off in the middle of February, the Canadiens traveled to Lewiston, Maine, for an exhibition game. Arranged at the urging of Lewiston's Alderic "Bucky" Gaudette (an outfielder with the Montreal Royals baseball club), the team's visit promised to be a social highlight of the city's winter sport calendar.

As their special railcar rolled toward south-central Maine, the Canadiens spoke the way they learned when they first began to play hockey as boys. Their need to tell and to listen was persistent. See-saw discussions that fluttered between English and French storytelling were how they educated each other in the culture of the game.

On the way to Lewiston, Howie Morenz told rookie Art Lesieur about being on the ice when Georges Vezina played his last heroic period of hockey in goal for the Canadiens, just as Vezina could have told Morenz years before about the last period of hockey played by Bad Joe Hall. Those kinds of stories became advice about how to respect the history and traditions of the club and the game.

Those kinds of stories also drew the newer players into a fellowship with current and former players. The stories knit players into the "anecdotal pageant of the game." The stories became a cavalcade of cultural understanding.[1]

There were etiquettes and privileges attached. If Howie Morenz was in the room, he would be the only one who could tell a Howie Morenz story. They were unapologetically self-deprecating: he would not tell stories about how he outskated Eddie Shore in last year's Stanley Cup final, nor would he marvel about his jumping goal against Boston earlier in the season. Those stories would emerge later, from the men who witnessed his greatest triumphs.

When Morenz began in the NHL, this tradition taught him that his true legacy would eventually be measured by the number of stories he could create for others to tell. Long before the days of mass media and on-demand content, oral histories would become the storehouse and measure of his greatest contributions to the game.

While a newspaper writer might have collected Morenz's stories in a book, such compendiums didn't exist in his time. In 1931 the full-length player biography was still nearly a generation away. Dean Robinson's *Howie Morenz, Hockey's First Superstar*, the first proper Morenz biography, was a full half-century away. Instead, the only biographical monuments that he could expect would be the ones that he made the effort to erect himself, day by day, and game by game, in the minds of others.

On that Thursday in mid-February 1931, when he might have taken a night off in front of 1,800 strangers at the St. Dom's arena in Lewiston, Howie Morenz put on a show. In a half-hour scrimmage against the Maine All-Stars, and with a grin on his face, he helped Biddy Poulin of Lewiston enjoy his "life-long ambition" to play goal for the Montreal Canadiens.[2]

When the Canadiens retired to a post-game reception at the Lewiston Music and Literary Club, Morenz created even more memories. He spoke about the game as a relationship, an experience, as something he shared with the hockey fans and players of Lewiston, and which he hoped to enjoy again. He understood his task on that night was to create a memory for those in attendance, both on and off the ice.[3]

The next morning, the Canadiens made the short day trip to New York in advance of their Sunday night game at the Garden against the Americans. In the first twelve minutes of the game, Morenz brought the puck to the New York end, passed to Joliat who then in turn passed to Gagnon, who scored the first goal of the night.[4]

Morenz dominated the offense that night and was prominent defensively too. He started another goal midway through the second period, and then, near the end of the third, did something that the *Montreal Star* proposed was even more remarkable: "He grabbed the puck in front of his net, passed the Americans' forward line, shot the puck down the ice and jumped over both American defencemen. He staggered for a few seconds when he came down on the ice, but kept his balance and the puck and continued his drive to the net. [Goalie] Roy Worters, however, left the net, met him in front of it and saved a shot that otherwise would have been a goal. The applauding and cheering at the feat of Morenz is indescribable, even the Americans being amazed at his performance."[5]

Two storytellers in particular engaged with what would become Morenz's narrative legacy. The first was English-Canadian novelist Morley Callaghan, who in 1928 installed Morenz as a haunting image in his first published novel, *Strange Fugitive*.[6] Morenz became both an incident in the plot as well as a stirring metaphor exposing protagonist Harry Trotter's struggle for social acceptance and respect. Callaghan's inclusion of Morenz in the book, by name, acknowledged the significance of his cultural impact after just five years in the league.

Novelist Hugh MacLennan also used Morenz as a cultural touchstone, but in a slightly different way. In *Two Solitudes*, first published in 1945, the memory of Howie Morenz's play served as the explicit measure used by the novel's protagonist, Paul Tallard, for his own success as a man. Tallard measured the worth of his life's choices by comparing himself with the Morenz ideal, and reflected that his own pursuit of glory had happened in "a good world when hockey was important in it."[7]

Callaghan and MacLennan's ability to use Morenz as a metaphor or simply as a cultural marker in their stories demonstrated how pervasive the narrative of the Morenz life was understood and appreciated as significant, even to the world outside of hockey dressing rooms.

***Canadiens* 2** at NY Americans **0**

Morenz: 2 assists

Game 32	GP	G	A	Pts	PiM	HG	AG	HA	AA	GWG	GWA
Season Total:	30	22	17	39	45	13	9	10	7	4	1

CHAPTER 33

Tuesday, February 17, 1931

Canadiens vs. Maroons in Montreal

The Explosiveness of Howie Morenz

HOWIE MORENZ WAS affable on the street with friends and fans. He engaged happily with children. Even before he became a famous hockey player, he was generous enough to think about how to anonymously make some random, unknown youngster's day happier.

NHL owners, managers, teammates, opponents, and fans described Morenz as a gentle, sportsmanlike, and unassuming man—a *bon sport.*[1] When he knocked out four of Bun Cook's teeth with his stick, Cook is said to have commented, "It was just an accident. Howie wouldn't pull anything like that intentionally."[2]

Officials would say that if there were more Morenzes, refereeing would be a job for children.[3] He was portrayed by some as a man who neither showed meanness nor was ever stirred by thoughts of retaliation.

However, many also knew that there was turbulence in his soul. As a youth he would get angry and petulant with teammates. The young Morenz could be easily goaded into penalties that put him off the ice. He remained testy and aggressive when he arrived at the NHL.

In one of the first games of his debut season in Hamilton, he made a mixed impression upon the *Hamilton Herald*: "It's quite in order for a lad just out of the amateur ranks to show the paid men that he doesn't fear them, but it's not necessary to go around with a chip on his shoulder. He appeared to be in a scrappy mood against the Bengals. He carried his stick a bit too high."[4]

In his first Stanley Cup final during his rookie season, he arrived at the Cup-clinching game against Calgary with a cocky attitude. His first act, after assisting on what proved to be the winning goal, was stickwork that left Bernie Morris of the Tigers with a six-stitch cut to the head.[5]

By 1931 he had learned how to harness his anger, and sometimes his attitude. He would still smoulder from being roughed up, but was more calculating about how and when to respond. Nevertheless, in his eighth professional season, his temper remained part of who he was. The more aggressively he played, the more goals he scored. He remained willing to take the physical initiative against tough men like Eddie Shore. His penalty totals were consistently among the highest, but never *the* highest, on the team. Any change in his approach after eight seasons was that he was now often able to create and protect his own space as much by attitude and posture as by overt acts of violence.

He still oscillated between being a feeler and a thinker on the issue of violence. He sometimes claimed to have sworn off fighting—but always retained a willingness to retaliate. He could suddenly erupt with fury. He would fight back even if he wasn't very good at it, on or off the ice. Even as his violence had become more tactical, adversaries knew there was a real and continuing risk that Morenz would deliberately come after them violently.

No game in his career demonstrated this breadth of difference between his two images as this mid-February contest against the Montreal Maroons. It was both a peak and a valley in his career, and it all happened in less than one hour.

The evening began with an extra touch of brilliance as the Canadiens arrived on the ice in new, bright red sweaters. The teams launched themselves at each other, and Morenz was visible early. "Howie had worked like a maniac throughout the first half," wrote *La Presse*. "His sensational runs down the length of the rink were uninterrupted, but also unsuccessful."[6]

The game continued scoreless into the second period, when Morenz took a puck to the face off a Babe Siebert shot. Then Jack McVicar "accidentally" hit him in the head with his stick. Midway through the period, with the teams playing four skaters aside, Morenz unleashed an explosive shot from the Maroons' blueline, beating goalie Dave Kerr along the ice. The shot had travelled sixty-four feet, from blue line to goal line, startling a goaltender who had otherwise been playing very well.

The goal that gave the Canadiens their 1-0 lead restored Morenz's lead in the NHL scoring race. It was also the 200th regular-season goal of his professional career—in his 289th game.[7] No Canadien had ever scored 200 faster than that.[8] The goal showed him at his best.

The Maroons were in no mood to celebrate another Morenz milestone. As the game moved into the third period, Dave Trottier was matched against Morenz. Trottier had already mixed it up with Lepine, Gagnon, and Leduc. He was also the one who had pierced Morenz's lip with his stick just twelve days before.

An archetype of the checking forward, Trottier had an abrasive style. He was not shy about using his stick as a weapon. Six weeks earlier, Baz O'Meara of the *Star* suggested that Trottier should actually "chuck" some of his opponents "under the chin" more often.[9]

As the game moved into the final couple of minutes, Morenz pushed the play back down into the Maroons' end. Trottier chased. Referee Odie Cleghorn explained the violence that ensued: "Morenz was coming fast along the boards when Trottier made a lunge at him with a high stick, just missed him, but threw Morenz off balance and then caught him with a butt-end in the chin."[10] Morenz retaliated with a drive at Trottier; as the latter was falling, Morenz swung his stick and caught him in the mouth with the blade.

Players can be killed by stick swings to the head. Even the toughest of tough players have always viewed stick-swinging as violent.

Morenz's reputation for good-natured sportsmanship could tear. Some remembered his conscious violence earlier in the season in Philadelphia. Some remembered Trottier's provocation from February 5. Others remembered Morenz's own stick-swinging against Boston's George Owen a couple of years before, and with Charlie Conacher in the middle of January, if not the playoff chop against Calgary's Bernie Morris in 1924. This was Howie Morenz's game at its ugliest and most dangerous.

Tonight, with only a minute to go, he headed directly to the penalty box. Trottier followed, keeping one hand to his mouth as if he was either counting teeth or staunching the flow of blood. *La Presse*: "When Dave Trottier arrived, [Morenz] paid no attention, but suddenly, without warning, the [Maroon] threw himself at Morenz and started hitting him with both hands. Furious at this cowardly aggression, the Canadien defended himself as best he could and managed to land several solid blows on his opponent."[11]

Whatever led to that "rash of socking" on the penalty bench,[12] the fighting spread into the stands and back onto the ice.

Hockey was a tough game in 1931. Boston's Eddie Shore could knock Morenz out cold without disturbing their mutual sense of respectful and legitimate athletic competition. They could scrape each other with the shaft or butt ends of their sticks and shrug off the bloody consequences, even in a hotly contested playoff game. It was when Morenz faced an opponent whom he resented, or did not respect, that he chose violence.

The game was over. No one celebrated George Hainsworth's second shutout in a row. None of the writers even mentioned that Howie Morenz had reached the 200-goal plateau.

Maroons **0** at ***Canadiens* 2**

Morenz: 1 goal
1 penalty

Game 33	GP	G	A	Pts	PiM	HG	AG	HA	AA	GWG	GWA
Season Total:	31	23	17	40	47	14	9	10	7	5	4

CHAPTER 34

Thursday, February 19, 1931

Canadiens vs. Bruins in Boston

The Statistically Invisible Portion of the Morenz Game

EVEN THOUGH THERE was a quarter of the season still to play, Howie Morenz anticipated that the Thursday night game at the Boston Garden would be the NHL championship preview. Pundits and fans agreed.

The Canadiens had not won a regular season game at the Garden since the night the building opened on November 20, 1928 nor gained even a draw since January 22, 1929—more than two full seasons ago. While last spring's playoff result proved they could win here, their inability to show it in regular-season play was getting into their heads. Only hard work would change that.

Morenz had been carrying the Canadiens. With twenty-two of the team's ninety-nine goals, and seventeen assists, he had officially been involved in nearly forty percent of the Canadiens' scoring. He had played in thirty-one of the Canadiens' thirty-three games and had at least one scoring point in twenty-three of them. Ten of those twenty-three had been multi-point games. He had taken at least one penalty, and sometimes two, in fifteen different games. There had been just four games in which Morenz had not been statistically involved.

Cecil Hart did not evaluate Morenz's contribution by statistics. The real measure was simply to consider whether he was *involved*.

"Right from the top of the bell, the famed old clash started to sizzle," wrote the *Boston Post*. In the game's opening minute, the Canadiens' Marty Burke, "from a scrimmage outside of the defence, passed a clean forward right onto the great Morenz, anchored a few yards out from Tiny [Thompson] with not a Bruin covering." Thompson quickly dove out, and Morenz was unable to take a shot.[1]

The Bruins responded immediately. Marty Barry eluded Morenz before splitting the defence and scoring the game's first goal. The *Post* identified Morenz as the one who prevented the Canadiens from falling into their habitual Boston funk: "Taking the burden mostly on his own shoulders, the wizard of the ice, Howie Morenz, dashed hither and non [sic] in his most spectacular manner and his presence on the ice meant everything in the poison line to the Bruins."[2]

When Dit Clapper took a penalty for tripping, Morenz stayed on the ice for the power play. He pursued the puck into a corner against Eddie Shore, stealing the puck and taking a shot on goal that Thompson deflected.

Morenz soon took advantage of Shore again and made another shot on goalie Thompson, "who kicked fast to barely save," reported the *Post*.[3]

The physical competition between Morenz and Shore became the chief delight of the opening period. The "galloping cowboy" Shore had arrived in the NHL in 1924, a year after Morenz.[4] They were the same age. Shore set penalty records from the time of his arrival, gave and received wounds, ended careers of opponents on slight pretexts, and freely slugged goal judges and referees. His physical stamina also became legendary. Shore was often expected to play sixty minutes a game. His game drew on raw athletic capability, physical endurance, and meting out vicious punishments on his opponents.

Morenz penned his own appreciation of Shore in 1928, calling him "the best defensive player on the line—as long as he stays on the ice, though. He's tough and he's very hard to beat, and you can bet I know a thing or two about that."[5]

The respect was mutual. Shore once said of Morenz, "He is not only a great forward offensively, but a powerful defensive factor on the team, because he skates back at such cyclonic pace. The work of the Canadiens defence is made much easier because Morenz is always breaking up attacks before they are really formulated."[6]

Joe Primeau knew that style, saying that his most vivid memory of Morenz required only two words: "constant pressure." Primeau said Morenz "never gave the other centre player a breather," and that "he never seemed to ease up and it was always top speed for him going both ways . . . always dangerous."[7]

Hockey fans everywhere wanted to see how Morenz and Shore performed against each other.

In the first period of this Boston game, Morenz made two electrifying rushes on goal that nonetheless produced no goals. As the period was ending, with Dit Clapper off for a penalty, Morenz leaped through the air to get behind the defence. Cooney Wieland caught up and knocked him sideways off his skates to save a shot on goal. Jumping up after his tumble, Morenz again secured the puck. The *Montreal Star*: "He started from his own blue line, swept down the right around the Boston net, down the left around his own net and back to centre ice without having the puck taken from him. This was the highlight of the game, which kept the crowd in a continual uproar."[8]

Morenz remained in charge into the second period. Shore blocked one of his shots with his shin. Midway through the period, when Shore had been penalized for charging, Cecil Hart gave Nick Wasnie his first shift of the night alongside Morenz and Joliat. Joliat passed to Wasnie, who shot the puck along the ice. It caromed off defenceman Red Beattie's skate and fluked into the net behind a surprised Thompson to make the score 1-1.

Where had Morenz been during that sequence? The editors of the *Boston Globe* chose to reproduce a photo, fortuitously taken at the very moment of Wasnie's score.[9] The photo captured Beattie about six feet in front of the Boston goal, the deepest man back for the Bruins other than Thompson. There is no one between Wasnie and the goaltender, but probably little room to find an angle that would allow him to score. Morenz is on Wasnie's left, heading eagerly for the open side of the net near the far goalpost. The only thing preventing Morenz from converting Wasnie's pass into a shot was Beattie.

The photo also shows the Boston defenceman with his back to both the puck and Wasnie as he focused on blocking Morenz from getting to the net. The puck arrived while Beattie was chest to chest with Morenz, and just as Morenz was pushing Beattie's skates into the path of the puck.[10] Even though

Morenz didn't log an assist on the goal, it was his ability to shape the game no matter where he was on the ice that made the goal—and showed how imperfect statistics can be.

Morenz expressed the view, perhaps original for the time, that "attack is the best form of defence."[11] That uncanny ability to anticipate opportunities freed Morenz from having any real "position." Aurèle Joliat explained the effect this had: "Howie didn't pay much attention to positional hockey; he took any open ice and it was up to his mates to scramble for their own spots or get caught in traffic jams he caused."[12]

The game continued knotted at 1 into the third period, and continued to percolate around Morenz. Shore stole the puck from him in the Bruins' end and led the home team to a flurry of chances at the Canadiens' goal. Burke was penalized for tripping Shore, who was injured on the play. The Bruins continued to crowd the Canadiens' net. George Owen seemed ready to score, if it hadn't been for a spirited defence mounted by Morenz. Leduc, and a splayed Hainsworth.

Morenz's appearance in the middle of the defensive action, his seeming ubiquity, gave opponents like Earl Siebert a sense of inevitability about his play. The *Gazette*: "Half the time Howie was carrying it up the ice, and then he'd be the first one back to check. When Howie was on the ice, it seemed like he had the puck all night."[13]

Shore returned from his knee injury, breaking up a Canadiens rush, and then started one of his own that ended in another pile-up at the mouth of Hainsworth's goal. Morenz plucked the puck out of that chaos and carried the play back up the ice. He passed to Mondou, but Mondou's attempt at a shot caught Shore in the arm, forcing him yet again to leave the ice with an injury.

With about eight minutes remaining, Shore returned. Again it was Shore who pushed the play into the Canadiens' end. Pit Lepine disrupted the initial drive but Shore recovered the puck with an interception defending a Canadien three-on-two.

Wil Larochelle took a tripping penalty. Morenz returned to the ice as Boston sent four men inside the Canadiens' blueline for a final assault. Morenz broke through and made a pass to Burke, who managed a last shot on goal before the bell sounded for ten minutes of overtime.

Morenz started the overtime on the bench, but with a penalty to Lepine, come on again. The *Gazette* said he "held the fort." The overtime tension continued with a minute to go when the *Gazette* reported how Morenz "jumped a Bruin sortie and started down the left." He appeared to have "clear sailing," but as he reached his blue line he was checked by Chapman into the penalty box door, which sprang open and caught Howie for a fall.[14] After a pause that allowed his head to clear, Morenz finished the game on the ice.

The struggle between Shore and Morenz played out shift by shift, period by period, game by game. It kept audiences coming back. Who would prevail this time, and who the next? Tonight, both Morenz and Shore had been at the centre of the contest and both had been ravaged by it, even though both had been nearly invisible to the statisticians. Their duel represented the entire game and concluded in a draw.

***Canadiens* 1** at Boston **1**

Morenz: Nothing

Game 34	GP	G	A	Pts	PiM	HG	AG	HA	AA	GWG	GWA
Season Total:	32	23	17	40	47	14	9	10	7	5	4

CHAPTER 35

Saturday, February 21, 1931

Canadiens vs. Americans in Montreal

The Integrity of the Morenz Game

THE CANADIENS WERE a winning team. The idea that they would fix a game and purposely lose was anathema. And yet, there was an awareness through the day on Saturday that the Canadiens might have an incentive to "lie down" in their home game against the visiting New York Americans.[1]

The Canadiens had not lost to the Americans all season. The Canadiens had outscored their opponents 50-21 in their last sixteen games and given up just one goal in their last 240 minutes of hockey. The Americans had been shut out ten times in their first thirty-five games, most recently just six days ago by these same Canadiens. New York owner Willliam V. "Big Bill" Dwyer, along with every rational hockey observer, understood there was no favourable statistical angle for the Americans against the Canadiens. The Americans would be lucky to hold the Canadiens close.

Not many people in 1931 would have been too surprised, or too scandalized, by the idea that Dwyer's Americans might be looking for an angle. Gambling was a habit for hockey professionals. For the last decade, match-fixing had been a recurring feature on the sports pages.

There were a number of classic risk factors for a fix, the most significant being the fact that "Big Bill" needed his NHL team to provide more than a cover for his liquor and gambling businesses. He needed actual cash flow.

A win against the Canadiens would brighten the chances of some playoff ticket revenue—in addition to whatever he could make on the long odds for tonight's game.

Dwyer's alleged efforts at match-fixing were normally associated with games at New York's Madison Square Garden. The chance to fix an out-of-town game, against a team with such a disproportionate statistical advantage, would have been a different kind of undertaking. Even attempting it might have seemed foolhardy—except that Dwyer was becoming increasingly known for his fits of gambling recklessness.

There were known gamblers on the Canadiens. Howie Morenz was one of them. Even though it is always difficult to tell the difference between an unsuccessful effort and a deliberate failure, Peter Gzowski's suggestion that "no breath of gambling scandal ever touched his life" was kind—but inaccurate.[2]

Morenz arrived in the NHL fully aware of the opportunities gambling offered. In his teens he had been smuggled into a rink in Kitchener to mislead the city's gamblers about his availability. When he emerged on the ice, he changed the odds simply by showing up.

He had also gambled as a teenager himself. When he joined the Canadiens he quickly became adept at betting on horses. There were several stories of his approach to track betting. Some recount catastrophic losses in advance of his wedding in 1926, and others recount a day of salvation when he tore up his tickets on a loser, but then recovered them under a grandstand when the results were changed.

Those stories were all of a piece with the man Leo Dandurand said had "the soul of a gambler. He'd take all sorts of gambling chances in hockey games, and he was inclined to do the same in money matters."[3] Mike Rodden of the *Globe* said Morenz "craved action and gloried in flirting with danger."[4]

Speculations around Morenz turned to suspicion when he was either absent or didn't play up to (admittedly huge) expectations. There were anonymous grumbles about his unexpected failure to score in the 1928 playoffs, with losers assuming that he had been paid to throw the series.[5]

There is also a superficially innocent story about Morenz attempting, on ice, to arrange a result with Toronto's Joe Primeau rather than playing out the final few seconds of a match.[6] That Morenz would even contemplate that kind of arrangement, let alone invite an opponent to share responsibility for it, justifies close analysis of his behaviour, and this game against the Americans in particular.

The game started with a surprise. After just three minutes, Morenz came onto the ice for a faceoff just to the left of the Canadiens' goal. Instead of running away with the puck like he usually did, he let the Americans' Normie Himes snatch it. With only two strides to the net, Himes went around Hainsworth and scored a goal.

That same period, the Americans' Johnny Sheppard scored two goals in forty-five seconds, both with little to no interference from the Canadiens. Sheppard had only scored three goals in his first thirty-five games, and now suddenly had two more on the sudden against the Canadiens.

More incredulity followed: Joliat shot the puck over the top of an open net at the Americans' end. Then New York's Billy Burch scored. After less than eleven minutes of play, the Americans had a 4-0 lead at the Forum.

Expressions of disgust and disbelief erupted from every fan in the building. Some yelled "Fake!" and walked out.[7] Neither the furious fans nor the press felt any of this was happenstance. It appeared clumsily obvious that the Canadiens had arranged to give the game to the Americans. The *Herald* wrote, "The Doubting Thomases smell a rat."[8]

Howie Morenz heard the contempt in the crowd's jeers. He saw the sense of betrayal in the fans' faces. In addition to the weak and the porous defence, Morenz understood it all began with him losing that early faceoff to Normie Himes. The fans had seen him let Himes skate away alone with the puck. Their disdain was as personal as it was raw.

Although Aurèle Joliat was morally equivocal about dealing with gamblers, both he and Morenz understood that allowing the outcome of a game to be arranged in advance would corrupt the whole concept of the game as a contest of skill and effort. Games required an uncertain outcome. Competitive uncertainty was the unique selling proposition of professional sport. In order for any league to survive, its games had to have that integrity.

While the English word "game" had a flexible meaning, in French the phrase *être en jeu* meant "to gamble," and the phrase *être dans le jeu* meant only to be "in on the game." The English and French ideas of integrity, of something being *intègre*, were unequivocal and identical. To speak of the "integrity of the game" required something moral. Halfway through the first period, it had quickly become obvious that instead, this was an odd one.

Howie Morenz knew how improbable the first period seemed. He understood how his own history exposed him to moral suspicion. He accepted that the legitimacy of the night's result would come down to an evaluation of his play alone.

The *Montreal Star*'s Andy O'Brien knew this was out of character. He saw Morenz as a player who never shirked from effort, even when a game had become a lost cause: "It mattered not if it was a bad night and Canadiens were trailing by a seemingly impossible margin," he wrote. "Then Howie would decide to go it alone. He'd dig and fight and hurtle and crash and come back for more until the whole team took fire."[9]

Morenz needed to clear any whiff of a fix from the arena. So less than a minute after Burch's goal, Morenz netted a goal for the Canadiens. After another ninety seconds, he scored again. Georges Mantha scored a third before the end of the first period. But that response, while a relief to the local fans, sowed even more doubt according to the *Gazette*: "Their revolutionary change of form was as remarkable as their victory."[10]

Morenz missed a chance to score his third goal in the second period, but Mondou succeeded. With the game now tied and the dubious start perhaps forgotten, Morenz created the go-ahead goal by Gagnon at the start of the third period. Finally, with just over a minute left, the crowd was electrified as Morenz stole the puck inside the Canadiens' zone and set up Joliat for the nail-in-the-coffin goal.

Morenz, the *nonpareil*, again wore the hero's mantle. He had salvaged the game, his own reputation, and that of his team. Elmer Ferguson proposed that he had also rescued the reputation of the league. Morenz was very near the apex of his career that night. It was his biggest scoring night of his season. He and the Canadiens had done the improbable after having appeared to do the inexcusable.

It is difficult to fully understand this game without challenging our inherent bias. As Declan Hill wrote in his book *Fix*, about soccer and organized crime: "We do not want to believe that human frailty lurks within them. We do not want to believe that they, who can do what we cannot, would stoop to sully themselves. We do not want to believe, when so much in our lives is so corrupt, that the garden of innocence that is supposed to be sport could also be corrupt."[11]

Morenz's ultimate performance in this game seems to confirm his personal integrity. He did not limit himself to a gesture, a token nod to legitimate effort. He made the athletic and mental commitment to produce his greatest offensive display of the season. Consistent superiority had become the minimum required to keep his reputation above suspicion.

NY Americans **4** at ***Canadiens*** **6**

Morenz: 2 goals
2 assists

Game 35	GP	G	A	Pts	PiM	HG	AG	HA	AA	GWG	GWA
Season Total:	33	25	19	44	47	16	9	12	7	5	5

CHAPTER 36

Thursday, February 26, 1931

Canadiens vs. Falcons in Montreal

Wil Larochelle, Yves Gabias, and the Healing Power of Morenz

ON FEBRUARY 24, 1931, eleven-year-old Yves Gabias was up early to help serve Mass at his parish church in St-Henri and then dashed off to school. A CNR freight train crossing Vinet Street had been too slow for the impatient child. He tried to clamber over a coupling between two of the moving cars, but in his haste he slipped. The train crushed both legs. Doctors amputated one leg above the knee, the other above the ankle.

Yves was a fond admirer of Howie Morenz. The boy and his father, a city councillor and one-time deputy mayor, had seen him play live at the Forum. On February 27, the night after the game against Detroit—which of course Yves had missed—M'sieur Morenz came to visit him at the Western Hospital (now the Montreal Children's Hospital) before the Canadien left for Toronto.[1]

The boy in the bed was about as old as Morenz had been when his own legs were showered in scalding water in a household kitchen accident. The pain had been terrible but the idea of being unable to move his legs, stand, walk, or skate had been intolerable. Yves's plight seemed worse than intolerable.

Morenz recovered because he always believed that he was a skater. His recovery was supported by his mother's devotion. He returned to the ice and surpassed even his own lofty expectations during his recovery. Yves was going to have a harder time.

The visit was more spiritual than verbal. Expectations were tempered: not much more than a touch, a handshake, a souvenir game puck from the night before, a photograph for comfort and courage. That would be enough. Yet the photo appeared to wrap them all in a shroud—the visitors apparently reluctant to make eye contact with the boy and his missing limbs.

The boy wanted to know how the Canadiens had managed against the Detroit Falcons. Morenz recalled how Wil Larochelle had missed four games earlier in the season with a separated shoulder and been unable to even shoot.[2] Larochelle had been hospitalized too, but last night had assisted on one goal and scored another. The Canadiens won 5-0 for their first victory over the Falcons this season. It was as hopeful a story as Morenz could think to offer.

The boy's eyes asked eagerly for more, about M'sieur Morenz himself. What had he done? His father had already stirred the boy's imagination with coverage from *La Presse*, about how well Morenz had played despite "missing unprotected goals on one occasion and coming within an inch of scoring on another."[3]

The boy's assumptive admiration did nothing to alleviate the frustration that Morenz still felt about those unsuccessful chances and the repeated rough play from Stan McCabe, Ebbie Goodfellow, and stick-wielding Leroy Goldsworthy.

Even if the visit to Gabias had originally been engineered by Dandurand as a publicity event, afterwards other hospitalized children in Ontario and Quebec began to ask for Morenz's presence at their bedsides, too. Morenz knew that Babe Ruth had done this kind of thing, but it was his own visit that established the demand for hockey players to visit children in Canadian hospitals. It became a tradition within the Canadiens' family and an enduring part of broader professional hockey culture.

Morenz struggled with this kind of role. He understood the adulation of crowds and the fleeting handshakes with anonymous individuals. The hospital visit required something different. It required his attendance and attention. He was going to the fan instead of the fan coming to him. It was a visit to one fan, not to a group.

There was no hockey rink on which he could wow the kid with skills or tricks. Hockey, the most important thing in his own life, seemed utterly unimportant when contrasted with what was keeping the child in hospital. Talking with Yves, he could not even explain how he scored or assisted on a goal, or successfully fought off and overcame an opponent.

In a game he had been well-paid to play, Morenz failed to meet every opportunity offered to him. The *Montreal Herald* spared nothing in comparing his effort against the Falcons with his lack of accomplishment: "Seldom has Morenz fought harder to get a goal or two than last night, but ill-luck dogged his trail from beginning to end. Times without number he went blazing in on the Detroit defence, only to have his shot blocked or deflected . . . Howie couldn't even amass an assist."[4]

Morenz felt the chasm between the boy's admiration and the reality of last night's failures on the ice. Hockey itself seemed meaningless compared to the plight of a boy who had just lost two legs at the age of eleven.

Morenz did not yet recognize that by taking his own time to create a relationship with a sick child, he was doing two important things: acknowledging the child as a person important enough for a hockey superstar to visit, and giving the child a connection to the normal, healthy world outside the hospital's walls. He didn't need to be a physician to fill those needs.

Double goal scorer Wil Larochelle understood, based on his own hospital experience, how isolating health care facilities could be. Visits couldn't so much cheer up the afflicted as keep them connected with a life that was not controlled by their illness.

Larochelle also knew what Morenz could offer in a relationship. As his teammate, Larochelle measured his career in terms of when the two of them played together. Morenz had provided the fire that lit his own career. In recalling that career later, Larochelle would unconsciously erase whole NHL seasons of effort, remembering only the times when he played with Morenz.

Like Gabias, Larochelle believed that Howie Morenz was the greatest hockey player he had ever known. Like Gabias, Larochelle also regarded Morenz as more than a hockey player. For each of them, Morenz was a spiritual, energizing force and a connection to a larger world.

Morenz's relationships with some of his teammates, like Marty Burke and Wil Larochelle, should have made him more alert to this positive promise of celebrity. In late February 1931, his limited capacity for that kind of self-awareness confined him. He still believed his legacy would be based entirely on what he was able to do on the ice.

Detroit **0** at ***Canadiens* 5**

Morenz: 1 penalty

Game 36	GP	G	A	Pts	PiM	HG	AG	HA	AA	GWG	GWA
Season Total:	34	25	19	44	49	16	9	12	7	5	5

CHAPTER 37

Saturday, February 28, 1931

Canadiens vs. Maple Leafs in Toronto

Howie Morenz and the Role of Officials

IT WAS TIME for a show.

Howie Morenz had not had a standout game in Toronto all season. The Canadiens had lost both previous matchups. He hadn't registered a point. This time his father was coming from Stratford to see the game.

Mary would be able to listen to the game on the radio back in Montreal. There was a chance that she and Howie Jr. would eventually be able to watch the game, too. The Canadian Movietone Company and Fox Films were attempting to make the first live, sound film recording of a professional hockey game.

The game started out brutally. Morenz took on both Red Horner and Lionel Conacher at the same time, only to land on his back. He had separate exchanges with Harvey Jackon and Joe Primeau. The *Toronto Star* said the Leafs were "too busy trying to crash Frenchmen to play real hockey."[1]

Morenz got his first point on a mid-period power play, wading through a no-man's land of conflict described by *La Petit Journal*: "Morenz is put down by Horner and Conacher and the referees say nothing. Morenz retaliates with a 'six inch' and the crowd roars . . . Morenz grabs the puck and throws a shot ten feet from the goal that Chabot stops, but Georges Mantha takes the return and scores."[2]

Minutes later, after a goal by the Leafs and after referee Bert Corbeau had put the Canadiens two men short, Charlie Conacher flopped Morenz and was given a penalty.

Morenz managed to get himself alone in front of goalie Lorne Chabot, but again the opportunity was lost. *Le Petit Journal*: "Morenz, alone in front of Chabot, had his legs lifted by Horner and the referees still said nothing."[3]

The tone changed at the start of the second period. The sound system burst with "Happy Days Are Here Again." The audience sang along and gave a rare salute to Morenz, who was treated to huge applause. The Canadiens scored again.

The beckoning silver screen had become an opportunity for Morenz to dash across centre stage with a permanence that teletype and telegraph machines, even radio broadcasts, would never be able to provide. The *Toronto Star* described the star turn that Howie made while the cameras rolled at the start of the third period:

> *Less than two minutes after the period opened, Morenz pulled the best individual play of the night when he took the puck from mid-ice and walked through the Leaf defence and leaped in on Chabot in the Leaf nets. Shappy [Chabot] shadow boxed with the Canadiens star but was finally beaten with Morenz's last shift. Morenz pulled the puck away from him as he dove and lifted it into the net waist high.*[4]

The Toronto defence had been caught watching.

What no one knew at that point was that the film experiment was unsuccessful due to lighting issues.[5] Like almost every other effort to capture Howie Morenz with motion picture technologies, this experiment would fail. Some short segments of film do exist that catch him in motion, skating and playing the game. Each is frustratingly brief and of disappointingly poor quality.

The Canadiens continued to play with unruffled competence through the middle of the third period. At one point the players themselves "hoisted the flag of truce" to rescue Andy Blair after he accidentally spiked himself on his own stick.[6]

Bert Corbeau, the night's lead referee, was a former member of Les Canadiens. He had been traded away by the club to the Hamilton Tigers, before ending his NHL career in 1927 with four seasons as a member of the Toronto St. Pats and Maple Leafs. *La Presse* had openly questioned his impartiality in the past, and tonight *Le Petit Journal*'s P. de St-Georges described him as possessing "*une hostilité ouverte aux Canadiens*," offering the example of "Blair hooks Morenz, who is about to fall between Corbeau's legas . . . Corbeau still can't see him."[7]

A Canadiens' game was a rare assignment for him, not so much because of his previous team affiliations, but because of his antipathy for the Canadiens. In December Corbeau had kicked Lepine out of one game for arguing and then given Joliat a major for "defiance" in another. He harboured a specific dislike for Morenz. Morenz had embarrassed Corbeau in their very first on-ice encounter as players. Nevertheless, he had been given the whistle for tonight's contest.

Corbeau's time as a player had earned him high penalty minutes. He was generally known for letting rough play go. The Leafs took advantage of that tolerance.

With about five minutes remaining, Charlie Conacher crashed Marty Burke into the boards. While being penalized for that, he started a fight with Burke as well. Conacher then held Burke while Jackson hit him—as did some members of the crowd. Other paying customers prevented Burke's teammates from coming to his rescue. Soon the whole arena was hurling programs, newspapers, and peanuts onto the ice, including a knife apparently directed at Corbeau.

Corbeau claimed not to have been disturbed by the fights, the knife, or the capacity crowd that had exploded around him, but he was locked inside a pressure-cooker. There was so much garbage on the ice that play had to be delayed several times. When play did resume, Conacher sat on top of the boards at the penalty bench, with at least one leg dangling inside the playing area, waiting to get back on. He was buoyed by the rabid braying of the fans around him.

What happened next was the game's turning point for the *Toronto Star*: "On the next Leaf rush Burke met Jackson's dash on the nets with a cross check—and the fat was in the fire. Jackson came back with a cleancut right that dropped Burke on his back. The referees rushed in and broke up the fight and gave both players major penalties."[8]

Some thought the encounter deserved no more than coincidental roughing or cross-checking minors, but the major penalty rendered the Canadiens' best defenceman unavailable for the rest of the third period. Corbeau and fellow referee Vic Wagner threatened both Jackson and Burke with match penalties if they continued their feud. As soon as play resumed, Conacher and Jackson attacked Burke on the penalty bench. The *Toronto Star* witnessed how "a policeman behind the bench grabbed at the battling trio and over went the bench and down all four went in a heap."[9]

The fighting continued for several minutes before the game was again stopped, and the warring factions were separated. It was not the first time Charlie Conacher decided to insert himself into a fight in the penalty bench, nor the last time that Toronto management would encourage the tactic. In addition to the players, several fans and three policemen were eventually counted as participants in the brawl. When the referees arrived at the penalty bench, Corbeau gave match penalties to both Jackson and Burke, but did not penalize Conacher at all.

Conacher was back on the ice about ten seconds later and rushed down the boards. He dodged a check from Morenz and took a shot on goal, stopped by Hainsworth. "A second later," wrote the *Gazette*, "Corbeau blew his whistle and waved the Canadien centre off the ice for an offense that was not apparent. The timer's clock showed some three to four minutes to go."[10]

Morenz had been penalized "for taking a clout at a Leaf player."[11] As he recited the Morenz penalty to the timekeeper, he observed a fan approaching, insulting him about his call. Morenz glanced toward the approaching fan with sudden apprehension. It was his own father!

William Frederick Morenz was, in his time, as well-known as Walter Gretzky would be in his. Howie remembered the legendary stories about Sprague and Odie Cleghorn's unhinged father Bill. Howie's own father had also beaten him, once badly enough that "he didn't go to school for a day or two."[12] The two had apparently reconciled, but as William advanced on Corbeau, Howie couldn't predict what would happen next. Corbeau imperiously directed the police to remove the man from the arena.

It must have infuriated Corbeau that no one paid attention to his edict. Instead, several fans sided with the angry dad emerging from the crowd and then made fun of Corbeau for trying to kick Howie's father out of the Arena Gardens. Whether the moment was the result of William Morenz's own fame, or the crowd's contempt for Corbeau, is hard to discern. Corbeau had simply lost control of his game.

Corbeau's penalty call on Morenz still had real consequences. Morenz squinted at the clock and asked the timer how much time was left in the game. He was told four minutes. He glowered across the ice but didn't say a word. In the two minutes that followed, Sylvio Mantha was penalized, and on the two-man Leaf advantage both Charlie Conacher and Ace Bailey scored within eighteen seconds of each other to tie the game at 3.

The Gazette: "Leafs, flushed with excitement, again tore in anxious to score the winning goal. Out of the flurry, Albert Leduc broke away clear. At the same time Morenz jumped out of the penalty box and the two were speeding through the centre area with no one except Chabot in front of them when the gong sounded the end of sixty minutes, while the clock above indicated some two minutes to go."[13]

Howie Morenz, knowing how volatile Corbeau could be, shook his head in frustration. A watch was thrown into the vicinity of referee Vic Wagner. Morenz shrugged. There were ten minutes of overtime to play and he was determined to dominate the Leafs.

Four minutes into overtime, Morenz and Joliat broke out of their own zone and Morenz scored. "The play left the Leaf defence anchored," wrote the *Toronto Star*, "and Morenz had all the time he wanted to feint Chabot out of position while he buried the bootheel. His effort on that goal was outstanding."[14]

When Gagnon put Canadiens up 5-3 a minute later, the win appeared to be within grasp again—until an Andy Blair shot caromed off Morenz into the net behind Hainsworth.[15] With an inevitability that seemed to transfix the Canadiens, Conacher scored just forty seconds later to tie the game once again.

Up in the stands, the *Gazette*'s L.S.B. Shapiro was already contemplating a futuristic idea, writing, "A sound moving picture record of the entire game was taken. It will be interesting to watch the film unwind in slow motion during some of the strategic moments."[16]

Another game at the Arena had ended in disappointment for the Canadiens. Morenz's effort was ruined by home-ice shenanigans and another dubious performance by Bert Corbeau at the expense of the Canadiens. Corbeau's failures were as much a fundamental betrayal of the official's role as the timekeepers' fiddling with the game clock. *Le Petit Journal* concluded that "Corbeau's negligence led to the Tricolore's defeat in a game they had won three times."[17]

On Monday, NHL president Calder imposed the same $15 fine on Conacher that he imposed on Jackson and Burke for the penalty-box fracas. The league also ensured that Corbeau never officiated another game involving these Canadiens again.

***Canadiens* 5** at Toronto **5**

Morenz: 2 goals
1 assist
1 penalty

Game 37	GP	G	A	Pts	PiM	HG	AG	HA	AA	GWG	GWA
Season Total:	35	27	20	47	51	16	11	12	8	5	5

CHAPTER 38

Tuesday, March 3, 1931

Canadiens vs. Senators in Ottawa

Her Half-Life as Mrs. Howie Morenz

MARY LOUISE STEWART was born in early 1908. By the time she was a teenager, she was known as Mary Louise McKay. At the age of seventeen, she had become enraptured by a young hockey player, an emergent star playing in the National Hockey League. She had turned his head as well. With her mother and stepfather's permission, Mary Louise made a giddy plunge into adulthood and marriage shortly after she turned eighteen.

When Howie Morenz first signed with the Canadiens, the local clergy in Stratford complained about the team "luring an underage boy to the wicked city of Montreal."[1] It was true. Morenz arrived in Montreal as the city's youth were being swept up into the carnal indulgences of the 1920s, and he dove in happily. His temptations were pursued under the morally suspect guidance of fellow Canadien Sprague Cleghorn: gambler, card player, adulterer, and team captain.

Mary was smitten with Howie for the same reasons Zelda had been drawn into the orbit of novelist and jazz-age chronicler F. Scott Fitzgerald. Howie was Mary's opportunity to enter a world of fame, excess, and high places that she could not otherwise have hoped to enter. On the first day of summer 1926, while still under legal age, Mary married twenty-three-year-old Howie and became Mary Louise Morenz.[2]

On March 1, 1927, just a little short of nine months of marriage, she became the mother of a boy named after her husband. Still a few months short of her nineteenth birthday, she was ready to embark on a life at the centre of everyone else's attention. A raucous lifestyle of youth, energy, sex, and alcohol beckoned to them both. Now, as their fifth hockey season as husband and wife moved into its final month, they remained in the vortex of that whirlwind.

Mary attended her husband's games at the Forum, leaning forward on the boards at rinkside in Box 22, without any glass or netting to protect her. She had a front-row seat for the crowd's roars and jumped and yelled with everyone as he dashed across the ice. It was in the heady moments when her husband rode the roars of thousands, his legs driving him into, around, and beyond his opponents to reach his target, that she knew she really had become a Morenz. Sometimes she even brought young Howie to the games.

Mary's connections to the game were such an ecstatic, enthusiastic, and ceaseless celebration that it was quite impossible to notice how, or when, it might ever come to an end. Neither she nor Howie ever thought of that. After all, in February 1931 she was still only twenty-two.

She could not avoid the fact that she had become a hockey wife, a fate coldly described in Leo LeSieur's new "*Ah! le hockey!*" song of early 1931:

My wife is a little woman
Just as she should be
She is pretty, kind and gentle
She has no faults
But when the hockey season comes
There's nothing better for her to do
Than to look after the house.[3]

That song described the other half of her life, when the Canadiens were away. Except for the odd road trip to Toronto to visit with her in-laws, she stayed at home. She could still read about her husband in the newspapers and sometimes hear him talked about on the radio. She could savour the solitary experience of brief separations and the excitement and anticipation of his returns home.

Home was where Mary stayed for the Canadiens' mid-week trip to Ottawa on March 3, 1931. It wasn't much of a road trip at all, since the Canadiens would be travelling back to Montreal immediately after the game. As the Canadiens took to the ice at the sparsely attended Auditorium, the Senators decided that they would neutralize Morenz by whatever means necessary.

Art Smith tumbled Morenz three times in as many minutes during the first period—hurtfully, but legally. Nevertheless, Morenz set up the best chance of the period, and also vaulted himself into one of his famous end-to-end rushes. He circled the Senator net with a flourish but was blocked at the finish by goalie Alec Connell.

The game continued in the same vein through the second period. The Canadiens opened a lead on a goal by Leduc, when Morenz suffered perhaps his hardest crushing of the night. He tried to split the Senators' defence, but was hit hard enough by both defencemen that the impact even broke his stick. Morenz appeared to fade after that. Cecil Hart decided to be cautious, and Morenz's shifts became fewer and shorter as the game moved to its conclusion.

The game in Ottawa ended with a confused pile-up around the Canadiens' net. A puck that wandered into the net was called off as a goal, sealing the Senators' twenty-sixth loss in thirty-eight games. Ottawa had been focused on stopping Morenz, but tonight he had not been necessary for a Canadiens' victory. It was another unnoticed step in the descent from who he had been: still skilled, still dangerous, but neither overpowering nor essential.

At home, Mary was about to become pregnant again. The idle days of indulgence, made possible with a grandmother babysitting for a single child, would soon evaporate like the morning dew.

Morenz's true heart was committed to playing hockey, a devotion also fed by love. That meant that for half of every hockey season he was out of town. When he was home, hockey still consumed him every day.

Decades later Guy Lafleur spoke of the same tension: "Hockey is the most important thing in my life. It even comes before my family, my wife, my son." Lafleur said he hadn't worked like a madman for fifteen years with the goal of being a model husband, or an exemplary father, "but to be a great hockey player."[4]

Igor Dmitriev, once the coach of the Soviet Red Army team, went further, expecting that his players accept that their relationship with the game was as exclusive as a marriage: "The artist has to be locked up for a month or so to get in the frame of mind to produce his masterpiece. If hockey is to be treated as the creation of a masterpiece, one must live with, and in, hockey. One has to refuse everything else."[5]

That reality meant that however much he loved Mary, Howie had to let go of her to pursue a more insistent love, the pursuit of which was essential to making him feel whole. Nancy Marshall, who was married to famous Montreal baseball player (Mike Marshall of the Expos), said that sports wives had to "avoid the fairy tale and recognize the reality," and that they should "make lives for themselves outside of their husbands' careers . . . The same ego that enables husbands to perform well on the field may prevent them from performing well in their relationships."[6]

The fates that had promised so much to Mary McKay at the age of seventeen had completely defined her as a Morenz by the age of nineteen, and drained her of any real ability to establish a persona of her own. Mrs. Howie Morenz was now fully bound up in the rhythms of her husband's life. Instead of hitching a ride toward brighter skies, hand in hand across the cosmos with Howie Morenz, Mary was on the cusp of becoming Gloria of F. Scott Fitzgerald's *The Beautiful and Damned* instead.

***Canadiens* 1** at Ottawa **0**

Morenz: Nothing

Game 38	GP	G	A	Pts	PiM	HG	AG	HA	AA	GWG	GWA
Season Total:	36	27	20	47	51	16	11	12	8	5	5

CHAPTER 39

Thursday, March 5, 1931

Canadiens vs. Rangers in Montreal

The Icarus Mission of Howie Morenz

DURING THE LATE winter of 1917, a young Dr. Norman Bethune arrived in Stratford, Ontario, to provide vacation relief for Dr Lorne Robertson. Robertson was about to take on the presidency of the town's midget hockey team and its emergent star, fifteen-year-old Howie Morenz. It is unknown if Bethune was called upon to treat Morenz, or even if he met the kid hockey player.

Now, about fourteen years later, Bethune was working as a surgeon in Montreal, struggling with the final separation from his wife, Frances. His forty-first birthday had just passed on March 3, and Bethune was still searching for his life's purpose. He would sometimes distract himself from that anguish by going to the hockey games. If he had seen this particular Forum game against the Rangers, it would have been both a challenge and a prophecy for him.

Early in the first period, Howie Morenz provided an extravagant and almost defiant demonstration of his athletic prowess, described by the *Montreal Herald* as a flash of brilliance:

> *Morenz broke away from the Canadien end and blazed up the left wing. [Joe] Jerwa moved over to meet him, but Morenz leaped nimbly, flipped the puck ahead, cleared Jerwa's feet in his stride but stumbled as if he might fall. But with a great*

> *effort he regained his balance, swerved sharply to avoid the thrusting stick of Bill Cook, and swinging like a flash around this obstacle, whipped a backhand shot that travelled like a bullet and tore across [goalie John Ross] Roach's ankles.*[1]

His rush caused the crowd to jerk to its feet even amidst his initial charge. Once every fan was standing, they burst into an exclamation of louder, exultant hollering when the puck snapped into the back of the net. It was as if Morenz had conducted a choral accompaniment to his own performance.[2]

It was a sound new to "Buddy" Elmer Maracle. The New York Ranger was playing his first—and only—career NHL game at the Montreal Forum. Growing up in Brantford but playing in North Bay, Ontario, Maracle had never heard that kind of thunder. He heard it now, six minutes into this game in Montreal. It was awesome. Maracle had heard about Morenz, but seeing him up close, and with the aural accompaniment, was indeed different.

Morenz was able to *think* the game faster than his opponents. Even as he rushed the puck, sorting through opportunities, he transformed ideas into performance faster than opponents could respond. Tonight, when he had been off-balance, and perhaps entirely off his skates by the end, Morenz still retained enough core strength to propel the puck into the Ranger net as he tumbled to the ice.

Late in the opening period Morenz was chasing down a Ranger counterattack being carried by Bun Cook. Cook fell and took Morenz down with him. In trying to free himself of the moving entanglement, Morenz then fell over sideways, wrenching his leg. It was an "accident," but the inevitable had, in an instant, finally caught up with him.[2]

The most exciting player on the ice limped off to the Canadiens' dressing room. The Forum crowd was silent in suspense over cause, blame, and consequence. Every hockey player in the rink already understood what they had seen. Dr. Sir Henry Gray left his seat for the dressing room as soon as he saw Morenz's response to the tumble.

Morenz didn't return to the Canadiens' bench for the start of the second period. Instead, he was lying on the trainer's table surrounded by four men: trainers Eddie Dufour and Jim McKenna, as well as the two physicians: Sir Henry Gray and John Corrigan.

On a couple of occasions during the season, Morenz had been subdued in the course of play. Each time, McKenna had been able to get him back on the ice: on December 30 when Morenz returned to score the tying goal late against the Maroons, and in Philadelphia on January 13, when he had done much the same. This situation looked worse.

Sir Henry arrived in Montreal in 1923 with emergency medicine experience acquired in the trenches of the First World War. Dr. Corrigan was the team's second travelling physician. As the second period began, both doctors continued to examine Morenz's right ankle. In time, they agreed that the injury appeared to be a sprain rather than a break. What they didn't know was the severity of that sprain.

The game was tied 1-1 when Morenz had been injured. The Rangers took the lead early in the second. The doctors were cautious about him returning to play. There was no compelling reason to do so other than that Morenz insisted on doing so.

Morenz hobbled back to the player's bench and onto the ice for the start of the third period. The crowd rose spontaneously in admiration. Their welcoming roar sounded like the medicine he needed. It restored his faith in himself.

Dr. Bethune would have been impressed by the emergency medical aid that had so quickly repaired Morenz and readied him, like a soldier, to return to the fight. Some doubted that it had really been Morenz's choice to strap up, but his commitment to such an effort had been part of his character ever since he was a teen. His own junior history hinted that he was willing to, and could, play through pain. Scientists would eventually learn that athletes were less sensitive to pain than non-athletes—and particularly on game days.

The results of Dr. Gray's efforts at wrapping the ankle were not encouraging. Morenz was slower, and the *Montreal Herald* reported that he "was plainly distressed."[3] His appearance was short, at best limited to boosting morale. Despite his belief that he could contribute, the early cheers soon became shouts of apprehension, disappointment, and disapproval as the third period continued. The Canadiens lost a home game for only the third time that season.

Morenz's commitment to soldiering on was as cultural and philosophical as Norman Bethune's commitment to medicine. For both men, staying on the job was how you demonstrated you were still devoted to the cause. Bethune would articulate that credo for himself during his tour through the Spanish

Civil War and later—and most famously—in China. "Every leader starts by first leading himself," said Bethune.[4] It was an attitude that could prove fatal.

The initial injury report suggested that Morenz needed only a brief rest before returning to the team.[5] But it got worse. Morenz was kept in Dr. Gray's hospital and did not make the team's trip to Detroit. The playoffs, and his chance for a repeat Stanley Cup triumph, were just three weeks away.

Rangers 2 at ***Canadiens* 1**

Morenz: 1 goal

Game 39	GP	G	A	Pts	PiM	HG	AG	HA	AA	GWG	GWA
Season Total:	37	28	20	48	51	17	11	12	8	5	5

CHAPTER 40

Sunday, March 8, 1931

Canadiens vs. Falcons in Detroit

The Friendship of Aurèle Joliat

WHILE MORENZ WAS in a Montreal hospital, the Sunday night game in Detroit began with Pit Lepine taking his place. Wil Larochelle replaced the injured Johnny Gagnon on right wing. Aurèle Joliat, the little guy in the black cap, was the only one in his usual place on the left.

There was a peripatetic poet from Selkirk, Ontario, who eked out a living in the early 1930s by writing and performing popular verse and selling collections for his audiences to take home. Wilson Pugsley MacDonald traveled on a circuit primarily through southwestern Ontario and the states bordering the Great Lakes. His opportunity to see Aurèle Joliat came when he and the Canadiens overlapped in Detroit.

MacDonald watched Joliat trail a rush toward the Detroit end which produced a loose puck, then pick it up to score the game's first goal.

A couplet formed instantly in MacDonald's mind:

De rest of players seem asleep
As he was going pas'.

Joliat had a reputation for predicting how a play could unfold. Morenz himself was in awe, once saying of his friend: "Personally, I used to call him the brainiest player in captivity, with the most knowledge of hockey. And although he has had to overcome the difficulties of a lack of weight and small stature, he makes everyone forget all that, both himself and others, with his ultra-fast thinking and quick, supple and marvellous manner of execution."[1]

The writer Ron McAllister recalled how Joliat's "dizzy pin-wheel turns and spectacular pirouettes" brought "ballet to the hockey arenas of the thirties."[2] MacDonald saw all of that too:

Garcon! he's slippery; oui, oui—
Lak' leetle piece of soap. . . .

He weegle jus' lak' fish-worm do
Wen eet ees on a hook;
An' wen he pass de beeg defence
Dey have one seely look.

Speed, changes in pace, shifts and weaves, and pivots were integral to how Joliat skated and played. No other player in the league had such an ability to dodge the opposition.

Having victimized the Falcons' defenceman Harvey Rockburn for inattention on the opening goal, Joliat then induced him into a penalty midway through the period. The Canadiens used the power play to extend their lead to 2-0. That would complete the scoring, but not Joliat's work.

Joliat had arrived in Detroit on a mission to prevent Ebbie Goodfellow from overtaking the narrow lead that Morenz worked all season to build in the NHL scoring race. As a consequence, he spent much of the second and third periods by getting in the Falcons' way:

He's small but 'e ees bothersome
Lak' ceender in de heye.

He showed off his ability to stickhandle around and through the best of the league's defences. He controlled the puck:

He's good on poke-heem-check, he is;
He's better on attack

The *Gazette* described Joliat's shot "as deadly as that of any player in the game."[3] MacDonald understood:

. . . An wen he shoot de wind from her
Eet knock de hompire down.

Falcon goaltender Dolly Dolson felt its impact late in the second, when Joliat led a four-man thrust and made a shot on goal from fifteen feet away.

Joliat emerged for the third period with visible intensity. He became as dominant as MacDonald imagined him to be:

Morenz he go lak' one beeg storm;
Syl Mantha's strong and fat.
Dere all ver' good, but none ees quite
So good as Joliat.

He subdued the notorious "hanger een hees eye" to avoid any chance of a penalty that would give an advantage to the Falcons. The Canadiens took the win at 2-0.

"Aurèle Joliat played one of his best games of the season last night," wrote *La Presse*. "In fine form, Joliat gave a masterful display, constantly keeping the Detroit defence on its toes and breaking up a host of the home side's rallies. Joliat took very little rest throughout the game, remaining on the ice for most of the time." Not only that, *La Presse* continued, Joliat was so "sensational, he made us forget the absence of the famous Towie [*sic*]."[4]

Performances like this were perhaps why, for more than a generation, Joliat's admirers viewed him on par with the great Morenz.

Ron McAllister evaluated the relationship between the two men the same way, writing that the two "functioned as a *unit.* It is impossible to estimate the smaller man's contribution to the meteoric career of the 'Stratford Streak' and it is fitting that their names stand together for posterity in Hockey's Hall of Fame."[5]

As a co-operative meshing of uncommon skills involving an Englishman and a Frenchman, their relationship was unique. The fact that they claimed to have been best of friends was notable as well.[6]

Their chemistry was not always demonstrable with neat statistics. Even this season, Joliat was credited with assisting on just three of Morenz's twenty-seven goals to that point. Of the thirteen goals that Joliat scored that season, Morenz was similarly credited with assisting on only three.

Joliat's own word was more important than the statistics and opinions of non-players. Never shy about enlarging the dimensions of his own legend, Joliat consistently deferred to his famous teammate from Stratford, calling him "the greatest hockey player of all time. I've never seen another player get fans off their seats the way Morenz could. From what I've seen of 'Rocket' Richard, he was like the owl from the opposing club's blue line, watching for his chance to go up and score. But Morenz was going to carry the puck to the net from one end of the ice to the other and I saw him go through the opposition three times in a row to go and score."[7]

Besides, Albert Laberge had already seen the fans decide who was superior during training camp that November: "Joliat wows the crowd with his zig-zagging runs, while Morenz goes 100 miles an hour."[8]

***Canadiens* 2** at Detroit **0**

Morenz: Did not play

Game 40	GP	G	A	Pts	PiM	HG	AG	HA	AA	GWG	GWA
Season Total:	37	28	20	48	51	17	11	12	8	5	5

CHAPTER 41

Tuesday, March 10, 1931

Canadiens vs. Black Hawks in Montreal

Rehearsal and Preview: His Evolving Game

WHILE THE CANADIENS played Sunday night in Detroit, Howie Morenz was lying in his Montreal hospital bed after a day full of visitors and well-wishers. Dr. Gray's prescription of rest was an attempt to repair injured ankle ligaments. For hockey purposes, they had a week to fix damage that might normally take six.

On Tuesday, Dr. Gray released Morenz to watch the game against the Black Hawks. It seemed a generous concession, given that the ankle still ached when he shuffled across his hospital room. He made his way awkwardly along the Forum promenade that evening, leaning heavily on his crutches and visiting with fans. When the game began, he sat with his teammates on the Canadien bench, watching intently.

The game he had learned on the frozen river was a game of possession and dispossession. Whole afternoons of playing keep-away created his ability to monopolize the puck, to stickhandle through opponents, to skate through or away from an opposing defence line, all the while trying to create yet another way to score. After Victoria coach Lester Patrick's innovative strategy of cycling a succession of players against him in the Cup playoffs of 1925, the "no substitution" style of play had been exhausted.

Over the next five years teams began to promote "combination play," a liberated passing style of game that moved the puck toward a particular scorer, often through diagrammed plays. Those teams—such as the Rangers, Maroons, and Bruins—were the ones who began winning Cups.

The Canadiens persisted with their game of opportunity created through possession and imagination. They opened the scoring midway through the first period, before Chicago tied it in the first minute of the second. By the midpoint of the third, the score was still stalled at ones. With fifteen minutes gone, no one was taking command.

Morenz understood that regardless of the system, strategy, or style, a player needed to make the emotional and physical commitment to score each goal, to create or exploit any advantage. Despite the Canadiens' loss in the Cup final series of 1925, he recalled how he had scored three goals in the Canadiens' only win in that series.[1] Six years later, he still had the confidence that he could put the puck in the net himself.

He had also always been capable of playing the passing, set-up game. He learned it as a teenager, though it took a bitter loss in the Memorial Cup to crystallize the lesson.[2] Butch Kelterborn, one of his long-time Stratford wingers, remembered Morenz playing a generous passing game. Teammate Toe Blake rejected out of hand any suggestion that Morenz was ever a "hog."[3]

A few weeks earlier in Boston, Morenz was asked if he would get a kick out of leading the league in scoring. "Sure I would," he replied. "I'd rather lead the league by virtue of making a large number of assists than do it by scoring goals. When you get the goals without the assists it looks as if you were trying to hog the puck."[4]

He had already set an NHL record for assists during the 1927–28 season. This season his assist numbers had exploded upwards: from the ten recognized in 1929–30 to a new high of twenty, with three games left to play.

Since he had joined the Canadiens, he was regularly involved in more than thirty per cent of the Canadiens' scoring. He achieved a career-best participation of 43.9 percent of the Canadiens' offence in 1927–28.[5] That season was better than Rocket Richard, Jean Béliveau, Bernie Geoffrion, or even Guy Lafleur achieved in each of their best years.[6] This year, having played only thirty-seven of the team's forty-one games, his forty-seven points with three games remaining in the regular season still represented a touch above 39.1 percent participation in the 120 total goals scored by the Canadiens before tonight's puck-drop.

The Canadiens' trouble tonight was that Morenz wasn't on the ice. Sitting on the bench, he rocked forward against the lip of the boards in an impatient rhythm. He was restless. The Canadiens' style required one or two of their best offensive players to create the result. The Hawks expected their relative freshness, based on strictly timed player rotation would eventually produce a strategic advantage. There had been no finish for either club.

With less than four minutes to go, two Hawks broke through centre. Marty Burke intercepted the puck and turned the play back. Burke ripped a shot at the chest of Gardiner, who moved the puck away. But Nick Wasnie was suddenly there and ready for the opportunity. He made a lightning shot into the empty net.[7]

Morenz was ignited by Wasnie's moment of anticipation and finish. Forgetting about his injured knee, he leaped upwards with the same excitement as any fan. That moment of exhilaration passed the instant he landed—when the pain of his injury flooded back. He lowered himself gingerly to the bench and contemplated his return to his hospital bed.

Chicago **1** at ***Canadiens*** **2**

Morenz: Did not play

Game 41	GP	G	A	Pts	PiM	HG	AG	HA	AA	GWG	GWA
Season Total:	37	28	20	48	51	17	11	12	8	5	5

CHAPTER 42

Thursday, March 12, 1931

Canadiens vs. Maroons in Montreal

The Most Valuable Apparition

FREED FROM DR. GRAY'S hospital on Wednesday and tossing aside his crutches in favour of a cane, Howie Morenz was murmuring about being "fully recovered" for Thursday's contest with the Maroons.[1] He arrived at the Forum intending to play, but Cecil Hart once again confined him to a spectator's role.

The Canadiens had already claimed the Kendall Cup—just as often known as the "Kennedy Cup"—named in honour of the Canadiens' first owner, George Kennedy (his last name at birth was Kendall). It was a local trophy awarded to the winner of the season series between the Canadiens and Maroons. This year's triumph represented Morenz's fourth of five wins since the trophy's inauguration in 1926.

The Canadiens had also already secured the fifth O'Brien Cup of Morenz's career, for first-place finishers in the NHL's International Division.[2] The "O'Brien" carried the name of a man who had never taken the time to watch a hockey game. It was originally donated to the precursor of the NHL in 1910 by Senator M. J. O'Brien in honour of his son, Ambrose. Like the Kendall, the O'Brien trophy had no space for the names of anyone who had actually earned it—much like the Prince of Wales Trophy.[3]

Morenz had already won the Prince of Wales trophy twice: first because of the Canadiens' victory at the opening of Madison Square Garden in New York on December 15, 1925, and their designation as the NHL champions in 1924–25 (before the New York game, and despite the better record of the striking Hamilton Tigers).

The Maroons needed to win this game, being only a single point ahead of the New York Americans for the final playoff spot in the International Division. They began aggressively. The *Montreal Star* wrote that Morenz could be observed on the players' bench beside Cecil Hart, and had the coach "black and blue from nudges in the ribs and arms."[4]

No matter how much he swayed in his seat, kicked against the boards, and slammed his cane, Morenz felt helpless. The Canadiens seemed helpless, too. They fell behind in the second period. Morenz alternated standing and sitting but never stopped glaring out at the ice. "At one time," wrote the *Star*, "it looked as though he was ready to jump over the side using the hooked end of the cane he was carrying, to heave a long shot or two goalwards just to relieve the tension."[5]

Every teammate, every opponent, and the whole of the crowd knew what he could do. Yet his absence from the ice seemed to demonstrate how inherently temporary hockey greatness could be.

The great monuments of the First World War that were being created during Howie's hockey career memorialized the names of the dead and lost heroes in stone. The NHL had barely started the process of establishing its own silvery pageant of individual awards when Morenz joined the league. There were few opportunities to permanently stamp his name on the game.

His closest peer in his rookie season (1923–24) was Red Green of the Hamilton Tigers. Green had eleven goals and twenty penalty minutes on a last-place team against Morenz's thirteen goals, three assists, and twenty penalty minutes on the league championship and Stanley Cup team. But there was no Calder Cup rookie award until 1937.

During Morenz's original Stanley Cup campaign in 1924, he counted seven goals and two assists in six undefeated games—leading all scorers as a rookie. He scored three game-winning goals in the six games. He counted one hat-trick as well as another two-goal game. But there was no Conn Smythe Trophy for most valuable playoff performer until 1965.[6]

Montreal jewellers Mappin & Webb took the initiative to provide Morenz with the equivalent of both the Calder and Conn Smythe in the spring of 1924. The firm gave the *bébé de la ligue* a trophy carrying the following misspelt inscription (translated from the original French):

Presented by Mappin & Webb to Morentz, as a reward for his good efforts during the final games for the NHL championship, 1923-1924.[7]

Howie Morenz scored the most goals in the league during the 1927–28 season (thirty-three). The first impromptu award for that feat went to Ace Bailey in March 1929, but there was no Rocket Richard Trophy for top goal scorer until 1999.

In the same 1927–28 season, Morenz also captured the NHL scoring championship for racking up the most points. He was in position to capture the scoring championship for a second time this season, despite missing five games. But there was no Art Ross Trophy for being the leading points scorer in the NHL until the 1947–48 season.

Morenz did establish a firm claim to the Hart Trophy. Originally donated by coach Cecil Hart's father David, it had been awarded since 1924 to the NHL player most valuable to his team during the regular season. It provided a tangible recognition of the player who most made his teammates better. No player could predict the outcome of the Hart voting. Morenz won it for the first time in 1928 and was about to win it again this season.[8]

The paucity of individual awards at the time ensured that he would focus on the only trophy where his name could appear, and where he had some control of the outcome: the Stanley Cup itself.

Morenz continued to sit grimly through his teammates' mistakes and frustrations in the second period. Everyone saw how they missed his speed, as well as his ability to organize their attack. *La Presse* said, "The Canadiens were a shadow of themselves. The club seemed to be completely disorganized and their teamwork was lacking throughout the evening."[9]

Albert Laberge noticed the true significance of Morenz's absence: "It was easy to see at any moment that the great Howie Morenz was not there."[10] Without Morenz in the line-up, the Canadiens had no soul.

Despite his accomplishments, Morenz had no serious expectation that his career would get any post-career recognition. There were no statues of hockey players then. The game's culture did not yet include the naming of parks, streets, and arenas in a player's honour. League and community "halls of fame" were unknown. No one except family curated shrines containing personal awards, keepsakes of equipment, and jersey collections. There were no banners in arenas.

When the Canadiens emerged for the third period, Morenz was leaning forward anxiously at the boards, following every turn of play. When the Maroons scored a short-handed goal less than a minute into the period to make it 3-0, Morenz flung himself back from the boards, stood without help from his cane, and marched away. Some thought he was consumed with anger.

The writers preparing to vote for the 1931 Hart Trophy soon saw Morenz reappear on the upper concourse of the Forum. He had lifted himself from enforced idleness to a place where he felt he could have some better influence on the game. The *Montreal Star*: "Independent witnesses state he must have worked out his injured leg a quarter of a mile during the period at least."[11]

In 1927–28 Howie Morenz had convinced the voting media that he deserved the Hart Trophy by dominating the league offensively. Tonight the writers could not rid themselves of the vision of him marching around the upper concourse of the Forum. Still obviously injured, but also bursting with a sparking, frustrated energy, as he urged his teammates on against their city rivals.

Morenz had taken himself to a place where everyone could see him. The fans and his teammates and the Maroons could hear every bellow he shouted down at the ice. He commanded better efforts from his teammates. More important, he commanded everyone's attention without even being on the ice.

If Howie Morenz's legacy had been limited simply to how well he played on the ice, he may not be any more important today than Bill Cook. Morenz's place in the pantheon of the game has endured among elite players as it did even among the casual fans of his own day, because he influenced how others played.[12] Tonight, he confirmed to everyone that he would become the first of the ghosts, the first of *les fantomes du Forum*.[13]

His teammates actually rallied in response to Morenz's commands from the stands. The Maroons glanced up from time to time, relieved that tonight they did not have to face his particular fury on the ice. They still took five penalties, and five penalty-kills, to contain the Canadiens until the final whistle.

In the last days of the 1930–31 season, those same writers who watched his third-period display made Morenz the clear winner of the Hart Trophy for the second time in his career. Having already gained elite status among his peers, he made winning the NHL's most valuable player award a personal, signature accomplishment.

The ability of Morenz to affect the play of the Canadiens from beyond the ice surface might have been accounted as ephemeral inspiration, but the more general belief in Montreal was that his influence was spiritual, even supernatural. Roch Carrier explained the idea while describing Rocket Richard's first goal at the Forum:

> *The sparse crowd at the Forum is on its feet. They have recognized the Messiah they've been hoping for. They howl their pleasure. In seats at the rear, old fans with white hair under their flat caps remember Howie Morenz, the greatest hockey player of all time. The old champion is at the Forum. He saw this goal. Morenz has heard the clamour. He remembers. He knows that the crowd doesn't make mistakes.*[14]

Despite the pain from his injury, Morenz remained furious—at the Canadiens' defeat, at the missed scoring opportunities, and at his inability to play. He waited until the crowd cleared from the building, then made his way to the office of Forum manager Art Cayford.

***Canadiens* 0** at Maroons **3**

Morenz: Did not play

Game 42	GP	G	A	Pts	PiM	HG	AG	HA	AA	GWG	GWA
Season Total:	37	28	20	48	51	17	11	12	8	5	5

CHAPTER 43

Saturday, March 14, 1931

Canadiens vs. Senators in Montreal

The Best Instincts of Howie Morenz

HOWIE MORENZ'S POST-GAME visit to Forum manager Art Cayford after the Maroons game Thursday night resulted in personal ice time on Friday morning. In addition to testing his recovering ankle, he spent time lining up pucks and shooting them at the new, inch-thick unbreakable glass enclosure at the north end.[1]

As he tried different angles, speeds, distances, and power, the tell-tale tink-tink-tink sounds of contact echoed through the empty building. He began to learn how the puck might react after contact—how it would carom, turn, ride, or bounce back to the ice, based on different kinds of shots. Morenz wanted to understand how to make this new glass part of his game.

The difference between just having a superior aptitude for the game, and continuing to be its most valuable player, was this corresponding willingness—eight years into his professional career—to continue to imagine the game differently and to put in the hard work to stay ahead of his opponents.

Morenz had not been pegged as the most likely to succeed by his coach in Mitchell. In Stratford there had been another kid, from New Hamburg, by the name of Berger. Both Morenz and referee Bobby Hewitson thought Berger had been better.[2]

Throughout his career, Morenz remained modest enough to know that without that work ethic and some good fortune, he would never have become the player he was. He also knew, as an aging player, that he still needed to put in that work.

He had some powerful professional incentives to play on Saturday night. Being out on the ice was a way to calm his anxiety. After a week of bed rest without skating, he needed to restore game fitness. He needed to work out against actual competition before the playoffs. He also needed to protect his slim four-point lead over the Falcons' Ebbie Goodfellow in the scoring race.

Cecil Hart watched Morenz's skating with more interest than his puck play that Friday morning. He had been inclined to continue to let Morenz rest and heal, but respected that his star knew his own body better than anyone else. If Morenz accepted the judgment of others about whether he could play, he would have abandoned control of his own destiny. Morenz had earned the privilege of making this decision. He was prepared. A terse media release late Friday night announced that he would be in uniform on Saturday. Hart's only real choices in coaching Morenz were whether to use him as a starter or a substitute.

Howie's second-most favourite task as the most famous hockey player in Canada called for his attention on Saturday morning. He arrived at Eaton's to sign autographs and to give away his souvenir picture. Three thousand kids invaded the Montreal department store. These were his purest fans, the ones he enjoyed the most.

Armand Jokisen at *L'Illustration Nouvelle* believed that this was the kind of event that would fuse him with the game in their imaginations: "He was a role model for young people. Who hasn't seen a toddler on the city's ice rinks, in the streets, dressed in the tricolor sweater with the now famous number 7 on the back?"[3]

As he had done in Lewiston, with Yves Gabias at the hospital, and now at Eaton's, he made each personal encounter seem unique and genuine. As the kids crowded him out of his own news photo, he took time to speak with any child who came near.

He enhanced this fan relationship-building with random acts of generosity: giving away his sticks, signing others, encouraging Eddie Dufour to pass along the club's worn equipment to fathers and sons who couldn't afford their own, and offering those precious moments of his time on the streets and in the hospitals of Montreal.

Hugh MacLennan understood how youngsters' lives were affected by witnessing Morenz in his prime at the Forum. In *Two Solitudes,* protagonist Paul Tallard remarks: "I guess it was the first professional game I ever saw. I was sixteen. Joliat, Morenz and Boucher were playing. After that I was willing to slave eight hours a day training just on the chance of being half as good as they were."[4]

Without a younger brother of his own, Morenz approached every one of his young fans as if each of them might become just that. The kids certainly responded to him that way. They wrote letters asking him to visit them in hospital or to meet him when he travelled out to Trois Rivières and Chicoutimi on exhibition tours. They sent him get-well cards. Once, some kids walked two hours to visit with him in the hospital, where Morenz chatted with them for another three. Kids were part of every public hockey event of his NHL career.

At the same time, he understood that he owed each of the kids something more. He owed them effort and performance on the ice. As Claude Larochelle expressed it, in commenting on Guy Lafleur: "Extolled to the skies by his adoring public, Guy was already imbued with the feeling of responsibility . . . He put everything he had into the kind of performance he wanted to deliver on the ice." Larochelle said Lafleur had never heard of Howie Morenz, "but he behaved in the identical fashion of the man who belonged to the Canadiens' legendary past."[5]

There was another unusual demand on his time before that Saturday night game. An hour before the puck dropped, he was interviewed live on the CKAC radio station. He found the interview stressful, both in terms of its expectation for comment, while disrupting his focus on the start of the game. It was going to become an unavoidable part of his new game-day routine. Over the next week, he was scheduled to participate in three early mornings of talk radio on CFCF and then return to CKAC as a guest announcer for the Aylmer Musical Line-up.

That night he was not in the starting lineup, and the crowd waited respectfully until he actually stepped into the game before bursting into cheers. In his first two minutes on the ice, he scored with what the *Gazette* called "a rising shot that actually caught [goalie Alec] Connell napping."[6]

The Senators tied the game on a goal by Bill Touhey. With just over a minute left in the opening period, Senator Art Gagné managed to evade

Morenz and score with a fast backhand shot. Morenz was stung by losing such an obvious step to Gagné. It was an omen.

The game was tied in the second period. Morenz not only lost two good chances to make amends for his earlier miscue on the Gagne goal, but missed his own open net chance on a set-up from Wil Larochelle. There was a slight atonement when he assisted on Larochelle's go-ahead goal with about fourteen minutes gone in the second period, but the teams were tied at 3 after forty minutes.

While Morenz had played the first two periods somewhat like his usual self, by the third he found it increasingly difficult to maintain the game's pace. His infirmity was evident enough that Senator Joe Lamb held back on their faceoffs. The *Herald* inferred that "he did not wish to inflict further injury on Morenz's still-painful ankle."[7] As time passed, Morenz's ice time dwindled even more.

The Forum's out-of-town scoreboard showed that the Bruins and Falcons had also gone to overtime. Ebbie Goodfellow had an assist on Detroit's second goal, and in overtime scored one and assisted on another. He finished the night just two points behind Morenz for the overall scoring lead. Morenz would have to play better against the Quakers in the season-ending game. Happily, that was still a week away.

Ottawa **3** at ***Canadiens* 3**

Morenz: 1 goal
1 assist

Game 43	GP	G	A	Pts	PiM	HG	AG	HA	AA	GWG	GWA
Season Total:	38	29	20	49	51	18	11	12	8	5	5

CHAPTER 44

Saturday, March 21, 1931

Canadiens vs. Quakers in Montreal

His Best Shot

THE FINAL GAME for the league's most inept team ever was in Montreal, against Howie Morenz and the first-place Canadiens. Some of the Philadelphia Quakers may have seen the French press describing the game as more of a "practice" for the Canadiens. More may have realized they were likely playing their last NHL game. A few may have hoped to help Detroit's Ebbie Goodfellow, a fellow Ottawan, overtake Morenz for the scoring championship.

Resentments began erupting from the Quakers during the warm-up. Crowding the Canadiens' net early, they opened the scoring. With about five minutes left in the second period, the game was tied 1-1. For nearly two full periods, these Quakers had made Howie Morenz nearly invisible.

But suddenly he was open, leading a rush with Gagnon to his right. Fifteen feet away from goalie Wilf Cude, Morenz fired a forceful shot. Cude took it on the chin and collapsed "like a lump to the ice, like a boxer collapsing to the floor," wrote *La Presse*.[1] Morenz was first to rush to his side, just before the Quaker was carried away to be revived by the Canadiens' medical staff. Officials called the end of the period early, while the ice-keepers came out to scrape Cude's congealing blood from the rink's surface.

Morenz had a reputation for injuring goaltenders, sometimes even ending their careers.

His shots were commonly described as weapons. Maroons goalie Dave Kerr said Morenz's shot had "the same effect as a bomb dropped in the middle of a party."[2] Others likened it to a "cannonball," or a "torpedo," with the puck arriving at its destination with "thudding," or "stunning force." Players who saw it regularly, including Eddie Shore, spoke of it "travelling like a bullet."[3] Americans' goalie Roy Worters evaluated Howie's wrist shot as heavier than even the mid-century NHL slapshot.[4]

That power came in part from how Morenz would use his stick. Instead of merely sweeping the puck like many of his contemporaries, hockey historian Stephen Cole says that Morenz leaned down into the puck and "put all of himself into a shot, bowing the shaft of his stick before letting the puck fly."[5]

Joe Choquette made Morenz's sticks by hand, using ash sourced in Quebec's Eastern Townships for the shaft. Hickory and elm from nearby Brockville, Ontario, were used for the blade. The ash came from only younger, straight-grained wood, which ordinarily was capable of withstanding a lot of abuse. Unfortunately, the lighter shaft tended to break when slashed against a target, or when hacked by another player—as would happen on faceoffs. Morenz was not dissuaded from his preference. Instead, according to Choquette he set a trend: "Howie Morenz was the first man to use a light stick. He was such a great player that everybody copied him."[6]

With the light, straight-grained elm, he leveraged his own strength by leaning down on the stick, creating torque, and used the reactive spring of the wood to supercharge the release against the puck with a characteristic snap.[7] The physics of the technique sometimes caused him to shatter his own sticks, and sometimes snap the shaft of an opponent's stick with an erupting shot. Whether forehand or backhand, he had the ability to turn that flex in the stick shaft, and the snap of his wrists, into sizzling puck speed.

His shots stymied goaltenders. They often remained motionless, mesmerized, hypnotized, or simply bewildered. He could make the puck behave unpredictably even after it left his stick. He could make it go straight, curve, or even flutter up and down like a knuckleball.[8] More disconcerting for goaltenders, Morenz could effectively render his shot invisible. Game reports regularly described goaltenders unable to actually see his shots even when they should have. Whether forced to guess about where the puck would be going, or unable to react, opposing goaltenders often did not move at all.

"Babe" Dye, a prolific scorer himself, remarked how even among the league's best shooters, Morenz "stands alone in his ability to get the puck away while in full flight."[9] He would shoot from unexpected places like centre ice, or just inside the blue line, even though he preferred to be between ten and fifteen feet in front of the net.

Morenz exploited yet another advantage that distressed goaltenders: ambidexterity. Joseph C. Nichols of the *New York Times* wrote, "Like most outstanding players, Morenz prefers to carry the stick left-handed, but he is at no disadvantage when forced to wield it from the right side. His ability to shoot from any angle with blinding speed has made him the most feared forward on the ice."[10]

His shots hurt goalies in many ways. Play was often paused to allow a goaltender to recover from injury, if they could. Just a season earlier, a Morenz shot gashed the low forehead of the Maroons' Clint Benedict and caused the goalie's nose to disintegrate.[11] Howie's own son saw it as a definitive characteristic of his father's offensive power:

> *How he travels!*
> *How he goes!*
> *How he socks*
> *The goaler's nose!*
> *Howie!*[12]

"Praying Benny" was an experienced, four-time Stanley Cup winner when his face was on the wrong end of a Morenz shot in January 1929. The blast put him out for seven weeks, but his NHL career only lasted two more games. Now the same kind of shot appeared to have done incalculable damage to a nineteen-year-old rookie, playing goal for a terrible hockey team in a nothing game.

Early in 1931, *Le petit journal* described Howie's development of the "bean puck," similar to or modelled on the "bean ball" pitch in baseball. Both were designed to appear directed at the target's head, creating a fear that would provide strategic advantages and opportunities later in the game.[13]

Had the head-shot or head-scare been intentional? It was just the second time Morenz faced this rookie. Having been stoned by Cude in their first encounter, Morenz would still have been trying to figure out how to play him.

There were those who faulted Cude for jumping on the shot. Yet if he had remained still, it might have barrelled into the kid's eyes or forehead.

Cude wanted to return after regaining consciousness. He started to march out toward the ice surface but collapsed en route. The pause in the game continued until he regained consciousness again.

Morenz seemed to shrug off the Benedict accident. Now he was reminded how dangerous the game could be—because of his own potential to create serious harm. The Cude situation was going to radically change his own approach to the game. The same skills that distinguished him as a unique and elite player also condemned him as dangerous.

It was, perhaps, some consolation that Cude was revived a second time and against physician's advice re-emerged to take his place in the Quaker net. Morenz immediately assisted on a Johnny Gagnon goal to give the Canadiens the lead for the first time. The Quakers tied it five minutes later, and then took a lead themselves. Georges Mantha tied it up again, but the Quakers took another lead.

The Canadiens' game stalled. The *Montreal Star* thought Morenz started to consciously hold back, "taking pains to keep his shots low, and once jumped clear from a contending position when Cude slid out to make a save."[14]

The reckless abandon the Forum crowd expected of his play had suddenly been replaced by caution. The competing psychological burdens—winning the scoring race versus his capacity to harm others—pressed on Morenz. So too did his reputation for creating important goals that actually made a difference in games.

With five minutes remaining and the Quakers still leading, Cecil Hart moved to his five-forward offence. Then, with less than a minute left, there was a last, frantic rush by the Canadiens. The *Gazette* said the puck "flew high in the air in front of the nets. Mantha swung at it with his stick but missed, and then Morenz got it with his hand. The puck fell at the goalmouth and Georges Mantha scooped it in with his stick. Morenz apparently had his hand open at the time, and his action was held legal by the referees, despite the protests of the Quakers."[15]

The referee ruled that the Canadiens had their draw, and that Howie Morenz had his second assist of the game.[16]

He finished the regular season as the league's leading scorer with fifty-one points, the best total of his career. For the sixth season in a row, he was the goal-scoring leader for the team.[17] But in the actual moment, those accomplishments tasted of ashes. He tangled with D'Arcy Coulson in overtime, and both of them were penalized for fighting. That closed out Morenz's season, Coulson's NHL career, and the Quaker franchise.

Morenz had been far from his best. The gnawing worry about what he might have done to Wilf Cude remained in his head. Howie Morenz would never be as prolific a scorer, nor as electric an offensive player, again.

Philadelphia **4** at ***Canadiens*** **4**

Morenz: 2 assists
1 penalty

Game 44	GP	G	A	Pts	PiM	HG	AG	HA	AA	GWG	GWA
Season Total:	39	29	22	51	53	18	11	14	8	5	5

PART III

The Playoff Season

CHAPTER 1

Tuesday, March 24, 1931

Canadiens vs. Bruins in Boston

A Challenge to Faith

THE CANADIENS LEFT Montreal on Monday evening to give themselves a full day in Boston to prepare for the opening game of the playoffs. Lodged at the Copley Plaza Hotel, the team wanted no distractions. Meeting in the playoffs for the third straight year, the Canadiens and Bruins were never spiritually complete until each had had the opportunity to measure themselves against the other over the course of a playoff series. This year, that contest would be a best of five.

The *Boston Globe* said Morenz had the first good chance of Game One: "Joliat had carried down the left while Shore and S. Mantha were having words behind the [Canadiens'] net. Joliat got well through and fed Morenz a perfect pass three feet in front of [Tiny] Thompson. Howie shot for the corner, but Tiny slid his stick out just in time to send the puck up and outside of the near upright."[1]

In the second period, with Eddie Shore penalized for tumbling Albert Leduc, Morenz set up Gagnon for the first goal of the game. While Shore was still off, Nick Wasnie made it 2-0. With less than three minutes remaining in the middle period, Dit Clapper scored for the Bruins, but the Canadiens responded on a scramble in front of Boston goal with less than a minute left.

The *Boston Globe*: "Morenz, Burke and S. Mantha rode down on the Bruins goal, and all seemed to get through on Thompson. Tiny stopped thrusts by Mantha and then Morenz' stab failed to clear Tiny's prone body. Burke dove headlong into the tangled mass of players and the red light went on."[2]

After two full periods the Canadiens led the startled Bruins by a score of 3-1.

Shore and Joliat started the third period with sticks swinging. During a scramble for a rebound behind the Canadiens' net, Dutch Gainor drew a minor penalty for charging Morenz into the fence.[3]

Morenz had led with his left arm to protect himself from the collision, but the contact still bent his wrist. The flash of pain across his face prompted yet another penalty call against the Bruins. On the power play, Morenz feigned an attack at the blueline before feeding Sylvio Mantha for the Canadiens' fourth goal. There were just over seventeen minutes left to play.

The Bruins clawed their way back. Shore put the puck in the net while Cooney Weiland was lying on top of Hainsworth at the right side of the Canadiens' goal to make it 4-2.[4] Then Hainsworth stopped Shore point blank from twelve feet out. The Bruins proved unstoppable. Weiland and George Owen scored to tie the game just past the halfway mark of the third.

Play became tense and fierce—and scoreless. The referees stopped calling penalties. The Canadiens had a last chance to win in regulation time when Joliat broke loose. Thompson stopped him, while Shore prevented Morenz from following up.

When overtime began, the referees began to call penalties again. Morenz and Shore came to the fore both in terms of hard checks and scoring attempts. Morenz played nine straight minutes during one stretch of overtime. Shore only missed the time when he was penalized.

Morenz was on the ice as the game reached its seventy-ninth minute. His play had been intense. He broke four sticks during the game—three of his own, one of Harry Oliver's. Now he had the chance to win the game.

The *Boston Globe* reported that on his first effort, "he raged through the Boston defence with a brilliant display of stick handling which carried him into the open, ten feet in front of Thompson. Then he let drive with all his might. The shot was waist high and on the post. Thompson kicked like a ballet dancer, the puck going off his thigh to safety."[5]

Almost immediately, Morenz went in again, alone, down the middle. Shore, however, extended his stick from behind and prevented a shot. Undaunted, Morenz came back a third time and passed to Mondou, who took a shot. "Thompson stuck his hand out helplessly," Morenz told the *Gazette*, "and the puck hit his wrist and bounced out. An inch higher and the game would have been ours. And just after that happened, Tiny looked at me as I swung by and pursed his lips, and shook his head as if to say, 'That was a narrow one.'"[6]

Then the Bruins took the game the other way. With Sylvio Mantha off for his third penalty of the game, the Canadiens twice cleared the puck down the ice. The third charge was led by Shore, whose shot was easily caught by Hainsworth, who flung it out of the danger zone. His effort was foiled.

The *Boston Globe:* "Cooney Weiland was directly in the path of the high-flying puck, twenty feet out, directly in front of the goal. Cooney reached up with his right hand and speared the puck, shortstop or centrefield fashion, dropped it on the ice in front of him, took two or three steps and let it drive. The puck went off the ice, rebounded off Hainsworth's chest and into the net."[7]

The Bruins left the ice in celebration. The stunned, outraged Canadiens continued to mill around the ice, unwilling to concede the result, and contesting the outcome with referee Mickey Ion until Morenz tapped Leduc on the shoulder and persuaded the rest of the team to head to the dressing room.[8]

Morenz had played "a sparkling game": leading the power plays and killing penalties. He created chances and assisted on three goals. He participated in every aspect of the game, at each end of the ice. The failure of all that effort would haunt him.

According to the *Montreal Herald*, Howie's humiliations were not yet over: "When the players were trooping off the ice on Tuesday night, one sporting Boston fan took a close range shot at Morenz and socked him in the eye with a hard-rolled program. Howie gave brief chase to his annoyer, but found that skates are a slight impediment for running on a wooden floor, and gave up after being badly distanced."[9]

The Canadiens made their way back to their hotel, where Elmer Ferguson found Morenz "crying like a child" over the loss, and wandering from room to room all night, wanting to go over the game with anyone who would listen. "Your correspondent hung on grimly until four," wrote Ferguson, "after which Howie went into a fresh huddle with Leo Dandurand."[10]

***Canadiens* 4** at Boston **5**

Morenz: 3 assists

CHAPTER 2

Thursday, March 26, 1931

Canadiens vs. Bruins in Boston

Cut Down

GAME TWO APPROACHED with high odds favouring the Bruins. The gamblers and many of the writers theorized that the Canadiens' collapse in Game One would have demoralized the team. Sprague Cleghorn was in town and betting on Morenz.

Morenz started with a determination and panache that surprised the Bruins. In the three minutes of play before the Bruins could manage their first shots at Hainsworth, he set the tone. On his first rush he carried the puck directly at Eddie Shore, even as he was being chased by Weiland. Shore's hit on Morenz knocked Weiland down as well. Morenz recovered the puck and drove directly at the Boston defence again. This time both Shore and Lionel Hitchman floored him, but the puck had made its way to Sylvio Mantha and then Joliat, who took the first shot of the game.

Shore and others made attempts to bully Morenz, but the Canadiens hit back hard. The pivotal moment of the opening period came when Pit Lepine intercepted a pass on a three-man Bruins rush. Just inside the Bruin blue line, Shore rattled Lepine into the boards. Despite the contact, Lepine was able to release his shot, allowing the unchecked Georges Mantha to bat in a rebound for the game's first goal.

In the early moments of the second period, coach Hart put Morenz on the wing with Pit Lepine at centre. Lepine gave him a chance on a pass from behind the Bruins' net. Thompson saved.

When Sylvio Mantha was penalized for holding the puck—a less egregious infraction than Weiland's catch of two nights before—Shore and Clapper produced the Bruins' best chance of the period. Morenz was the one to clear the rebound left by Hainsworth's save.

Coach Hart was double-shifting Morenz on offence, and relying upon him for penalty killing and back-checking. Dit Clapper had a partial breakaway in the early minutes of the third, but Hainsworth made a dive and then brushed the puck away while lying on his back, for his most spectacular save of the game.[1]

Every moment Morenz was near his own end, he was intent on wrestling the play away in the other direction. When he did break away, he got between Shore and Hitchman and received a heavy pounding.

Later, while playing left wing with Lepine at centre, he found himself chasing a Bruins rush led by Hal Darragh. Darragh swept around behind the Canadiens' net and drew Hainsworth out. Morenz worried that Hainsworth had gone too far, so he dove and then turned while sliding toward his own goal. He braced himself on the goal line—facing out with an ankle against each post. "He sailed into the nets," wrote the *Montreal Star*, "went to his knees and took a blistering shot from [Marty] Barry right in the stomach, a drive that almost knocked his wind out but saved a goal."[2]

Howie's load increased when Lepine took a butt-end to the face from Barry's stick during a goalmouth scramble. Toronto's *Globe* wrote that "Morenz was playing one the best games he ever provided on Boston ice, but the Bruins' defence was much too much for him."[3]

The Bruins started sending four men up the ice with about four minutes remaining. The Canadiens remained solid and defiant. Morenz remained at the fore. Five Bruins crowded into the Canadien end. Morenz broke out twice; the first time Shore overtook him, and on the second George Owen nabbed the puck with a hook check.

Burke and Barry collided along the boards at speed. As they bounced off each other they whirled around with their sticks high. Both were penalized for hooking. Johnny Gagnon hesitated on a play at centre, turned back toward his own zone, and made a pass that Morenz chased but couldn't catch soon enough. Gagnon was penalized for stalling. Morenz objected, but the penalty stood. With the Canadiens two men short, Morenz stayed on the ice, this time more on defence, intercepting rushes by Weiland.

It was Shore, however, who remained the main rival. Morenz "skated round Shore four times and away from him twice in racing for the puck," said the *Montreal Star*.[4] The *New York Times* remarked on this sequence as demonstrating both Morenz's superior qualities as a clever back-checker, and his perfect harmonization with his defencemen.[5]

In the waning minutes of the third period, Morenz's penalty killing still drew on his capacity for speed. Breaking away from a jam, he "raced down to beat Shore," reported the *Boston Post*, "but Big Ed wouldn't be fooled and forced the wizard to overskate his shot and lose at the back boards."[6]

Burke and Barry returned, and Burke immediately became involved. The *Montreal Herald*: "Burke broke away when all Bruins but Shore were up on the attack. Morenz went with him, took the pass and easily circled Shore, but George Owen made a phenomenal save. He hurled himself at full length along the ice and slid right into Morenz's stick, ruining his shot."[7]

The Bruins changed, still on the power play. Morenz remained in charge defensively. What happened next was a climax created by a confluence of speed, confrontation and sudden violence. "Morenz got a swell break, catching everyone but Shore down the ice," reported the *Boston Globe*. "At last the fans were to see the duel they had waited for so long. The world's greatest forward against the world's greatest defence man. As Morenz approached Shore, he bore to the right and half got past the Bruins' star. His angle for the goal was not too bad and he was ten feet out. Then two things happened at once."[8]

The play exploded like a pinwheel. The *Montreal Herald*: "Shore backed up slowly watching intently the speeding figure which flew toward him. Five feet away from Shore, Morenz swerved to the right like a flash. Shore lunged desperately with his stick and either his own stick jabbed Morenz in the forehead, or he lifted Morenz's own stick. On that point Morenz himself is not quite clear, so kaleidoscopic was the play, but at any rate, Morenz flashed around Shore and raced for the nets. Thompson flung himself straight out in a last desperate effort. Morenz blazed his shot, the puck hit the post and Morenz catapulted into the sliding form of Thompson. Going at blinding speed, the impact threw Morenz high in the air spinning end over end and he crashed face downwards on the ice with a stunning thud and laid there."[9]

Morenz was unconscious on the ice, "out cold as a mackerel," said the *Herald*, and bleeding from a head wound.[10]

A photograph of the next moment in the *Boston Post* shows Shore skating away from an unconscious Morenz, and the puck just inches from Thompson's near (left) goal post. George Owen is standing behind the right goal post. The referees have not yet arrived at the scene.

When the referees did arrive, they gave Owen the major penalty for injuring Morenz—a call so erroneous that it brought the Boston fans to riot. The *Gazette* reported that the twenty-minute furor that followed was "one of the most violent demonstrations in the history of the NHL."[11]

While the crowd was distracted by the referees, Morenz was recovering from being stretched out. He had been led to the side, but brushed off support and skated back toward centre ice—despite blood trickling from his forehead.

He returned to his post, ready to finish the final four minutes of the game with a man advantage. Morenz stole the puck from Shore again. They raced against each other toward the Boston goal. Shore managed to hook the puck, but the Bruins found themselves with just forty seconds left.

Coach Art Ross motioned for Tiny Thompson to leave the ice and sent Shore, Beattie, Clapper, Art Chapman, and Weiland out to play without a goaltender. The Bruins managed to keep the play within the Canadiens' zone for the rest of the game, but never managed a shot on goal. The match finished 1-0 for the Canadiens.

Morenz had a headache, but the important thing was that the series was tied. It had taken every available ounce of him, as well as his teammates, to leave Boston on even terms. He had had no goals and no assists. But he had been essential.

***Canadiens* 1** at Boston **0**

Morenz: Nothing

CHAPTER 3

Saturday, March 28, 1931

Bruins vs. Canadiens in Montreal

Nearer Death

THE CANADIENS WERE numbed by the physical cost of the first two games. Georges Mantha, Sylvio Mantha, and Albert Leduc each suffered head injuries during the first game. Howie Morenz was knocked unconscious in the second.

Art Ross believed the Bruins could win by reducing the Canadiens to physical wrecks. Eddie Shore would be the core mainstay of this strategy. Shore began Game Three by catching Johnny Gagnon with an elbow that was hard enough to take the Canadien off his feet. Referee Mickey Ion stopped play so that Gagnon could be helped off the ice, but assessed no penalty. Soon after play resumed, Ion penalized Shore for attempting to demolish Sylvio Mantha.

Mantha shrugged off the collision. Still on the ice for the power play, the captain skated end-to-end, finishing with a backhander that got behind Thompson for a 1-0 Montreal lead. Père Mantha had produced one of his statement goals.

Morenz managed a couple of close-in chances during the first period. Just as he was in mid-deke in front of Thompson on a third, Shore managed to sneak the puck away from him. With ten seconds left in the first period, Dit Clapper tied the game.

Early in the second, Joliat resumed his own feud with Shore. Joliat knocked him down in the Canadiens' end, then carried a rush toward

Thompson. Shore caught back up and "hit Joliat with a perfect body check, catching the midget Habitant wide-open, and Joliat went down like a poled steer," wrote the *Montreal Herald*. "He hit the ice with the broad of his back, his famous black cap flew off, and he seemed to be completely knocked out." However, he was conscious enough to make a fabulous play. "He had slid the puck straight in front of him," the *Herald* continued, "and passing between Shore's feet, it had slid across to the front of the Boston nets. Almost before Joliat's back had crashed the ice, Gus Rivers had flashed in, batted the rubber and driven it home."[1]

In that moment when the Canadiens took their 2-1 lead, a few noted that Rivers was playing where Morenz might have been.

Morenz took his regular turn through the second period, as well as on the penalty kill, but seemed more cautious than he had been in Boston. He played as if he was hurt.

When Joliat was later penalized for tripping Clapper, Morenz was on the ice to kill the penalty with Pit Lepine. Their efforts limited the Bruins to a solitary, unsuccessful shot. Morenz appeared to be back-checking effectively.

His offensive initiatives were more sporadic, with just a couple in the second period.

On one of those he dodged another attempted open-ice hit by Shore so nimbly that Shore's own momentum plunged him ten full feet out of the play. Instead, Morenz was shuddered to his knees by Percy Galbraith. That hit was hard enough to put him back on the bench, where he looked pale and obviously unwell.[2]

Morenz watched as Joliat knocked Eddie Shore to the ice again, bringing the Forum crowd to its feet. When Art Chapman was penalized for tripping Gagnon, Morenz watched as Shore shouldered the responsibility for the penalty kill. For a full minute, Shore played keep-away with the whole Canadien team. Shore appeared to have control of the game until his conceit of competence was interrupted by Georges Mantha. Mantha carried the puck through Shore's zone and then looped the puck over Thompson for a 3-1 lead.[3]

When the third period began, it was evident that the Bruins' violence was taking its toll on Morenz, Joliat, and Gagnon. Boston seized an initiative and cut the Canadiens' lead to one in less than a minute when Weiland, Gainor, and Clapper all crashed the Canadiens net on a power rush.

The game resumed with only eight skaters on the ice. During the regular season, this would have been a grand opportunity for Hart to unleash Morenz—if he had been healthy. Instead, Hart's Canadiens played defensively, sending only one man forward, while the rest of their skaters remained on the home side of the Bruins' blueline.

The game moved into the final five minutes. Morenz returned, but then made the rare decision to take a rest. As he stepped to the bench, the crowd cheered with appreciation.[4]

The teams were at full strength. The atmosphere in the Forum was raucous. Fans were anticipating victory and in full voice. The optimism wouldn't last. *The Montreal Star* said the team was "dead tired, and they were sorely beat by injuries, but their unflinching spirit kept them going when tired nature rebelled, and a breakdown seemed inevitable."[5]

With Morenz off, Shore created a series of panics in the Canadiens' end. They concluded with a Bruin goal in the midst of a scramble. Hainsworth's claim that Barry had kicked the puck across the line was ignored by referee Ion. The score was tied with less than four minutes left in regulation time.

The Canadiens appeared to be no closer to winning than they had been when the game began. Cec Hart gave Morenz a final turn on the ice, and he managed a chance from the left side, which may have been the only challenge Tiny Thompson faced in the third period. It had not been enough.

The flame of the Canadiens' candle was flickering. In the intermission, the Canadiens looked entirely incapable of playing any more hockey at all—as the Bruins had planned and hoped all along.

Hart felt that there was only one strategy for the overtime: "Skate them dizzy."[6] Use speed. Score as quickly as you can.

The *Gazette*: "Joliat, Morenz and Gagnon for Canadiens, and Weiland, Clapper and Barry for the Bruin, six of the greatest forwards in hockey, past or present, vied with each other in brilliant displays of hockey brains and speed for four minutes without result."[7]

Morenz's reserves were nearly spent, and he devoted most of his efforts assisting the defence while seeking an opening. Thompson saved three shots: two from Morenz, one from Sylvio Mantha.

Cec Hart then replaced his starters with his younger subs. They roamed eagerly inside the Bruins' zone, outshooting the visitors 6-2. Instead of fear and apprehension, fans now sensed anticipation and opportunity as Burke weaved his way up the ice, only to be faced with a body check from Owen—but not before he passed to a rushing Larochelle at the Bruins' blueline. Larochelle took a shot. Thompson batted the puck away.

The *Montreal Star* followed the puck: "Larochelle darted in behind the nets, came out to the right, and hammered another startling shot that Thompson cleared with his chest, and [Georges] Mantha, coming in as gracefully as a figure skater, picked it up almost off his boot tops and sliced it back into the unprotected part of the net."[8]

The Canadiens had prevailed 3-2, by an effort of will.

A crisis remained on the ice. Marty Burke dropped to his knees and lost consciousness. The check from Owen as Burke passed to Larochelle had included a butt-end to Burke's chest. Reports differed on where the blow had landed in relation to his heart. Barely able to speak, he needed assistance to get to the dressing room, where he was blanketed with hot towels on the rubbing table.[9]

While the medical team worked on Burke, the goalless Morenz told the *Gazette* of his appreciation for the substitutes who had pulled the game out for the Canadiens: Georges Mantha, Rivers, and Larochelle.[10]

Then he, like the rest of the team, returned to their vigil. The exhausted Canadiens stayed in the room together in a communal refusal to abandon their teammate while he appeared to be teetering on the edge of life itself.

As he waited, Morenz was reminded of Judge John Augustus Barron of Stratford, a former hockey player and organizational force in the Ontario Hockey Association. Judge Barron had drifted away from the game, at first because he felt it had become too rough, but particularly after his son Fritz died playing the game in Winnipeg. Fritz's heart had stopped after he had been hit with a puck in the solar plexus and could not be revived.

Now Burke had the team breathing in with every gasp he made, grimacing with each phlegmatic cough that wracked his body as air came back out. Whatever darkness he had to endure, his roommate Howie Morenz and the rest of the Canadiens needed to endure it with him.

Boston **2** at ***Canadiens* 3**

Morenz: Nothing

CHAPTER 4

Monday, March 30, 1931

Bruins vs. Canadiens in Montreal

Fear

IT WAS NEAR midnight on Palm Sunday morning when Marty Burke stabilized, began to breathe more consistently on his own, and a patina of colour seeped back into his skin. An appearance of relief—instead of a fixed stare of fright—softened his eyes. An hour's work by the team doctors and trainers had managed to restore a regular heartbeat. His teammates then felt able to disperse, comforting themselves with the thought that this had just been a scare, nothing that would interfere with their ability to eliminate the Bruins on Monday night.

Howie Morenz and Eddie Shore each expected that the game would be another challenge of wills. It began early in the first period, at high speed, with Morenz coming within a hair's breadth of scoring, followed by Shore practically breaking his stick over Morenz's head (just as he had in game two) to prevent a second shot.[1]

Gagnon was penalized for tripping, but Morenz kept control of the game as a penalty-killer.

Morenz showed himself to be a good stickhandler in his club's defence, when he kept the puck for a good half-minute before taking it out of his zone.

The Bruins sensed that Marty Burke would be struggling. When Eddie Shore sprang a four-man attack toward the Canadiens' end, he purposely launched toward Burke's side of the ice. Burke managed to turn that attack aside, but he later told the *Herald* he was playing with "intense pain . . . I felt all right while quiet, but it was like a knife cutting me when I moved."[2]

Despite his bravado of Sunday morning, Burke's night was done after just twelve minutes of effort in the first period. Before this, he'd been regarded as the biggest barrier to Bruin success in the series. Now that he was replaced by Albert Leduc, the Bruins saw an opportunity.

An early hit on Morenz by George Owen was just the start of his greatest ever playoff performance. Owen's next opportunity came on a near-full-team rush against the Canadiens. A pass from Owen to Weiland resulted in the first goal of the night.

Morenz tried to initiate a brief rally in the last minutes of the opening period, but was dogged by Shore. The *Boston Post*: "At the jag end of the period Morenz nearly did it. He all but passed Shore, who worked like a Trojan to topple him and was successful to the degree that Morenz had little left to his shot."[3]

The fans remained anxious and uncertain about Morenz's health and were keyed to overreact at any apparent misfortune. When another Canadien was sent sprawling, the crowd clamoured for a Boston penalty. When that didn't happen, they showered the ice with programmes.[4]

The teams traded chances in the second period until Eddie Shore and Pit Lepine began to trade hits, stick slashes, and punches. Penalties to both provided Hart with an opportunity to give Morenz more room without the menace of Eddie Shore.

Morenz carried the puck across the Bruins' blue line with Sylvio Mantha open on the far side of the ice. Marty Barry disrupted the play and was penalized for tripping—giving the Canadiens an actual power play. Morenz and Joliat were ready to pounce. Instead, the Bruins, and Art Chapman in particular, prevented them from getting a single shot on net.

In fact, the Canadiens never managed to break the Bruin blue line during their man advantage. Although Leduc eventually retrieved a rolling puck inside his own blueline and moved to the attack, flanked by Morenz and Joliat, that was the moment that Shore was liberated from the nearby penalty box, with Lepine right behind him. Shore then "skated right across Leduc's stick, dislodged the puck and broke with it down the ice," said the *Boston Globe*.[5]

Neither Morenz nor Joliat nor anyone else caught up with Shore, who tucked his shot into the left corner of the net.

The Bruins' 2-0 lead provided a psychological boost, reflected in their play. Leduc fell on a miscalculated defensive chance. He lay on the ice, dazed, for thirty seconds before a whistle was blown. Having replaced Burke, Leduc was now replaced by rookie Art Lesieur.

The Canadiens' efforts to get a grip on the game continued to falter but Morenz remained their offensive bright spot. In the second period. Morenz was shoved around by Shore, but was "all over the ice," said *La Presse*. "He's everywhere. He makes impetuous attacks. He's 'checked' and returns to the attack."[6] Frustration overflowed. He tripped Shore and was penalized for the first time in the series.

The Bruins were strong and in charge. Art Ross was rolling three fully rested and injury-free forward lines. Each cut loose with their finest and most robust hockey of the series. They extended their lead on a George Owen shot that was deflected into the net by Sylvio Mantha's stick or Hainsworth's own arm.

The Canadiens' efforts during the first forty minutes had none of the precision, good fortune, nor success, of the Bruins' attacks. Instead, they skated impetuously. Even when they got close to Tiny Thompson, the goalie rebuffed them. Toronto's *Globe*: "Nick Wasnie burned two hot shots from close in, one on a pass from Morenz, and once from a scramble. Morenz himself broke through the Boston defence with a swerving dash, but Thompson sprawled and saved from his back-hand shot."[7]

A few trademark rushes by Morenz had no effect, nor did some dashes by Mantha, and a run or two by Leduc and Lepine. These efforts were not going to be enough to overcome a Bruin team facing elimination. The Bruins were dominant, while the Canadiens seemed spent. After two periods the Canadiens seemed already beaten—except that at the close of that session, Art Lesieur brought Shore to his knees with a solid hit.

When the fans next saw Morenz, he was running from the tunnel and through the gate to get to the ice for the start of the third period. Morenz believed that the remaining twenty minutes gave the Canadiens a chance to achieve something. He appreciated the defiance in Art Lesieur's humbling of Shore and yearned to do the same.

As soon as the puck was dropped, Morenz launched the first attack. The *Boston Post* reported how he "just flew across centre and looped around Shore for the first time in the series to get inside to give Tiny the stop of the evening, and Tiny handled it in masterful form."[8]

The Bruins responded with a trio of glittering passing attacks, each repelled by Hainsworth. The Canadiens pushed back. Percy Galbraith was eventually penalized for tripping Larochelle. That created the room Morenz wanted. Though again slammed by a series of rough body checks, he managed to break away with Wasnie at his side. Morenz shot him a pass, and Wasnie scored.

That goal changed the game. Morenz's first scoring point since the first game also brought a sense of relief that energized his play.

Cec Hart made the radical decision to play five forwards in front of Hainsworth, with Morenz at right wing and Lepine at centre. Hart also accelerated his line changes, attempting to keep his forwards fresher than the Bruin defenders. That created a raucous contest for the rest of the third period. The locus of the game became smaller.

The *Boston Globe*: "Morenz carried down and lobbed a shot in front of Thompson, then everyone piled in for the feature mix-up of the evening with eleven of the twelve players on the ice all skating, shooting, checking within the space of a few square feet in front of Thompson. Tiny kicked out two or three pokes and then finally Chapman cleared."[9]

The period continued with the same pattern of play until late in the period when Nick Wasnie and George Owen collided. Their sudden flurry of arms and sticks and angry voices resulted in a single penalty to Wasnie. The frayed and irritated nerves of Canadiens fans again erupted in shouts of anger and litter on the ice. Their protest had the effect of stalling any Canadien momentum. Morenz wasn't happy. As he crossed the ice to help clear the debris, he shook his stick in anger at the crowd. They paid him no mind and continued to howl. It took nearly ten minutes for the game to resume.[10]

The Canadiens tried to carry the game to the Bruins despite being a man short. A contretemps between Galbraith and Gagnon left the Canadiens on a short power play. Shore, Chapman, and Hitchman faced Morenz, Georges Mantha, Wasnie, and Joliat. The play was furious within the Bruins' zone. Weiland returned.

Owen got the puck away from Morenz at one point, and as he dashed off on a two-man breakaway a spectator was motivated to heckle Morenz for losing control of the puck. Albert Laberge thought it a cruel taunt.[11]

Hainsworth blocked the two Bruins. Soon enough he was called upon to stop another breakaway by Weiland, which the *Herald* thought was his "finest save of the night."[12]

The Canadiens brought a final play back down to Thompson. Wasnie made a clean shot, and Morenz took the rebound. Thompson tumbled and made the stop, ending Morenz's final chance of the game.[13] It was a limp end to a game where Morenz had given it his all—but by that point, said the *Herald*, he was only operating on "half a cylinder."[14]

Fear now gripped the Canadiens. They were one loss away from playoff elimination, while a jubilant Bruin team believed that they had finally rendered the Canadiens physically incapable of winning. Morenz kept his fear at bay with the knowledge that the Bruins still faced the same Sisyphean threat of elimination that they had faced when the game began. In fewer than forty-eight hours the Canadiens would have another opportunity to break them.

Boston **3** at ***Canadiens*** **1**

Morenz: 1 assist
1 penalty

CHAPTER 5

April 1, 1931

Bruins vs. Canadiens in Montreal

Reprieve

MORENZ WAS UNSETTLED. He and Mary both wondered whose voice had called out, late in the third period, urging him to "play!"—as if he had done nothing for the first fifty-seven minutes of the game. After a day and a half of fretting, he surprised Mary by going to bed and sleeping soundly until late in the afternoon before the fifth game.

Shortly after 8 p.m. the Canadiens took to the ice for their pre-game warm-up. Mary was in the Morenz pew. Marty Burke was there. Albert Leduc remained in hospital.

Morenz didn't start the game, but as soon as he took to the ice he immediately played his tactical hand by clipping Hitchman on the head with his stick, which led to a two-minute penalty.[1]

It was actually more of a jab. It had been intentional—retaliation for a heavy Hitchman check on Lepine. Morenz wanted to give notice that the Canadiens would meet aggression with aggression. And more.

Part of the "more" was an unworried, freewheeling offensive attack. Just as his penalty expired the puck came loose in the Canadiens' end. Wil Larochelle tried to time a pass to reach Morenz as he burst from the penalty box. The crowd caught its breath, but he failed to pick up the puck.

He created other early grief for the Bruins by forcing them to take penalties. The first was a trip by Shore as Morenz tried to turn a Joliat pass into a shot. In the first moments of the power play, Morenz kept the heat on

Tiny Thompson and was waiting for a pass from Gagnon while scrambling with Owen. That's when he got hit in the mouth.

The Canadiens were now looking at a long, two-man advantage against Barry, Hitchman, and Chapman. The three managed to control the puck until Burke began racing around the net, distracting the Bruins while Morenz placed himself in front to receive a pass. He took a shot, but Thompson made a kick save. Burke turned the same kind of play into a goal by Johnny Gagnon just before Shore's penalty expired.

The Canadiens continued to press. Coach Hart was rotating his forwards at one-minute intervals to protect them from exhaustion. The Bruins found room to make a rush. Morenz overtook them with vengeance, pouncing on Clapper like a hawk for being too close to the Canadiens' net.

When Sylvio Mantha took his own penalty for tripping Shore, Morenz and Lepine killed it together. Owen came back on, giving the Bruins an apparent man advantage. Instead, Owen soon earned his second penalty, for tripping Morenz as he ragged the puck.

Morenz was on the bench when Shore allowed a Wasnie-Joliat pass to go through his legs. Lepine found the puck and easily feinted Thompson out of position for a 2-0 Canadien lead.

There was another sudden, unexpected Morenz moment in the period. He took a shot from centre ice that proved so powerful that it almost knocked Thompson over. But the puck did not go in.

The Canadiens' unrelenting wildfire speed, odd-man encounters, and forechecking made it difficult for the Bruins to get past their own blue line. In this one-sided period, the Bruins' first shot may have been recorded as late as the eighteenth minute. The Canadiens continued their onslaught at the opening of the second, led again by Morenz and joined by Lepine.

Marty Barry led a four-man Bruin rush. Hainsworth leaped into a dramatic spreadeagle pose for the save. Morenz and Lepine picked up the remnants of the play and broke back together. Thompson made saves on each of them in succession.

Sylvio Mantha, Armand Mondou, and Marty Burke each collided with Eddie Shore, sometimes exchanging words. Burke used his stick and was penalized. Morenz and the lightly used Art Lesieur were the penalty killers, with Lepine later replacing Lesieur. Both Morenz and Lepine managed short-handed shots on Thompson before Burke returned to the ice. Morenz seemed to be playing everywhere, not just on the attack line but in defence as well, blocking several passes.

On one of the Bruins' few second-period opportunities, Morenz's involvement was typical. In front of the net, he intercepted a pass between Darragh and Chapman and then made a run in which Shore roughed him up against the boards. It was Shore's second penalty of the game. Despite the battering he had received over the first four games, Morenz was still playing too quickly for Shore.

Shore returned and initiated a rush up ice, banging into Sylvio Mantha twice. Mantha's head bounced heavily off the ice. Although dazed and needing help to get to his feet, the captain remained in the game. Then Sylvio forced Shore into a delay-of-game penalty.

The pace of the Canadiens' attack slackened then, even as their defence remained unbroken. After two full periods of hockey, the Bruins had managed a meagre seven shots on goal.

Howie Morenz and Cooney Weiland met at centre ice for the opening faceoff of the third period. As they batted at the puck, Morenz's stick broke cleanly in two. The Bruins sent five men forward. Hainsworth stopped a flurry of four shots, but Weiland counted on the fifth to make the score 2-1.

Morenz continued to engage directly with the Bruins' attack, at one point throwing himself at Shore to halt a rush. The Bruins continued on the attack even when short-handed. Morenz interrupted a couple of chances by Oliver, controlled the puck, and tossed it to the far end of the rink.

Then fortune broke in favour of the Bruins with about six minutes remaining. After a series of nervous chances on both sides of the puck, the playoff's leading scorer, Cooney Weiland, tied the game.[2]

The Bruins seemed to relax. Morenz wondered whether it was exhaustion. He made a run on goal, but was laid out by Shore, who got his fourth penalty.

That removed Shore from the ice for the closing minutes of the third period. When play resumed, Hitchman and Sylvio Mantha collided so hard that both were forced to retire. Morenz surveyed the Bruins zone as he waited for the next drop of the puck. A man advantage, no Shore, no Hitchman.

He collected the puck off the drop and took a short turn through centre ice. Racing through the defence, he took a stick to the face from Chapman. While the initial stick contact might have appeared unintentional, Chapman left no doubt about his purpose, taking a swing at Morenz with his fist. Chapman got a major penalty, giving the Canadiens a two-man advantage for the third time in the game. Morenz was prepared to disregard his now-broken nose, but it needed bandaging. The power play would begin without him.

Morenz had been living in the heads of everyone affiliated with the Bruins for some time. After the obvious pain and blood from Chapman's cross-check, the media made snide remarks about how Morenz was just acting hurt, like "the old Eddie Shore act of writhing around," wrote the *Boston Herald*.[3]

Thompson thwarted the Canadiens in three chances out of a scrimmage around the Boston goal, before a bandaged Morenz returned to create yet another goalmouth scramble. Morenz and Gagnon forced Thompson and the puck into the net, and the goal light flashed red, but the referees ruled no goal. The game would go to an overtime session for the third time in five games. Chapman still had about a minute to serve.

At the overtime's start, the teams traded chances. Shore had the first, leaping down the ice to the Canadiens' goalmouth. Thompson stopped Gagnon twice. Morenz found a path to feed Mondou who went in on the Boston goal on his own, but Thompson saved again.

Hainsworth turned away shots by Galbraith, Beattie, and then Galbraith again. Oliver had a shot. The rebound from Hainsworth went to Beattie, but Sylvio Mantha got a piece of stick on Beattie's try and the puck rolled inches past an unprotected goalpost. The best of the Bruins' assault lasted for about ten minutes.

Morenz reappeared at the head of the Canadiens' attack. *La Presse*: "Morenz grabbed the puck from Joliat. He approached like a cyclone and fired with terrible force. The shot looked a certainty, but Thompson blocked and saved the game for Boston—for the moment."[4]

Morenz and Rivers then put on a passing exchange that put Morenz in alone. Thompson plunged to save. A third Morenz shot from a distance was stopped. Morenz set up Joliat for a shot that rang off the iron behind Thompson, and then Joliat returned the favour. Morenz's shot looked sure to score, but Thompson made a stellar save.

Mondou and Larochelle had chances, and then Morenz prevented Marty Barry from responding with a chance of his own. The crowd roared with approval at Morenz's defensive play, before he took a deserved rest from the ice.[5]

After that, the speed of the game slowed to a crawl. The *Gazette*: "Over seventy-eight minutes of breakneck hockey had stripped two mighty hockey machines of their trappings, the speed of Canadiens was fast failing them, and the ruggedness of the Boston Bruins was spent."[6]

Marty Barry swung slowly around behind his own goal with the puck. He gathered pace, emerging across his own blue line and through centre. He reached the Canadiens' blue line, but Marty Burke poked the puck away from him. Burke started up the ice. As in game three, Will Larochelle was on his right, with speed and vigor and ready to receive a pass from Burke. As it came, the crowd began to rise, anticipating a goal. It came before they finished standing.

The *Boston Globe*: "The shot was right on the right upright. Thompson kicked desperately with his left leg, but the puck caromed off his pads and went into the side netting for the winning goal."[7]

The Canadiens had won, 3-2.

La Presse: "[Morenz played] a phenomenal game. He didn't record a single point but he had done enormous work. He was as effective defensively as he was offensively. He thwarted, paralyzed and disorientated the visitors by going around them with the puck. Furious, the Boston players went after him and laid him out on the ice, but they couldn't subdue him and put him out of action. One could say with all justice that Morenz made an enormous contribution to the Canadien victory."[8]

Morenz remained on the ice when it was over, spending some final moments there with Tiny Thompson, and later several minutes chatting side-by-side with Eddie Shore in the Canadiens' dressing room. Shore hinted at the burden of his own losing experience, his gravel-voiced monotone adding potency to his claim that this had been "one of the hardest series I ever played in," as reported by the *Montreal Star*.[9]

Both Shore and Morenz knew how necessary the trials of these playoff confrontations were to their relationship and the relationship of their teams. Neither of them could know how good they were until they tested themselves against each other in the spring. The margin between victory and defeat seemed to be so narrow as to be within the realm of chance. Tonight, in their final playoff confrontation, chance and effort had favoured Morenz and the Canadiens.

Boston **2** at ***Canadiens* 3**

Morenz: 1 penalty

CHAPTER 6

Friday, April 3, 1931

Canadiens vs. Black Hawks in Chicago

Les Coequipiers

TWELVE HOURS AFTER their climactic victory over the Bruins, the Canadiens convened at Montreal's Bonaventure Station to board their train to Chicago. A throng of five hundred well-wishers saw the players off, who posed for movies and stills looking surprisingly rested and relaxed.[1] However, as the train moved west, Dr. Corrigan was gingerly patching, uncovering, and then repatching the wounds that had disfigured Howie Morenz's face.

The "inferior" Black Hawks had surprised Conn Smythe's Leafs by outscoring them 4-3 in their two-game, most-goals, series. The Hawks then defeated the New York Rangers in the Cup semifinal without allowing a goal. Charlie Gardiner had a goals-against average of about 0.70. Chicago's seven playoff goals had been scored by six different players. The Hawks were in good physical shape. Mike Rodden of the *Globe*, who had been assigned to referee the first game of the final, wrote that he liked the Hawks' chances.[2]

A turnout of 16,500 fans to the Stadium for the opening game was regarded as "something of a disappointment" by Major McLaughlin.[3] The fans who showed up were nevertheless expectant. The ice was clean and smooth. The Stadium had been decorated with the flags of the United States and France, giving the game *un cachet international*. When the Canadiens climbed up from the basement for their warm-up they were greeted with warm applause.[4]

The teams that looked across the ice at each other saw reflections of themselves: the only players left active who were playing for anything important. The Canadiens felt a special frisson of having returned for the second consecutive spring. Howie Morenz was three wins away from his objective. It was both time to begin and to conclude.

Howie Morenz opened the first period of the series on the bench. When he came on, it was with Johnny Gagnon and Georges Mantha. After a couple of quick shots from the Hawks, Morenz snatched at a rebound and carried the puck out of his own end. His surge into the Chicago end created temporary chaos among the Hawk defenders. Morenz caught Gardiner off guard with a shot into a scrum at the goalmouth. Gardiner fell in making the stop, but

Gagnon caught the rebound, passed to Mantha, and Ti-Georges tallied over top of the fallen Gardiner. Some reports made no mention of Morenz on the play at all.

Cecil Hart rested Morenz after that. Lepine made himself ubiquitous. Burke banged Rosario Couture hard into the boards for the first penalty of the series. Then the Canadiens began to play more cautiously, throwing the puck the length of the ice. Their caution continued when Burke returned.

After holding Joliat and Morenz back for much of the first period in favour of some of the younger forwards, Hart gave them both another shift in the late minutes. Joliat made a shot from the left side that was stopped by Gardiner. Morenz created another chance off the rush, but time ran out on him. Hawk coach Dick Irvin wondered why the Stadium had seen so little of Morenz and Joliat, when they had looked so dangerous in flashes.

The Hawks started the second period assuming that their eventual control of the game was inevitable. Morenz made several attempts on goal but couldn't get a clean shot on Gardiner. Lepine, Rivers, Gagnon, and Georges Mantha made most of Montreal's scoring attempts.

Any time that Chicago made an attack, Lepine was nearly inescapable in the middle of the ice. He disrupted rushes with his poke-check as well as fancy, imperturbable stickhandling. The surprising Canadiens kept Gardiner busy in the second period, while Hainsworth cooled each of the few Hawk shots with aplomb.

Chicago's first penalty of the series was taken by Tommy Cook. After it expired, the Canadiens really came to life. Sylvio Mantha, Morenz, and Wasnie each took hard shots at the Chicago goal. Mantha missed the net by an inch and hit the boards. The puck rebounded to Morenz, who shot again and was stopped.[5] The Canadiens also began to clearly outskate the hometown Hawks.

Georges Mantha was penalized for dumping Frank Ingram. Hart defended with Lepine at centre, while Morenz patrolled both wings. The two centremen spent the Mantha penalty stickhandling and passing the puck back and forth. They kept the puck from the Hawks with such skill that when the Hawks finally gained possession, they sent four anxious men on a furious attack. The Canadiens were all back. There were some moments of worry inside the Canadiens' blueline, but Morenz blocked Mush Marsh in front of the goal on the Hawks' best opportunity.

George Hainsworth was both engaged and imperturbable. Even for those who saw him play regularly, several of his stops seemed miraculous. He ended one Hawk attack by clearing the puck from the zone himself.

When the second period closed, the Canadiens had outshot the home team and continued to lead 1-0. Unlike the nervous tension that had threatened to consume them in the Boston series, the Canadiens were playing with a posture of patience—as if they already knew the game's outcome.

The third period, like the first, began with Morenz on the bench. In the first minute, Couture of the Hawks had an excellent shot, but was met by just as excellent a save on the part of Hainsworth.

Joliat set up one chance by Lepine that was stopped by Gardiner. Gottselig recovered the puck but Lepine snicked it off his stick at the Canadiens' blue line and turned the game back in the opposite direction. Lepine squirmed through the Chicago defence and surprised Gardiner from a difficult angle to boost the Canadiens' lead to 2-0. It was a play of such elegance that the *Chicago Tribune* remarked how "Big Pete Lepine, who shoved across the Frenchmens' second goal with nary a bit of assistance, was as good as Morenz last night."[6]

There was just 2:20 gone in the third period.

The Hawks began to break toward the Canadiens' end of the ice in groups of three, and sometimes even four abreast. That gave them chances, but Hainsworth was impenetrable.

Hart sent Morenz on to back-check the Hawks.

Morenz did steal the puck off a poor Hawk pass in the Canadiens' zone and was gathering momentum toward the Chicago end of the ice when he was tumbled by Helge Bostrom. Morenz got himself back to his feet and continued. Bostrom then cross-checked him, knocking him down again. Bostrom was penalized for the second disruption. Georges Mantha soon joined Bostrom for tripping Gottselig.

With a player each in the penalty box and the teams playing four-on-four, Dick Irvin decided to play four forwards. He supplemented the line of Gottselig, Ripley, and Couture with Tommy Cook. The change produced immediate results, with Vic Ripley scoring to close the gap to 2-1.

The goal whetted the Hawks' offensive appetite. The Canadiens' defence stiffened. The Hawks' three- and four-man rushes of the earlier minutes now became five-man attacks. The Canadien forwards backchecked with a diligence that impressed even the *Chicago Daily Tribune*: "The Chicagoans played one of their best games of the year, but what can be done with a forward line that is hammering your goal one minute and is back helping defend its own a half minute later?"[7]

The leader on the ice remained Pit Lepine, who *La Presse* thought was playing "one of the best parts of his glorious career."[8] Hainsworth remained essential. Morenz continued to contribute. Twice it appeared that the Chicago attack was getting a step away from him. Once, Gottselig stole the puck from him and almost scored. Short seconds later, Gottselig had the puck in front of Hainsworth, but Morenz managed to snatch it away from him before firing the puck to the other end of the ice.

Coach Hart was relying as much on Morenz's veteran experience as his physical capacity.

Late in the period, Morenz was on the ice with Joliat and the young legs of Nick Wasnie. He broke out from the Canadiens' end. The crowd half-stood with worry until their rush was pushed to a corner by the Chicago defence. Less than a minute remained. The Hawks returned up ice. Morenz overtook the puck carrier at centre, stole the puck, and immediately turned the attack again, whipping a quick pass to Wasnie.

The Manitoban broke free of the Chicago defence but, in his haste, missed the net with his shot. Gottselig had just enough time to bring the puck up ice a final time. He shot. Marty Burke caught the puck with his hand just as the final gong sounded.

There was a pause, as if the crowd and the Hawks were waiting for something more. The game that began with such anticipation was now part of history.

It had been a team victory for the Canadiens. The *Gazette* said it required "yeoman work on the part of each French player."[9] The Canadiens "may have undergone some punishment at the hands of the Bruins," said the *Chicago Daily Tribune*, but "they could skate just as fast on crutches if necessary."[10]

Despite his failure to score, and his obvious weariness, the determined play of Morenz lingered in the minds of the Chicago fans and media as a highlight of the game.

***Canadiens* 2** at Chicago **1**

Morenz: Nothing

CHAPTER 7

Wednesday, April 5, 1931

Canadiens vs. Black Hawks in Chicago

Eteint

BY SUNDAY AFTERNOON a different expectation gathered around 1801 West Madison Street. The novelty of playing in the Stanley Cup final had faded. Chicago's mood was that it was time for the Hawks to win their first Stanley Cup game in franchise history.

When the contest began, Howie Morenz was centring the second line between Johnny Gagnon and Georges Mantha. After the Hawks carried the initial play, Sylvio Mantha tried to set up Morenz for a chance. Morenz was shoved off balance as the pass arrived.

His play brought the crowd on their feet with both fright and anticipation. First there were a series of chances with Nick Wasnie, but several of his passes missed. Then he created some unnecessary anxiety for his own teammates, and excitement for the Hawks and their fans, by carrying the puck across the front of Hainsworth's goal, nearly allowing Helge Bostrom to push the puck into the net.

As the first period wound to a close, he found the puck out of a missed shot opportunity by the Hawks. He turned and propelled himself through the middle toward the Chicago blueline. Something about Cy Wentworth's positioning encouraged him to choose the outside route, by the left sideboards. Wentworth pinched him there, squaring his stick against Morenz's left shoulder. Despite or because of a jolt of extra speed by Morenz in an effort to escape, Wentworth's stick shaft slipped quickly higher—first rasping Howie's neck, and then his jaw, and finally his ear.

Morenz turned and thrashed the chest and shoulder of the taller Chicago defenceman with his own stick. Each of them struck out at the other again. They were readying to club each other a third time when the referees interrupted and assessed the first penalties of the game.

The first period ended scoreless. As soon as Morenz's penalty expired, he struggled to ignite the Canadiens' attack. He skated the length of the ice only to make an unsuccessful shot. Then he missed a pass from Joliat. He failed on a pass attempt through centre ice. He and Larochelle approached Chicago's goal but were unable to shoot. A pass to Sylvio Mantha led to a shot on goal that Gardiner saved with a pounce.

Slick line changes by the Hawks, player by player, and on the fly, made the game so fluid that fans and had little sense of the actual passage of time. Then Chicago's Stew Adams scored into the top left corner over Hainsworth's shoulder.

The Hawks' first lead of the series electrified their fans. Between the grand organ and the crowd noise, the Stadium became a vortex of noise that pushed into the heads of the players with a kind of deafening disorientation.

Being in the unfamiliar position of leading on the scoreboard, the Hawks began protecting that lead instead of attempting to increase it. The Canadiens took advantage of that psychological shift. For the rest of the period they became the aggressors.

Hawks defenders Clarence "Taffy" Abel and Cy Wentworth took every opportunity to hit the Canadiens. Rosie Couture paid particular attention to disrupting Morenz, who remained relentless. Graham cross-checked Morenz and was penalized.

Morenz led the power play, which began majestically. The *Montreal Star*: "In one sweeping assault Morenz went hurdling through and gave Joliat a great pass to the wing and the atom whipped in a driving shot that spun off Gardiner's pads and he knocked it to safety with his free hand."[1] The puck was then kept in the Hawks' zone, though a nervous Morenz, in front of the goal, missed a gift of a pass from Joliat.

After forty minutes, the teams remained separated by the single Adams goal. When Sylvio Mantha was penalized early in the third, coach Hart sent Morenz out to kill the disadvantage. He remained bound to his own zone as the Hawks pressed to add to their lead. When Mantha's penalty expired, Morenz stayed in the thick of the battle, joining Wasnie and Larochelle to sift through the Hawks' defence. Morenz took a shot on goal, which was saved by Gardiner.

Morenz seemed to begin playing better. He and the Canadiens again displayed that intimidating confidence. There were no flashes of frustration. They were methodical, determined, organized, and relentless. That discomfited the young Hawks, who were becoming more apprehensive with each moment, as were their fans. No one dared look away.

Hart replaced Sylvio Mantha with Nick Wasnie near the middle of the period so the Canadiens would be playing four forwards. As soon as space became available in the middle of the ice, Wasnie abandoned his defensive assignment. The *Globe* described how he "battered his way through, refusing to be checked and staggered up to Gardiner, driving desperately and scoring. It was a gallant piece of work."[2]

With fewer than eight minutes remaining in regulation time, the Canadiens were now in a position to win. Hart chose his next five skaters. That group included Morenz. Play resumed.

As he led one rush, then another, Morenz's performance was tipping the Hawks' fans from anxiety into an angry kind of fear. Their defenders appeared powerless to anticipate where Morenz was going to go, whether he might pass or just shoot. On defence, he was stealing chances back from the Hawks. His play seemed equal parts frenetic and magical. Sometimes Joliat was with him, sometimes Wasnie, sometimes Larochelle. When he began his third consecutive rush toward the Chicago end, the crowd actually started booing him, which only inspired him further.

On that same charge up the ice, Morenz attempted to get by Helge Bostrom. He suddenly tumbled into a "rolling fall," having been snagged on Bostrom's stick, which flew into the crowd. Bostrom was penalized.

Moments later, on the powerplay created by Bostrom's foul, Morenz confronted Hawk defenceman Taffy Abel as he crossed the blueline. Abel compelled him to move toward the outside. Abel stayed close enough to push Morenz away from the net, and then behind the goal line. The puck dribbled off Morenz's stick, allowing Gardiner to swat it to the far side of the ice. Abel was oblivious to that, continuing to drive Morenz toward, and into, the end boards.

Morenz may have tried to slow down, to duck away from the worst of the impact as his skates skidded across the broken and rutted third-period ice.

His feet may have lost contact while his left shoulder slammed off the boards at an awkward angle.[3] Morenz ended up flat on the ice behind the Chicago goal with no feeling in that shoulder. The game carried on with no penalty. The teams remained tied after sixty minutes.

At the start of the overtime Morenz again led the charge, regaining momentum and making several runs. He set up a chance for Larochelle and had more chances of his own. However, there were also signs that he was suffering. When he tried to shrug off coverage from the Hawks' Teddy Graham, he needed two hands rather than one to push Graham away.

After having seemed already *trop fatigué* at the end of the third period, Morenz's early overtime brightness dimmed quickly. His shoulder injury was getting the better of him. Of three open shots, he twice lost the puck. Gardiner repelled the third. Morenz may not have been playing at all, except that Hart's bench was getting short.

Pit Lepine was increasingly unavailable because of a broken finger. Sylvio Mantha had been concussed again. Johnny Gagnon, in a decision that rankled him for decades, had been pulled back from play because news had arrived that his father had just died in Chicoutimi. Major McLaughlin's Hawks were starting to reap unexpected advantages from their strategic management of playing time within their roster.

The Canadiens struggled to keep up in the second overtime. They looked *pitié a voir*, dead on their feet.[4] Morenz had been extinguished and was no longer involved at all. The Hawks ran into Hainsworth with impunity. The game came to an end when Johnny Gottselig intercepted a too-slow Canadiens pass in the Chicago zone. The *New York Times* said he "drove a shot that whistled past Hainsworth's right arm. He made no move to stop it, apparently having failed to see the puck."[5]

The Hawks won 2-1.

Hours later, in the dark on the train, Morenz awoke with severe shoulder pain. He was treated with hot towels, but the diagnosis was grim and travelled faster than the team. Monday's headline in the *Montreal Daily Star* struck Mary Morenz like a blow to the chest:

Howie Morenz May Not Play Again

In a special dispatch from London, Ontario, Baz O'Meara reported that Morenz's injury from the previous night was "similar to one he suffered in the Stanley Cup playoff in 1924," and that he would be rushed to hospital upon arriving home in Montreal.[6]

As the train rumbled across southern Ontario, Morenz continued to suffer the consequences of his lacerated shoulder muscles. He couldn't lift his arm. He couldn't sleep. When the Canadiens arrived at Bonaventure Station, Leo Dandurand ushered him swiftly into a waiting car to take him directly to Sir Henry Gray's hospital. He received an electrical treatment that very afternoon.[7]

***Canadiens* 1** at Chicago **2**

Morenz: 1 penalty

CHAPTER 8

Thursday, April 9, 1931

Black Hawks vs. Canadiens in Montreal

Broken

MORENZ REMAINED IN hospital undergoing intensive treatment. He arrived late Monday "unable to move his arm or twist his shoulder," reported the *Montreal Star*.[1] The injury was now thought to involve the collarbone as well. Armand Mondou and Albert Leduc, who had been concussed and in hospital since before the end of the Bruin series, were so shocked by the appearance of Morenz being settled into his bed that both insisted that they would get back on the ice Tuesday morning. When they did, they looked utterly incapable.

Sir Henry's lived up to its reputation as a field hospital. By Wednesday, Morenz's condition seemed sufficiently improved. He appeared on the ice, in full uniform, at the Canadiens' open practice. Once it became thinkable that Morenz might be available for Thursday's game, and that Johnny Gagnon would be back from the family funeral in Chicoutimi, the physical complaints of the other Canadiens were quieted.

The newspapers turned immediately to the question of why Morenz was experiencing the longest scoreless streak of his career. The variety of explanations offered were troubling. One moment he'd admit: "Just a slump, but I hope to make up for it in the next two games," he told the *Star* on April 7. "We are due for some good breaks, and some of us boys who have been missing should be hitting the twine from now on."[2]

And then he'd start to rationalize: "You only get about four or five real good scoring chances in a game when you can work right in on the goal tend," he told the *Star* on April 9. "When you are tripped and charged on nearly all these attempts it becomes difficult to score."[3]

Questions about his scoring drought still irked. Despite the completeness of every other aspect of his game, despite not getting credited with uncounted but real assists, he was still expected to put the puck in the net himself. It irked him even more because he also expected that of himself.

On Thursday Joe Cattarinich assured fans: "Morenz is perfectly fit to play and will be in his position this evening."[4] That night, as promised, Morenz skated into position for the opening faceoff in front of a sold-out Forum crowd.

Leo Dandurand had been more circumspect about the team's chances based on the overall injury situation. Regarding Morenz himself, Dandurand said: "Morenz is much better and his treatment with electricity has done him a world of good."[5]

As had occurred earlier in the regular season, Morenz had been outfitted with a special shoulder protector. This game would be a test of how well it would work.

The Hawks had the first chance, but Johnny Gagnon finished an early passing rush started by Marty Burke to give the Canadiens the early lead. Morenz took his regular turn through the first period, maintained the same skating pace as his teammates, and even got some penalty-killing time with Pit Lepine. His shots were weak, but he wasn't alone among the Canadiens in that respect. He did have one dangerous shot from the blueline, which hit the crossbar and bounced behind the net. That was his only shot of note in the period.

The second period began with a Hawks rush into the Canadiens' end, and a Tommy Cook shot that bloodied the face of George Hainsworth. A pause of a dozen minutes for stitching followed. Morenz and Joliat, rejoined by Gagnon, faced off for the resumption in play. *La Presse*: "Morenz made a sensational run, rounded the goal and shot, but Gardiner blocked. Joliat grabs the puck but shoots over the net, missing a certain goal."[6]

Morenz then shared a chance with Sylvio Mantha. The *Globe*: "On the next play, Morenz and Sylvio Mantha sandwiched Taffy Abel, and Morenz dashed headlong to the goalmouth, but could not get his shot away."[7]

After an exchange of unsuccessful chances, Pit Lepine calmed the pace behind the Canadiens' net, carried the puck through centre, and set up

Georges Mantha for a low shot that got past Gardiner. The Canadiens felt a flickering sense of triumph. Leading 2-0 close to the halfway point of the game, the fans filled the Forum with the sound of singing.

Morenz took control of the puck behind his goal. Feeling more physically able as his muscles warmed over the first thirty minutes, he darted forward. The crowd's roar rose behind him. He chose the left side, Cy Wentworth's side, on the way to the Chicago goal. Wentworth responded with a hard body check that sent Morenz down to the ice with a thud. Wentworth was penalized.

Morenz picked himself up, ignoring the renewed howls in his shoulder muscles. He shrugged off the pain. He did not look toward the Canadiens' bench as he moved to face the puck. He won the faceoff and got the puck to Joliat.

The *Montreal Herald*: "Canadiens might have secured a winning margin in this period, if their scoring punch had held. Hawks lost two men in quick succession, first Wentworth for tripping Morenz, then Bostrom for hooking Joliat as the latter seemed to have a clear lane to the nets. With a two-man advantage the Canadiens cut loose a furious five-man attack."[8]

In the middle of that two-man advantage, Joliat was forced into a penalty to stop a shorthanded Chicago breakaway. The Canadiens retained a man advantage. In the final seconds of the period, Morenz rode a breakaway right up to Gardiner. The goalie made the stop in a horseshoe save. There was another chance when Morenz got into an excellent position past the defence, but he overskated the puck.

That misstep provoked more rumbles of disappointment from the crowd. Despite his injuries and his obvious effort, he was failing to produce what the fans and he expected. He left the ice incredulous, embarrassed, and exhausted.

When the third period began, Morenz and Wasnie squared off against Cook and Adams for some five-on-five hockey. Again, Morenz immediately took the puck, making a long run and a shot, only to be again blocked by Gardiner.

Morenz remained in possession of the initiative. *La Patrie*: "Morenz managed to clear the puck from a mess of sticks and raced down the ice at full speed . . . But Gardiner made another great save and Howie hit the ice with the blade of his stick in frustration."[9]

Morenz regrouped, leading two new attacks. The first resulted in a hurried shot, followed by a better one, but Gardiner still blocked both.

Sylvio Mantha and Art Lesieur then took penalties as the Hawks pressed. Cecil Hart defended the two-man disadvantage with Morenz, Joliat, and Burke. The three, with Hainsworth, managed to protect the 2-0 lead. The struggle was taking its toll, but with less than five minutes remaining, the game still felt like a certain win.

It was not. Three minutes and forty seconds before the bell, Mush March was on the right boards when he received a pass from Gottselig. He sped toward Hainsworth and landed a high shot in the top corner of the net.

Howie Morenz refused to unravel at this reversal. His Canadiens were still a goal ahead. Gardiner stopped a Lepine breakaway, and then Morenz had his own chance. Ten feet away from the goal, as he was preparing his shot, Wentworth appeared and prevented any shot at all.

The Hawks got their tying goal during a pretty play. The *Globe*: "Cook and Adams split the Canadien defence and Adams secured the puck a little to the left of the net. He burned home a true shot, waist high."[10]

The Hawks' comeback and the Canadiens' collapse had taken about a minute.

Howie Morenz did what he could in the time left. He forced Doc Romnes into a penalty. As time was expiring, he fed Joliat a pass in front of the net. Gardiner's block on Joliat's quick attempt allowed the game to move to overtime.

Play resumed cautiously on slow ice. At one point, Morenz and Larochelle were sent out with Joliat, who was playing on the knife-edge of self-control. When Larochelle's shot was unsuccessful, Joliat bawled him out.

The game carried on. During a three-man Hawk rush, Hainsworth made a double stop off Romnes and March. He then stopped Gottselig again as the first overtime expired.

The contest remained deadlocked into the second overtime. Morenz felt his strength and breath flagging, but buckled down. Five minutes into the new period, the heavyweight Hawks defenders took advantage of his obvious exhaustion. "They frequently stretched him out on the ice," wrote *La Presse*. "It was a miracle that he made it to the end of the game."[11]

Morenz was forced to take a rest. The *Montreal Herald*: "Howie Morenz was dead on his feet and didn't know it. On a couple of occasions toward the end of the stirring battle he fell on the ice and could hardly lift his weary battered bones."[12]

At the midpoint of the second overtime, Hart sent Morenz out again, still with Larochelle and Joliat. At first, the play went into the Canadiens' end. Morenz carried the puck into the Hawks' territory, giving Larochelle a chance that caused Gardiner difficulty. Soon they tried again. Again, they were unsuccessful. Tommy Cook crashed Morenz into the boards while chasing the play. Morenz made another end-to-end rush later, at surprising speed, but didn't make it past the Hawks' defence, and was once again crashed into the boards.

He struggled back to his feet and summoned a remarkable defensive check on Vic Ripley. Morenz then set up Larochelle for another chance and took another stick to the head from Cy Wentworth. By now he was almost unable to stand on his skates. He must have been playing almost entirely on instinct.

The second overtime period bled into the third, as the game approached Friday morning. It began with Morenz centring Joliat and Rivers. At first the Canadiens seemed revived, until another tumble precipitated by Wentworth provoked a snarky butt-end by Morenz against Mush March.

The resulting Morenz penalty squelched the Canadiens' early energy, but Hainsworth, Burke, and Sylvio Mantha successfully bore the penalty-kill burden. Morenz emerged from the penalty box with the score still tied and stepped into an opportunity. *La Presse*: "Morenz picked up the puck and made one of his sensational runs as the crowd cheered wildly. As he was about to shoot, Wentworth hit the tip of his stick and saved a goal."[13]

Taffy Abel was penalized. On the penalty kill, Mush March made it worse when he grabbed the puck with his hand and tucked it underneath him. It gave the Canadiens a two-man advantage for nearly three minutes. Johnny Gagnon missed an open net "by the width of a hand," said the *Star*.[14]

Both teams seemed to have nothing left. Howie Morenz was back on the bench. Adams, Cook, and Wentworth broke from their end and the crowd moved to the edge of their seats. The *Gazette* concluded the exhausted narrative at the pace of Wentworth: "The latter raced in through centre and as Hainsworth dived to make the save, he burned in a high shot that bulged the twine high on the right side."[15]

It was 13:50 of the third overtime, and 12:20 a.m. Friday morning. Chicago had won again in overtime.

Howie Morenz had driven himself beyond the limits of his own endurance—and it had not been enough. In each of the three overtime periods, Morenz led the Canadiens' attack, distressed the Hawk defenders, and forced them to take penalties. Instead of recognizing his endurance, he and his fans remained disappointed and dissatisfied.

A funereal mood now hung over the Canadiens' dressing room. Eddie Dufour and Doc Corrigan helped Morenz into the training room where they could get rid of his skates, strip him of his uniform, and undo the harness and padding around his shoulder. His skin was pale and clammy. Dr. Gray appeared and the three men grimaced above Morenz's still, naked body stretched out before them. Then Eddie Dufour found towels to cover him.

Chicago **3** at ***Canadiens*** **2**

Morenz: 1 penalty

CHAPTER 9

Saturday, April 11, 1931

Black Hawks vs. Canadiens in Montreal

Courage

HOWIE MORENZ WOKE on Saturday morning to the scent of spring. Three Montreal-area golf courses were opening, and the major-league baseball season was scheduled to open Tuesday. His Canadiens were now facing defeat and elimination again. His whole body was exhausted. He had already played the equivalent of more than ten full playoff games in about twenty-one days.

When he turned idly to the newspaper, the *Herald*'s Elmer Ferguson sharply reminded him that: "Canadiens, weakening before the steady parade of fresh Hawks which poured into the fray like the German waves of soldiery swept into Belgium in 1914, lost what may have been the crucial game Thursday night."[1]

Later that morning he heard the sound of bagpipes and marching feet moving along Sherbrooke Street toward Percival Molson Memorial Stadium. This was the anniversary weekend of the Battle of Vimy Ridge.

Ferguson's evocation of the recent war was cultural. It dictated how this generation understood conflict, adversity, and how to be victorious. Athletes, like soldiers, were expected to throw themselves into the fray. Like true soldiers, athletes were admired when they went to the edge of death—and, if necessary, beyond. Like Roman gladiators, an athlete was expected to live "for only as long as he competes, and yet in those few moments he lives more purely, more intensely, than any spectator," wrote Stephen Amidon in his book *Something Like the Gods*. "That is why we continue to value him. More than any other figure, he reminds us of the athlete's ability to perform with the utmost passion and dignity even as the clock runs out on him."[2]

That kind of purity of commitment was something people understood when they spoke about Stanley Cup winner "One-eyed" Frank McGee. It was what Montrealers understood when remembering Percival Molson. And although it would take two more decades for his words to be emblazoned on the Canadiens' dressing room wall, it was how this city's hockey people understood poet and soldier John McCrae's challenge, penned in 1915:

Take up our quarrel with the foe
To you, from failing hands, we throw
The torch: be yours to hold it high[3]

Reminders of the war haunted Morenz through the rest of the morning. Dr. Gray's soft encouragement to rotate his shoulder was grounded in skills honed on the Great War's Belgian battlefields.

Morenz signed up for that war when he was just fifteen. He hopped the train from Stratford to Toronto to join the Royal Canadian Dragoons—at least long enough to get a picture in uniform at the Stanley Barracks. Some reports say he returned to Stratford the same season. His military career had lasted just a day, or perhaps overnight. His mother followed him to Toronto and abruptly brought his underage soul home.

He remembered his chance to win the Memorial Cup, itself a touchstone of the Great War. He earned his chance to participate in that battle, then failed. There had been no second opportunity.

By mid-afternoon at the Forum, all the Canadiens learned how Johnny Gagnon had arrived home in Chicoutimi to find his father's casket taking up so much space in the family home that it was nearly impossible to sleep or eat or even live there. He had helped to carry the coffin out of the house, to the cathedral, and then bury it. Later that night he made it back to Montreal, just about game time. He put on his uniform and scored to give the Canadiens their first lead. The burial of his father had freed him from the paralysis of the death vigil.

Marty Burke echoed that same sense of release. Ever since George Owen had stopped his heart at the end of game three against Boston, he no longer needed to fear what could have happened. He was playing the best hockey, the most important hockey, of his life. Whatever happened next was always going to be better than being a battlefield casualty.

The Hawks now felt that they could not lose, becoming perhaps a team of destiny. In seven playoff games they had lost just once. In three overtimes, they had three victories. But if the Hawks believed winning was inevitable, they were doomed. Their hubris would become the coffin on their bench.

Someone mentioned that Ed "the Hatter" Michaud was running a promotion to give a new hat to every Canadiens player who scored in the series. Morenz was able to chuckle, responding that it was likely he will go collegiate and spend the summer bare-headed.[4]

He knew that he had become the big gun silenced. His scoreless stretch of eight playoff games actually extended to the first period of the March 14 game against the Senators. He was really riding a nine-game goalless streak, a failure that continued to sting.

The sold-out crowd assembling outside the Forum confronted the prospect of failure. Many wondered whether the Canadiens had the mental resilience for their task after they had watched the last game's chances evaporate in the last four minutes.

They had already failed like that against Boston, in games one and five. Morenz had been in a similar situation in 1928. After enjoying a spectacular regular season, the Canadiens had stumbled in their very first playoff game against the Maroons.

He had explained it then, to *La Patrie*, as a disruption of confidence: "First of all, I have to tell you straight away that I'm not at all satisfied with my performance this evening. I didn't feel at ease and my nerves, obviously, played a nasty trick on me. I tried valiantly to pull myself together several times, but nothing seemed to work. I went so far as to ask to stay on the bench in the last few minutes. Athletes, on the eve of and during an important event, quite often experience changes in condition for no apparent reason, changes that can only be explained by high nervous tension."[5]

Howie Morenz and the Canadiens had not been able to recover in 1928. Could they now?

Shortly before 8:30 pm, the Hawks took to the ice with bright faces and enthusiasm.

Cecil Hart changed his earlier lineup, opting to give his favourite a vote of confidence. George Hainsworth led the Canadiens onto the ice, followed defiantly by Morenz. When referee Alex Romeril took the puck to centre ice, Morenz skated into place for the opening drop.

The Canadiens' chances depended on a fast start. Instead, Johnny Gottselig poked a loose puck into the net before Sylvio Mantha had been able to clear it.[6] The Canadiens were down a goal on the game's very first shift.

The Hawks followed up the psychological blow of an early defensive failure and a soft goal by physically hammering the home team. The *Gazette*: "Howie Morenz, streaking between Bostrom and Graham, was sandwiched and sent flying over their crossed sticks."[7]

The staggering blow of the first Hawks goal was just the beginning. The Canadiens were caught looking at their own end boards for a second time as the trailing Chicago forward scored, putting the Hawks up 2-0 just before the fifteen-minute mark.

Fear gripped and stifled the home team's play. The *Montreal Herald*: "For the greater part of the first period Canadiens looked lifeless. They were outskated, seemed on the verge of losing their heads as taut nerves began to jangle, and rough play developed."[8]

As Morenz admitted in 1928, any anxiety among the fans in situations like this mirrored what was already being felt among the Canadiens: "Believe me, if you were uncomfortable, I was a thousand times more so than you."[9]

The Hawks sensed an opportunity to complete their quest. Ripley, Gottselig, and Couture swept up the ice. Couture, nostrils wide with anticipation, swung around behind the net. The *Gazette*: "When in rounding Canadiens' cage, he pulled Hainsworth from the side of his nets, and slammed him into the boards. That was too blatant to overlook."[10]

Hart sent Morenz out for the power play for Couture's penalty. Taffy Abel tripped Morenz and tumbled him to the ice almost immediately, without penalty. Cy Wentworth headed back into the Canadiens' zone, carrying the puck on a short-handed try. Burke dumped Wentworth just as Abel had dumped Morenz. But Burke was penalized.

Burke objected strongly, as did the crowd. He bumped referee Bobby Hewitson as a tumult of riot roiled through the Forum. The pandemonium disrupted Foster Hewitt's historic radio broadcast. The shattering of a gin bottle on the ice, among other missiles, served as the culmination of that moment.

Sylvio Mantha and Albert Leduc left the Canadiens' bench to speak with the referees. After lying helpless in hospital for weeks, where he lost eighteen pounds, Leduc remained on the ice when play finally resumed. Twice he was flattened while attempting to lead a rush. When he saw Mush March hit Pit Lepine in the head with his stick, Leduc retaliated. Leduc and March each received major penalties.

With those majors, and Burke's continuing minor, the Canadiens were defending three skaters against four in the dying minutes of the period. Hart turned once again to Morenz and Gagnon. They helped neutralize Chicago's offence and produced two short-handed chances, but no goals, to end the period.

The Hawks were forty minutes away from a Stanley Cup triumph. Leo Dandurand marched off to a radio interview to complain about the physical abuse of his players that started during the Boston series. Major McLaughlin held court rinkside with his wife, the dancer Irene Castle, anticipating a Hawk victory. NHL president Frank Calder made his way to the referees' room.

During intermission, Howie Morenz made an important speech in the hushed Canadiens' room.[11] According to both Wil Larochelle and coach Hart, Morenz was as magnificent a leader in the room as he was on the ice.

A refreshed attitude was unmistakable as Morenz took the opening faceoff of the second period. Both Morenz and Gagnon began leading *avec ardeur*. The team began to play in a cohesive and methodological manner, setting the pace from the outset of the period.

An early penalty to Gagnon had not changed the aggression in Morenz's game. He hit Bostrom on the head with his stick, which the referees ignored. Now none of the Canadiens had any reason to play shy or careful hockey. Cecil Hart also chose to play four forwards and just a single defenceman: Burke.

Gagnon emerged from the crowded penalty box, followed by Leduc. The *Montreal Herald*: "Leduc pounded inside the blue line, and feinting around, finally slid a pass to Gagnon. Morenz flashed inside, almost to the mouth of the cage, but Jonny crossed up Gardiner, for instead of giving Morenz the pass, he whipped away a stinging drive that hooked the far corner."[12]

It was Chicago 2, Canadiens 1.

Hart's four forwards continued to play inside the Hawks' blueline for most of the rest of the period. Chicago struggled to adjust to the different game now being called by the referees.

Morenz continued to be a commanding presence on the ice. The Canadiens now dominated play. The *Montreal Herald*: "During part of the second period Canadiens attacked with such intensity that for thirteen minutes Hainsworth didn't have a thing to do. Gagnon, Mantha, Morenz and Joliat stormed all over the Hawk defence and for a time Taffy Abel and his mates were bewildered. During those hectic moments Graham tossed Morenz and was chased. When he came back he was again waved out of action for spilling Joliat."[13]

Although the Hawks continued to hold their one-goal lead after forty minutes, the Canadiens had succeeded in moving the coffin.

Morenz and Joliat renewed the contest in the third period "like starving wolves," said *La Patrie*.[14] Gagnon was lifting himself to his best game of the year. When Bostrom took yet another penalty in an effort to stop Gagnon, Burke carried the initial rush. The *Montreal Star*: "Threading his way from his defensive position, he passed carefully to Wasnie. The latter slipped a neat pass to Gagnon and he whipped in another goal as Morenz sped toward the nets. The rink almost trembled with the ensuing uproar."[15]

The game was now even at 2-2. On the very next shift Lepine missed a chance and banged his own stick on the ice in frustration.

The Canadiens killed a penalty to Sylvio Mantha. Then Gagnon gave a perfect pass to Lepine from behind the net, a pass he would remember and savour for years. Lepine's shot was a dagger from twenty-five feet out, making the score 3-2 for the Canadiens.

The Canadiens continued to attack. Lepine found the net a second time, putting the Canadiens ahead by two. In a new mid-game ritual of success, every one of his teammates, now his Forum brothers, flooded over the boards to congratulate him.

There were three-and-a-half minutes left in regulation time. Hart kept Morenz on the ice. His words between the first and second periods had changed the attitude and effort of the entire team. The *Star* declared that his play in the second and third periods had been "a lion-hearted exhibition."[16]

Suddenly, with no one around him, Morenz stumbled while skating, made a brief arcing flight through the air, and crumpled heavily, head-first, into the bottom of the side boards. A penny protruding from the surface of the ice, perhaps left over from the riot of two periods before, was the cause.

A new pall of misfortune lingered around his empty chair in the dressing room. For an hour his body was again the focus of medical staff. He was wracked with pain.

The newspapermen returned to their cultural allusions about the war. There would be a final battle. The players would face more struggle and sacrifice.

Chicago **2** at ***Canadiens*** **4**

Morenz: Nothing

CHAPTER 10

Tuesday, April 14, 1931

Black Hawks vs. Canadiens in Montreal

The All-Time Forum Goal

WITH NEARLY THREE full days off before the fifth and final game of the Cup final, the Canadiens could finally relax at home with their families. There was a light skate for some at the Forum on Monday morning, while trainer Jim McKenna treated Morenz with hot towels and massage.

Major McLaughlin had returned to Chicago. Coach Irvin decided he would respect his veterans and not demand that they observe a curfew. Louis Letourneau invited the bored and idle Hawks to wrestling matches on Monday evening as his guests. If the Hawks felt suspicious of his motives, they didn't allow it to get in the way of a good time.

By early Tuesday morning a line of eager fans encircled the Forum, waiting for the sale of rush tickets. At the Windsor Hotel, Dick Irvin discovered some of the Hawks worse for wear from their night before. The official report was that Chicago's scoring ace Johnny Gottselig had come down with "the *grippe*."[1] The unofficial concern was that some of the Hawks had been induced to indulge in alcoholic excess during and after the wrestling. When Irvin arrived at the Forum, he gave a terse comment: "All our players are in good condition and we have no alibi. May the best team win."[2]

A national audience clustered around their radio sets to listen as Howie Morenz played for the Cup. His physical capacity to play remained the most significant concern for fans, coaches, opponents, and teammates. Baz

O'Meara reported the conventional wisdom that Howie would "toddle into action, as nothing short of bone breakages would keep him out."[3]

For the Hawks, even Gottselig, though under the weather, was dressed to play.

At puck-drop, Morenz was at centre. He and Gagnon initiated early chances, but it was the Hawks who held the upper hand through the first twenty minutes, accumulating a 10-3 shot advantage. Supported by the steady play of George Hainsworth and the imperturbable calm of Marty Burke, the Hawks were kept at bay primarily by the efforts of Aurèle Joliat.

Morenz was having a complicated game. At one point he fed Joliat with a pass as he crossed the Hawks' blueline. When he started to work into position for a return pass he became tangled with Tommy Cook. They then tussled again in centre ice until Morenz threw the much lighter player to the ice, injuring Cook's face. Cook appeared to have been holding Morenz so both were penalized for scragging. The referees ignored the Hawks' complaints that because Morenz had drawn blood from Cook, the Canadien should have been given a major.

Still cut and bleeding when he left the penalty box, Cook seized the puck inside his own zone and made two rushes. Burke and Hainsworth stymied the first. Morenz disarmed the second. The score remained blank at the end of the first period.

Morenz then began to sparkle more. The *Globe*: "As the second period opened, Morenz cut loose with one of his old-time rushes which carried him through the defence and in on Gardiner. The goaler made the perfect sliding save as Morenz's speed carried him past the goal and into the boards back first."[4]

Larochelle did the same, and then Morenz created another chance. The *Montreal Star*: "Twice [he] was able to race through an open defence and get his sights adjusted for a shot that would beat the almost invulnerable Gardiner. The first time he was swinging to the goalmouth when he missed the puck entirely in his anxiety."[5]

Rather than anxiety, it was actually a problem with his stick. As he turned away from the net to skate back down the ice, he looked in consternation at the blade. He carried on but yelled out to Eddie Dufour and shook his stick as he passed the bench.

Toward the midpoint of regulation time, Mush March was penalized. Johnny Gottselig attempted to kill the penalty all on his own. The *Gazette*:

"Johnny Gottselig was putting on one of his expert exhibitions of stickhandling at centre ice to waste time, but he was cornered on the east boards by Morenz and Joliat. The latter stole the puck while Gottselig and Morenz tangled."[6]

Joliat and Gagnon surprised and overwhelmed the Hawks' defence and solved Gardiner for the game's opening goal. The goalie broke his stick in disappointment.

The Hawks fretted that Morenz had interfered with Gottselig while Joliat and Gagnon slipped away. The referees were deaf to that. Morenz was still playing in the minds of the Hawks.

Morenz was also playing differently, with a serenity he hadn't shown since the bruising he suffered during the Bruin series. *The Montreal Star*: "Morenz, going forward and backward, was the same old whirlwind that stood the league on its head all the way through the season."[7]

It had become evident to those who knew Morenz best that he had adjusted the pitch of his play: despite the damage to his left shoulder, the head strikes he had suffered in the playoffs from the sticks of Cy Wentworth and Eddie Shore; the torn ligaments in his left knee and ankle; and the rib injuries that kept him out of five regular season games. He was psychologically committed to completing the pledge he had made to repeat as a Stanley Cup champion.

Athletes are in a privileged position to be able to recognize when the best among them rise to a superior level. Babe Ruth once told Leo Dandurand that Morenz played with "the biggest heart of any athlete he had ever known."[8] Morenz himself acknowledged that his "heart" was the necessary resource for escaping the traps of disappointment and failure in important games.

He and his teammates were now within sight of completing their quest successfully. It had taken an unstinting effort from him and each of those teammates. It had demanded determination and chance to overcome good and equally skilled opponents. His body and his game skills were now the only tools available to make the finish. What remained of either when the end came was irrelevant.

There was still half of the second period, and all of the third, to protect the slimmest of leads, but he and his team were playing from a position of command.

Albert Leduc became more visible as the Hawks attempted to come back. The Hawks eventually forced him into a penalty. The coaches chose their champions: for the Hawks, it would be Gottselig, Adams, Cook, and March attempting to force a break, while Lepine and Morenz faced them on the front line.

After two significant saves by Hainsworth, and an emergency disruption by Burke, Hart decided to change. The Canadiens would be better served if he used his best offensive line on the penalty kill.

The *Gazette*: "He threw three forwards on his depleted squad, leaving only Burke on the defence. The effect was instantaneous. Play swerved to the Chicago end of the rink as Morenz, Gagnon and Joliat set a terrific pace and the play was still humming around Gardiner when Leduc skated back into play."[9]

The tension on the ice became thicker, with tempers flaring and players being knocked down left and right—with no penalties called. "The managers quickly pulled the offenders to the side to avoid punishment," claimed the *Globe*. "Morenz and Cook were tussling, as were Joliat and Adams."[10]

The period ended with Hainsworth stopping Tommy Cook again.

During the intermission, Joliat marshalled all of his mental, emotional, and physical resources for the final twenty minutes of the game. Morenz sat silently beside him, admiring the stores of energy his friend held in reserve for just this moment. It comforted him and allowed him to relax with his own rediscovered confidence.

The game struggled for a climax through the third period. Nick Wasnie was penalized. Gagnon was injured by an unpenalized hack from Adams, compounded by a skate cut to his wrist, which forced Gagnon from the game.

As the pressure increased on the Hawks to equalize, each contact became a collision, each brush an abrasion. No one knew whether the referees were going to react.

The Canadiens were crowding their own zone, limiting the Hawks' room to skate, pass, or shoot, when "suddenly Morenz broke away from the milling pack around the Canadien nets when the teams were at full strength and had only Graham to beat," wrote the *Gazette*. "The Stratford star streaked around the defenceman but was hooked when he was ready to shoot and Graham drew a minor penalty."[11]

His sudden and surprising late-game speed created a chance and a power play.

But the Canadiens could not extend their lead. As soon as the Hawks regained full strength, Pit Lepine took two minors in quick succession.

Joliat made a few acidic remarks to his teammates as he skated past the bench. Having adopted the same commitment as his friend Morenz, Joliat was absolutely unwilling to lose this opportunity due to carelessness or inattention.

The Canadiens were again forced onto the defensive, but few Hawks shots actually reached Hainsworth. *La Presse* reported how Morenz backchecked effectively: "Not only did he fight furiously on the attack, but he performed wonders on defence and saved several goals by checking opponents at a critical moment or making them lose the puck as they were about to shoot. The whole time he was on the ice, Morenz did a tremendous job."[12]

Albert Leduc burst out of the Canadiens' end with time expiring on the second Lepine penalty. Bullying his way down the ice, he drove himself into Gardiner and the net. Play stopped. The score remained 1-0. Gardiner took time to recover.

From the next faceoff, Morenz reasserted his control of the ice. He made one rush that added to his legend, tearing down the left wing at such velocity "that everybody caught a cold in the dome from the draft he created," said the *Herald*. "His shot blazed in with such speed that it nearly went through the nets and came out on Atwater Avenue."[13]

Hyperbole would not complete the victory. Morenz had not scored. The Hawks' defence recovered and launched a four-man rush toward the Canadiens' end. Morenz circled back through the middle of the rink. He played with anticipation, as if he already knew that this moment, this game, could be the best of his life. He would meet it. He scrambled all over the Forum ice just as if he was back in his hometown on the frozen river.

The *Montreal Star* captured the next moments:

> *The puck went loose at centre, and he was on it like a hawk. Turning slightly to gain momentum he broke for the left boards at cannonball speed.*
>
> *Cook tried to waylay him, but he raced away, and Wentworth, one the fastest skaters in the league, as his name of "Cyclone" attests, raced over to head him off. Bending low on his skates, Morenz flew by him in a mighty stride, and as he did so whipped his shot with a sweep of the blade that almost put a curve into his stick. The puck rose in a dizzy streak and flashed under Gardiner's guard before he could upraise his arm, and whistled to the cords in the left-hand corner of the net.*[14]

The Gazette watched Morenz savour the moment, noting "there was nobody in the rink as pleased as Howie was himself."[15]

Aurèle Joliat remembered the moment as "the goal of goals," and "the all-time Forum goal." Not even a career of Rocket Richard goals could make him forget that moment.[16]

Chicago **0** at ***Canadiens* 2**

Morenz: 1 goal

What Happened After

IN FUTURE YEARS, Joliat would claim to have assisted on the goal, and Gagnon would claim to have scored it. But this final scoring play of the 1930–31 NHL season was only ever Howie Morenz, unassisted.

Eddie Dufour knew what had changed to allow that moment. He said Morenz had "changed his stick between periods, as the one he had been using wasn't bent enough. He went back to his old flail, and it was one of his favorite hickorys that sent the puck spinning behind Gardiner."[1]

Throughout the Forum there was bedlam. Across Canada, the effect on radio listeners was immediate. In St. Catharines, Ontario, John Downey jerked forward in his chair when he heard Foster Hewitt's urgent call that Morenz had captured the loose puck at centre. There was a roar. Downey heard Hewitt saying "score!" and while beginning to stand up and shouting back at the radio, Downey died.[2]

After the goal, while smothered by his teammates, Morenz staggered to the bench for a short rest before returning to the ice to finish the game.

The chant of victory, ignited by his goal, continued to the finish. The *Montreal Star*: "It was worth the price of admission alone to listen to the mighty chorus of victory as the fireflies, the matches that are lighted in the crowd when the end of the match is near, began to appear."[3]

Even though the Hawks managed to bounce a puck off the Canadiens' goalpost before the finish, there was no longer any doubt or fear. His goal became the final nail in the visitors' coffin. Howie Morenz and his teammates had repeated as champions, and he had reached his third in eight years.

He told the writers afterward: "I sure feel good about that goal. It worried me not being able to score in the whole playoff series. Everything is all right now, though."[4]

He kept a firm grip on the stick that had lifted him to the moment so he could give it to his nephew in Toronto. The puck itself, reputed to be a special-edition Spalding wooden insert puck, remains in the memorabilia auction market almost a century later.

The ice crew was already breaking up the playing surface with ice saws, but fans remained in the stands even as the celebrations clogged the Canadiens' dressing room. Even the corridor outside their room "was something else again," reported the *Ottawa Journal*. "Ushers and police were powerless in the press of well-wishers, all waiting to catch a glimpse of their heroes. There were many girls waiting for the chance of congratulating their particular choice of the world's champions."[5]

Fewer than twenty-four hours after that goal, the Canadiens gathered at the very crowded grand ballroom at the Windsor Hotel for a Stanley Cup banquet. The crowd that showed up was close to the advertised capacity of five hundred.

The Frolics' nightclub orchestra, under the direction of Billy Munro and featuring some of the Frolics' entertainers, provided a portion of the entertainment. Some of the Canadiens sang, and a new song: "Les Champions Canadiens," was heard.[6]

Cup trustee Bill Foran was on hand to officially present the Stanley Cup. Each of the teammates was given enough trinkets to fill a suitcase. The players' record share of playoff money had already been estimated at $3,000 per player. Morenz was personally singled out for the presentation of a painting which unveiled its own surprise: a Hugh Delaserre portrait of Morenz as he would ideally appear, ready to play hockey twenty years in the future, in 1950.[7] On nights like this he, and everyone else, wanted to imagine that he would be able to play hockey forever.

When the players were called upon to make speeches, Leslie Roberts of *Maclean's* noted that "Morenz eulogized the substitutes and his manager and declared that theirs is the credit for ultimate victory."[8]

His eyes darted out across the room, searching out faces that he knew, others he thought he knew, and some whom he wondered if he had seen somewhere else. His gaze moved to the faces of fathers and grandfathers in the room, seeing Molsons and Bronfmans—scions of two Montreal families which would, over the course of the next half-century, take custody of the hockey club.

Howie Morenz followed up that second consecutive Stanley Cup season by leading the Canadiens to another first-place finish in the Canadian Division of the NHL, and first place overall, in 1931–32. He appeared in all forty-eight regular season games and collected forty-nine points in the scoring race (twenty-four goals and twenty-five assists). It was his seventh consecutive season leading the Canadiens in goals scored—a record that endures to this day. He was again named the winner of the Hart Trophy as the NHL's most valuable player. By winning the Hart for the third time he achieved something that no member of the Canadiens has replicated. The Canadiens, however, were eliminated from the 1932 Stanley Cup playoffs in the first round, without Morenz scoring a goal.

On December 14, 1933, with his 239th goal, he became the top goal-scorer in league history and surpassed Cy Denneny as the NHL record holder for most points. A severe ankle injury during the 1933–34 season resulted in him missing nine games, and he netted just eight goals. Then he was gone.

The trade day, which had once seemed unimaginable, came abruptly at the end of an unsuccessful contract negotiation in October 1934. Morenz knew that Dandurand had been shopping him. Within a month of the Canadiens' playoff elimination that spring (at the hands of the Cup-bound Black Hawks), Morenz was being offered for the price of $50,000. No one was buying. A move to Chicago, with players and cash moving between three different clubs, was completed in time for Morenz to headline the opening night of the Hawks' own championship defence in St. Louis against the Eagles.

Although there had been contemplation of a three-year contract in Chicago, Morenz only played for McLaughlin's Hawks for about fifteen months. Time away from the Canadiens and Montreal had been unhappy, and even a trade in January 1936 to the Rangers provided only temporary relief to his estrangement from the game.

The NHL officially acknowledged the nature of that estrangement. In their 1937 league guide they wrote, "He had scaled hockey's highest pinnacle many times during his career. He had been hailed from all sides as one of the greatest players in the history of the game. He knew what it meant to be traded from the club he had learned to love in the way a patriot loves his country."[9]

Howie Morenz returned to the Canadiens in the fall of 1936 in an all-cash deal with the Rangers. Whether his late-career play that last partial season is seen as spirited, inspired, or even courageous, it can also be seen as frantic and dangerously desperate.

He pushed his body past the point of failure. Even if he should have known how to manage his increasing physical limitations, in the midst of play he could forget. Perhaps he really could not play any other way. On January 28, 1937, he confronted the consequence of that style when he broke his left leg in a collision against the Forum's south-end boards.

Morenz described it as an accident, as did others. Some tried to blame Chicago defenceman Earl Seibert, but Toe Blake attributed the whole unhappy event to too much speed. Johnny Gagnon had foreseen the likelihood of Morenz speeding past his physical capacity to play: "Morenz was a very fast hockey player, extremely fast. He'd skate so fast sometimes that you'd think he was going through the end boards."[10]

Novelist Hugh MacLennan's personal recollection of the final night echoed the same thought. "He had been playing marvelously and the little smile on his lips showed that he was having a wonderful time," MacLennan wrote in a 1954 essay. "But once too often he charged into the corner relying on his ability to turn on a dime and come out with the puck. The point of one of his skates impaled itself in the boards . . . Howie's head hit the ice with a sickening crack and he was carried out."[11]

Morenz knew his career was over from the moment he collided with the boards. In the Canadiens' dressing room, and as he was carried out of the Forum, he wept.[12]

Over the next six weeks there were hopeful newspaper stories about his recovery and possible return as a player. There were hospital visits from family, children, bon-vivants, and a teenaged Yves Gabias. Morenz panicked about the future. His own scoring records were already being overtaken even as he was immobile in hospital. There was a documented depression and mental breakdown in late February. It was reported to be lifting by early March.

Howie Morenz died on the night of March 8, 1937. Death from a broken leg seemed too trivial for the career that had preceded it. His community of fans developed fanciful ideas that he had died from a broken heart, what the local papers fancifully described as a *mort de peine*. Instead, the cause was more mundane. Morenz succumbed in his bed to an embolism, the result of blood clots[13] that may have led to a heart attack.[14] It was a fatal chain of events now well understood, and which should have been medically manageable even in 1937.

After he died at St. Luke's Hospital on the evening of March 8, kids set up a shrine of sticks and skates at the William Wray Funeral Parlour. There was an inquest into his death, and then he lay in state at centre ice of the Forum. John Leblanc of the Canadian Press commented that it was the first time that the "restless Howie" had been "still" in the Forum, and that the time he would spend in his grave would provide the long rest he would not take in life.[15]

There were claims that Howie Morenz's funeral at the Forum was the largest in Canadian history. Other services and memorials were observed in Stratford and in arenas hosting games at every level of hockey. It was a transitional time for Canadian society's reckoning with its relationship with Morenz.

"They gave him a funeral such as they would tender a prince of the realm or a dignitary of the church," wrote Baz O'Meara.[16] Horace Lavigne of *La Patrie* proposed the idea of Morenz being a spiritual figure: "It was Morenz who transformed his beloved tricolour club; he was its soul, its inspiration, its jet, its resurrection."[17]

Tommy Munns of the *Globe and Mail* described how the Canadiens "carried from the Forum the body of their comrade—carried it shoulder high, every bit as high as they might have borne him off the ice after a great victory in days gone by. To this writer, the way they carried him seemed to signify a triumph over death."[18]

Morenz's place in the culture of the Canadiens as a spiritual and religious figure, priest or spirit, remains unique in the history of the hockey club. A generation after Morenz's death, Rocket Richard's biographer Gerard Gosselin would still refer to the passing of Morenz as "*le depart de l'immortel numero 7*."[19]

Ken Dryden wrote that in order for a hockey player to have enduring significance, they need to occupy some imaginative space: "The people who are truly great players, there is something of them left in the imagination that is beyond statistics. If you close your eyes, you can see that person."[20]

Using Dryden's idea as a "hockey" idea rather than a "religious" idea, Howie Morenz made himself understood as someone larger and grander than just an especially skilled player. He had acquired the Canadiens' sense of tradition from Georges Vezina and become the club's next spiritual leader, taking responsibility for the team's soul until the torch could be passed to whomever might come next.

Howie Morenz provided a template showing how any hockey player, but particularly a Montreal Canadien, should approach the game. A true Canadien would play fiercely and passionately, even to the death, for the sake of winning. He bequeathed that to the club and anyone else who chose to follow him in the *Sainte-Flanelle*.

His hometown newspaper, the *Stratford Beacon-Herald*, wrote that when he died, Morenz "was at the zenith of his fame. He had already achieved all the success and glory that the hockey rink had to offer, but he had paid the full price for it by throwing the last ounce of energy into the game. Perhaps he overdid it—but Howie was built that way."[21]

The arc of Howie Morenz's athletic career also became the standard against which a century of Canadians would evaluate the impact of every subsequent hockey player's devotion, achievement, and contribution to the game. Charles Mayer of *La Patrie* anticipated that in 1937, writing: "It will never be seen again, but the long journey of a comet or a meteor is never forgotten, especially when, in its wake, this dazzling star has left indelible signs of great valour, heroic courage and countless glories."[22]

In December 1950, more than a dozen years after his death and a generation after his best season ever, Howie Morenz was named by Canadian newspapers as the greatest hockey player of the half-century. It was a testament not only about how he played the game, but how he had imbued more than a generation of Canadians with memories and a foundational understanding about the culture of the game.

APPENDIX

The Statistical Record

HOWIE MORENZ'S PERSONAL objective was to reach five hundred points before he retired.[1] Based on the statistics—as they were kept when he was still playing in late January 1937—he would have known that he was close to his target.

His desire to create scoring plays remained central to his game. His final goal at the Forum was the opening goal against the New York Americans in a 5-1 Canadiens win on January 2. His final goal in the NHL was at the Chicago Stadium on January 19. In his last three games he had five points: an assist on a tying goal against the Rangers, that final goal and an assist in Chicago, and then assists on two Joliat goals at Maple Leaf Gardens. Cecil Hart remembered those final games, on their last trip just before Morenz broke a leg: "I can say on good authority that Howie looked and played as well as at any time in his life."[2]

For much of the last century, the consensus appeared to be that Morenz scored 270 NHL regular-season goals.[3] Official NHL records have since added a goal for the 1924–25 season (28 instead of 27), and now *also* credit Morenz with nine goals during the 1933–34 season, rather than the eight normally shown in previous statistical accounts. Those adjustments raise his career regular-season goal total to 272.[4]

Traditionally, Morenz had also been credited with 197 regular-season career assists. Official NHL records now calculate that career assist total as 201.[5] With his 272 goals, that would grant Morenz 473 regular-season points. Adding in his playoff totals of 21 goals and 11 assists in Stanley Cup play, Morenz finished his NHL career with 505 total points.[6]

With the recent statistical adjustments, by the close of the 1930–31 season and playoffs, Howie Morenz scored 226 goals, with 93 assists, for 319 points.

That represented 83.1 percent of his career goal scoring and 62.7 percent of his career-total goal production in his first eight seasons.

That idea of a scoring decline attributable to a lack of enthusiasm for the Chicago style after his trade in October 1934 has remained common among hockey writers and was sometimes encouraged by Morenz himself. However, he had 26 assists to go with his eight goals in 48 games in the 1934–35 season. Playing on a supporting line rather than as a starter, Morenz remained involved in nearly 30 percent of the Black Hawks' scoring—close to the share he had in his years playing with the Canadiens. Then, when he was shunted off to New York for what has generally been regarded as the nadir of his career, he accumulated seven points (two goals, five assists) in 18 games, which was a contribution to the Ranger offence of 18 percent over those games.

His level of production in his final season with the Canadiens remained consistent with his earlier years in Montreal and Chicago. In the fall of 1936—allegedly washed up as an offensive force and seeing reduced ice time—he had four goals and 16 assists in 29 games for the Canadiens (he broke his leg early in the thirtieth game). Those 20 scoring points represented a participation rate of 32.3 percent in the Canadiens' 62 goals to that point in his final, partial season.[7] He remained an accomplished creator of goals until the very end.

He also remained an effective and valuable player. By the time of his final game, Morenz was only scoring about every eight games on average. At the same time, he was contributing four times as many other goals by the passes he made. He spread his 20 points over 15 different games during that partial 29-game season. Five times in those 15 he assisted on the Canadiens' winning goal. Twice he assisted on a goal that created a tie game. Five times he had two-point games—including in his last appearances at both the Chicago Stadium and Maple Leaf Gardens, both wins by the Canadiens. His contributions helped secure 15 of the 37 points his team had in the league standings at the time he was injured.

		Season					*Playoff*				
	Team	GP	G	A	Pts	PiM	GP	G	A	Pts	PiM
1923–24	CHC	24	13	3	16	20	6	7	2	9	10
1924–25	CHC	30	28	12	40	37	6	7	1	8	10
1925–26	CHC	31	23	3	26	39	DNP				
1926–27	CHC	44	25	7	32	49	4	1	0	1	4
1927–28	CHC	43	33	18	51	66	2	0	0	0	12
1928–29	CHC	42	17	10	27	47	3	0	0	0	6
1929–30	CHC	44	40	10	50	72	6	3	0	3	10
1930–31	CHC	39	28	23	51	49	10	1	4	5	10
1931–32	CHC	48	24	25	49	46	4	1	0	1	4
1932–33	CHC	46	14	21	35	32	2	0	3	3	2
1933–34	CHC	39	9	12	21	21	2	1	1	2	0
1934–35	CBH	48	8	26	34	21	2	0	0	0	0
1935–36	CBH	24	4	10	14	20					
	NYR	18	2	5	7	6	DNP				
1936–37	CHC	30	4	16	20	12	DNP				
TOTAL		**550**	**272**	**201**	**473**	**537**	**47**	**21**	**11**	**32**	**68**

Notes

This book is deeply indebted to the work of Dean Robinson in the late 1970s, particularly his book *Howie Morenz: Hockey's First Superstar* (Erin, Ontario: Boston Mills Press, 1982). That first proper biography collected the voices of Morenz's own generation: the people who grew up with him, who had the opportunity to watch him play, and who experienced his original impact among thousands of hockey fans across North America. That scholarship, so essential to understanding the phenomenon of Morenz, cannot be replicated. Robinson's work has ensured that his biography will remain a cornerstone of any serious appreciation of the cultural impact of Howie Morenz into the future. For that he deserves both appreciation and enduring thanks.

BOOKS:

Barrette, Rosaire, *Leo Dandurand Sportsman* (Ottawa: Le Droit, 1952)

Beddoes, Richard, Stan Fischler, and Ira Gitler, *Hockey! The World's Fastest Sport* (New York: Macmillan Publishing Co., Inc., 1973)

Benedict, Michael, and D'Arcy Jenish, eds., *Hockey on Ice: 50 Years of Great Hockey* (Toronto: Penguin Books, 1999)

Fischler, Stan, *Those Were the Days: The Lore of Hockey by the Legends of the Game* (New York: Dodd, Mead & Company, 1976)

Fischler, Stan, and Shirley Fischler, *Heroes and History: Voices from the NHL's Past* (Toronto: McGraw-Hill Ryerson, 1993)

Frayne, Trent, *Famous Hockey Players* (New York: Dodd, Mead & Company 1973)

Gzowski, Peter, *The Game of Our Lives* (Surrey, B.C.: Heritage House Publishing Ltd., 2004)

Liss, Howard, *Goal! Hockey's Stanley Cup Playoffs* (New York: Delacorte Press, 1970)

McAllister, Ron, *Hockey Stars Today and Yesterday* (Toronto: McClelland and Stewart Ltd., 1950)

McFarlane, Brian, *Clancy: The King's Story* (Toronto: McGraw-Hill, 1968)

McParland, Kelly, *The Lives of Conn Smythe* (Toronto: Fenn/McClelland & Stewart Ltd., 2011)

Mouton, Claude, *The Montreal Canadiens: A Hockey Dynasty* (Toronto: Van Nostrand Reinhold Ltd., 1980)

O'Brien, Andy, *Superstars: Hockey's Greatest Players* (Toronto: McGraw-Hill Ryerson Ltd., 1973),

Roche, Bill, *The Hockey Book* (Toronto: McClelland & Stewart, 1953)

Selke, Frank J., and Gordon Green, *Behind the Cheering* (Toronto: McClelland and Stewart, 1962)

Sullivan, George, *Faceoff: A Guide to Modern Ice Hockey* (New York: D. Van Nostrand Company Inc., 1968)

This work drew extensively on contemporary newspaper accounts in the *Montreal Gazette*, *Montreal Daily Star*, *Montreal Herald*, *La Presse*, *La Patrie*, *Le Petit Journal*, *Toronto Star*, *Globe*, the *Stratford Beacon-Herald*, *Ottawa Citizen*, *Ottawa Journal*, *New York Times*, *New York American*, *New York Daily News*, *Maclean's*, *Philadelphia Daily News*, *Philadelphia Inquirer*, *Boston Post*, *Boston Globe*, *Detroit Free Press*, and *Chicago Tribune*.

The *Montreal Star* is often abbreviated to the *Star*; the *Toronto Star* is always specified as such. Similarly, the *Globe* refers to the Toronto newspaper (which was merged with the *Mail* in 1934, to become the modern-day *Globe and Mail*); the Boston *Globe* is always specified as such.

PART I: THE BEGINNING

Chapter 1

1 "Morenz Sorry Hockey Season Is Rapidly Nearing Close," *Montreal Daily Star*, March 25, 1930, 28

2 "Send Donation to Morenz Fund," *Stratford Beacon-Herald*, March 11, 1937, 8

3 James C. Hendy, "Morenz the Magnificent, Part I," *Street & Smith's Sport Story Magazine*, January 1, 1938, 50, 58

Chapter 2

1 Robinson, *Howie Morenz*, 86

2 "Bolt of Lightning Almost Hits Morenz," *Globe*, August 7, 1928, 19

3 Mark T. McNeil, "From a Rink-Side Seat," *Montreal Gazette*, January 25, 1935, 12

4 Allen J. Abel, *But I Loved It Plenty Well* (Toronto: Collins, 1983), 203

5 McFarlane, *Clancy* 51, 53.

6 McParland, *The Lives of Conn Smythe*, 130
7 Elmer W. Ferguson, "The Last of Sports' Three Musketeers," *Montreal Star*, June 27, 1964
8 McAllister, *Hockey Stars Today and Yesterday*, 74. The facilities are described more generously by Mikael Lalancette, *Georges Vezina: L'Habitant Silencieux* (Montreal: Les Editions de l'Homme, 2021), 226
9 Sullivan, *Faceoff*, 116. Sullivan referenced the 1929–30 season, but it was the two seasons following when Howie Morenz would win consecutive MVP awards.
10 "Falcons Speed to Easy Win," *Globe*, March 25, 1921, 11
11 "Comes Back From Game to Find Mother Drowned," *Globe*, January 23, 1922, 3
12 "'Soo' Team to Meet Allan Cup Holders," *Globe*, March 7, 1923, 8x
13 Brian McFarlane, *The Stanley Cup* (Toronto: Pagurian Press Ltd., 1971), 59–60
14 Robinson, *Howie Morenz*, 45.
15 Liss, *Goal!*, 32; McFarlane, *Clancy*, 43. On occasion, Leo Dandurand actually agreed; see Beddoes et al., *Hockey!*, 306. See also King Clancy on Cleghorn in Trent Frayne, *Tales of an Athletic Supporter* (Toronto: McClelland & Stewart Inc., 1990), 184; and Cleghorn on himself: *Maclean's*, November 15, 1934; reprinted in *Maclean's*, December 25, 1995, 67.
16 Gzowski, *The Game of Our Lives*, 116; Vern DeGeer, "Malone Still Kept Busy Taking Bows," *Hockey News*, March 18, 1961
17 Joseph C. Nichols, "Players of the Game: Howie Morenz—Speedy Centre of the Canadiens," *New York Times*, April 6, 1931, 28
18 Barette, *Leo Dandurand: Sportsman*, 126
19 "Canadien Fans Eager to See Champs Play," *Montreal Daily Star*, November 4, 1930, 26–27
20 Robinson, *Howie Morenz*, 79
21 Doc Holst, "Another Morenz Looms as Future Comet of Ice Hockey World," *Stratford Beacon-Herald*, March 13, 1937, 10
22 "Champs Show Old-Time Gait to Trim Reds," *Montreal Daily Star*, November 6, 1930, 34
23 Ibid
24 "Un joli cadeau a Howie Morenz," *La Presse*, November 15, 1930, 44

PART II: REGULAR SEASON

Chapter 1

1 D.A.L. MacDonald, "Sports on Parade," *Gazette*, March 10, 1937, 14
2 "Origines des familles Mantha et Gagnon," *Le Petit Journal*, April 12, 1931, 36
3 Howie Morenz, "D'un bout a l'autre," *La Patrie*, March 27, 1928, 11

4 Dean Robinson, "Howie Morenz Was a Very Special Person," *London Free Press*, March 4, 1977, 10, 13

5 "Glancing Around the Forum As Canadiens Defeat Hawks," *Montreal Daily Star*, April 13, 1931, 29. It was a habit adopted by Wayne Gretzky, e.g., Wayne Gretzky with Rick Reilly, *Gretzky: An Autobiography* (Toronto: HarperCollins, 1990), 96

6 "Senators Fall Before Canucks Speed Waves," *Montreal Daily Star*, November 17, 1930, 23 See also: "Canadiens Score Decisive Victory," *Globe*, November 17, 1930, 11

7 D.A.L. MacDonald, "Canadiens Flash Brilliantly and Down Ottawa 5-1," *Gazette*, November 17, 1930, 29. See also: "Douze Mille Personnes Assistant au Glorieux Debut des Champions," *La Presse*, November 17, 1930, 22

8 Fischler and Fischler, *Heroes and History*, 41.

Chapter 2

1 Bruce Hood with Murray Townsend, *The Good of the Game: Recapturing Hockey's Greatness* (Toronto: Stoddart Publishing Co., 1999), 64

2 E.W. Ferguson, "The Gist and Jest of It," *Montreal Herald*, April 16, 1931, 8

3 J.W. Mooney, "Bruins Defeat World's Champs," *Boston Post*, November 19, 1930, 22

4 Bert Perry, "Detours through the Sport Maze," *Globe*, January 17, 1931, 11. See also: Dave Resnek, "Recalling Morenz: Babe Ruth on ice," *San Francisco Examiner*, April 24, 1977, 41; Andy O'Brien, *Fire-Wagon Hockey: The Story of Montreal Canadiens* (Toronto: The Ryerson Press, 1970), 41

5 "Flatteuse opinion sur Howie Morenz," *La Patrie*, March 24, 1928, 20. It was an opinion shared by Frank Selke in *Behind the Cheering*, 103.

6 Trent Frayne, "How They Broke the Heart of Howie Morenz," *Maclean's*, October 15, 1953, 25; reprinted in Benedict and Jenish, eds., *Hockey on Ice*, 63–72

7 J.W. Mooney, "Bruins Will Face Nemesis Tonight," *Boston Post*, November 18, 1930, 20

8 O'Brien, *Headline Hockey*, 42–43

9. L.S.B. Shapiro, "17,000 Look On As Canadiens Bow to Boston Six, 5 to 2," *Gazette*, November 19, 1930, 18

10 John J. Hallahan, "Bruins Topple the Champions," *Boston Globe*, November 19, 1930, 24

Chapter 3

1 D.A.L. MacDonald, "Canadiens Score 7-1 Victory Over Montreal Maroons," *Gazette*, November 21, 1930, 20

2 Charles Wilkins, Colleen Howe, and Gordie Howe, *When the Final Buzzer Sounds* (Chicago: Triumph Books, 2000), 8; Michael Ulmer, *Canadiens Captains* (Toronto: Seal Books, McClelland-Bantam, 1997), 146

Chapter 4

1 Edward Burns, "Hawks Whip Champion Canadiens, 3-0," *Chicago Daily Tribune*, November 24, 1930, 23
2 Paul Gallico, *Farewell to Sport* (New York: International Polygonics, 1990), 106–107; Charles Samuels, *The Magnificent Rube: The Life and Gaudy Times of Tex Rickard* (New York: McGraw-Hill Book Company, 1957), 2–4
3 John Ferguson with Stan Fischler and Shirley Fischler, *Thunder and Lightning* (Scarborough: Prentice-Hall Canada, 1989), 33; David McNeil, *In the Pressure of the Moment: Remembering Gerry McNeil* (Vancouver: Midtown Press, 2016), 49

Chapter 5

1 Vern Degeer, "Gazette Sports Good Morning," *Gazette*, April 22, 1964, 24
2 Doc Holst, "Another Morenz Looms as Future Comet of Ice Hockey World," *Stratford Beacon-Herald*, March 13, 1937, 10
3 Howie Morenz, "D'Un Bout a L'Autre," *La Patrie*, March 26, 1928, 9
4 Gordie Howe, *Mr. Hockey: My Story* (Toronto: Viking, 2014), 103
5 L.S.B. Shapiro, "Canadiens Hailed as History-Making Ice Aggregation," *Gazette*, April 15, 1931, 17; "Thumb-Nail Sketches of Canadien Players," *Globe*, April 16, 1931, 11. See also: "Les joueurs du club canadien se mettent a l'entrainement, ce matin," *La Presse*, October 21, 1930, 23. His career average was said to be 160 pounds: Claude Mouton, *The Montreal Canadiens: A Hockey Dynasty* (Toronto: Van Nostrand Reinhold, 1980), 246.
6 Baz O'Meara, "The Passing Sport Show," *Montreal Daily Star*, August 26, 1930, 23
7 M.J. Rodden, "On the Highways of Sport," *Globe and Mail*, December 27, 1937, 17
8 Ibid
9 L.S.B. Shapiro, "14,500 Look On As Detroit Six Beats Canadiens, 3 to 2," *Gazette*, November 28, 1930, 20. See also: "Le Detroit s'assure la victoire avec des joueurs du canadien a la cloture," *La Presse*, November 28, 1930, 30
10 M.J. Rodden, "On the Highways of Sport," *Globe and Mail*, December 27, 1937, 17

Chapter 6

1 Baz O'Meara, "The Passing Sport Show," *Montreal Daily Star*, December 1, 1930, 27
2 Robinson, *Howie Morenz*, 50
3 In this regard, the smooth style of young Lynn Patrick was particularly derided: Eric Whitehead, *The Patricks: Hockey's Royal Family* (Toronto: Doubleday Canada, 1980), 206
4 O'Brien, *Superstars*, 122

5 Trent Frayne, "Montreal's Grey-Flannel Hockey Cartel," *Maclean's*, December 3, 1960. Found in Benedict and Jenish, eds., *Hockey on Ice*, 12
6 "Lightning Legs" appeared in Stan Fischler and Shirley Fischler, *Everybody's Hockey Handbook* (New York: Charles Scribner's Sons, 1983), 43. The "Stratford Speedball" and "Canadian Comet" appeared in Al Parsley in "Meteoric Career Ends When Stratford Streak Is Fatally Stricken," *Montreal Herald*, March 9, 1937, 9. The "Stratford Bullet" appeared in "Howie Morenz is Returning to Game Senators Aim to Stop Speedy Rivals," *Ottawa Journal*, January 22, 1931, 22. "Flash" appeared in "Morenz Adds Four Points to Total," *Montreal Daily Star*, February 23, 1931, 22
7 "Canadiens Trounce Bruins With Great Rally," *Montreal Daily Star*, December 1, 1930, 26
8 Fischler and Fischler, *Everybody's Hockey Handbook*, 44
9 Milt Dunnell, "Howie's First Practice with Midgets Recalled," *Stratford Beacon-Herald*, March 9, 1937, 1
10 Roger Kahn, *Games We Used to Play* (New York: Ticknor & Fields, 1992), 36–37
11 Beddoes et al., *Hockey!* 178–179. That was first published in 1969, thirteen years *after* the Kahn version appeared in *Sport* magazine in 1956. Fischler, *Those Were the Days*, 81–82, paid homage to both Kahn and Morenz by simply quoting Kahn directly—though Fischler cited *Esquire* magazine rather than *Sport* magazine.
12 Don Gutteridge, *Bus Ride* (Tablo Publishing, 2019), 18–19. See also 143
13 Claude Larochelle, *Guy Lafleur: Hockey's #1* (Quebec: Lotographie Inc., 1978), 90–91
14 Robinson, *Howie Morenz*, 75.
15 L.S.B Shapiro, "Canadien Victory is Birthday Gift for Goerge Mantha," *Gazette*, December 1, 1930, 20
16 Ibid

Chapter 7

1 Stan Baumgartner, "Les Canadiens, Greatest in World, Morenz et al, Oppose Quakers Tonight," *Philadelphia Inquirer*, December 2, 1930, 16
2 "Le canadien defait le Philadelphie par 2 a 1 dans une brillante joute," *La Presse*, January 14, 1931, 24
3 L.S.B. Shapiro, "Morenz is Star as Canadiens Defeat Philadelphia, 2-1," *Gazette*, January 14, 1931, 16
4 e.g., Baz O'Meara, "The Passing Sport Show," *Montreal Daily Star*, April 9, 1931, 39
5 "Hainsworth," *Kitchener-Waterloo Record*, October 10, 1950, 2. No doubt in homage to his predecessor, Georges Vezina, the "Chicoutimi Cucumber"
6 Eddie O'Meara, "Flashy Canadiens Overwhelm Senators and Win By 3-0 Score," *Ottawa Journal*, January 23, 1931, 22

7 Roy MacGregor, *Wayne Gretzky's Ghost and Other Tales from a Lifetime in Hockey* (Toronto: Vintage Canada, 2012), 134

8 Trent Frayne, "Why Big-League Goalies Crack Up," March 19, 1955, *Maclean's*, in *The Thrill of Victory: Best Spots Stories from the Pages of Maclean's* (Toronto: Viking Canada, 2003), 26

9 "How Long Can a Player Last?" *Toronto Daily Star*, March 11, 1931, 10. A variety of dates have been proposed for George Hainsworth's birth: June 26 in either 1893, 1895, or 1898. See also: Vern Degeer, "Hainsworth, One of Hockey's Greats," *Gazette*, October 11, 1950, 16; "Geo. Hainsworth, 57, Killed in Auto Crash," *Kitchener-Waterloo Record*, October 10, 1950, 1; "George Hainsworth Former Ace Goaltender Killed in Auto Crash," *Globe and Mail*, October 11, 1950, 17; Dick Irvin, *In the Crease: Goaltenders Look at Life in the NHL* (Toronto: McClelland & Stewart Inc., 1995), 18

10 Vern Degeer, "Gazette Sports Good Morning," *Gazette*, April 22, 1964, 24

11 Vern Degeer, "Hainsworth, One of Hockey's Greats," *Gazette*, October 11, 1950, 16

12 Attributed to Charlie Conacher in Trent Frayne, *Famous Hockey Players* (New York: Dodd, Mead & Company, 1970), 10. Also quoted in Frayne, "How they broke the heart of Howie Morenz," *Maclean's*, October 1953, 25; reprinted in Michael Benedict and D'Arcy Jenish, eds., *Hockey on Ice: 50 Years of Great Hockey* (Toronto: Penguin Books, 1999), 63–72.

13 "Canadiens Defeat Quaker Six, 2 to 0, in Close Contest," *Gazette*, December 3, 1930, 20

14 "Joliat and Morenz Score Third-Period Goals to Win Thrilling Game at Arena," *Philadelphia Daily News*, Sports Extra, December 3, 1930, 1. Stan Baumgartner, "Tiny Joliat Proves Undoing of Locals," *Philadelphia Inquirer*, December 3, 1930, 18 described it as a clean breakaway

15 "Morenz's Goal In Overtime Defeats Chicago Hawks, 1-0," *Gazette*, January 31, 1930, 16

16 Stan Baumgartner, "Just a Moment," *Philadelphia Inquirer*, December 3, 1930, 16

Chapter 8

1 He had even written a bestseller about it: John S. Hammond and Dawson Olmstead, *Gunner's Handbook for Field Artillery* (New York: E. Dutton & Company, 1917). See also: Morey Holzman and Joseph Nieforth, *Deceptions and* Doublecross: *How the NHL Conquered Hockey* (Toronto: Dundurn Group, 2002), 341

2 Paul Gallico, *Farewell to Sport* (New York: International Polygonics Ltd., 1990), 323–324.

3 "Watching Umpires Doing Their Stuff," *Montreal Daily Star*, December 5, 1930, 38. Of course, talk of a bigger net has recurred at the NHL level, most recently during the 2007–08 season.

4 Doug Smith, "Winning is . . ." *Toronto Star*, October 17, 1999, E2
5 O'Brien, *Superstars*, 122
6 Robinson, *Howie Morenz*, 130
7 "Marty Burke Eulogizes Great Player, Fine Pal," *Stratford Beacon-Herald*, March 10, 1937, 9
8 Marc T. McNeil, "Canadiens Climb into Tie for Lead, Beating Rangers," *Gazette*, December 5, 1930, 20

Chapter 9

1 Harry Cross, "Garden is Opened in Blaze of Color," *New York Times*, December 16, 1925, 29
2 Fischler, *Those Were the Days*, 38; Fischler and Fischler, *Heroes and History*, 34. See also Frank Boucher with Trent Frayne, *When the Rangers Were Young* (New York: Dodd, Mead & Company, 1973), 11, about the dressing rooms at the Garden.
3 Gerald O'Carroll, "Super-salesman of Sport," *Montreal Standard*, undated, 16
4 Rickard's favourite expression: Samuels, Charles; *The Magnificent Rube: The Life and Gaudy Times of Tex Rickard*, McGraw-Hill Book Company, Inc. (New York: 1957), 4
5 Bill Slocum, "Worters Accidently Scores Winning Goal for Visiting Six," *New York American*, January 9, 1931, 9
6 Joseph C. Nichols, "Players of the Game," *New York Times*, April 6, 1931, 28
7 L.S.B. Shapiro, "Canadiens Defeat Americans Before Throng of 15,000," *Gazette*, December 8, 1930, 23
8 "'Flying Frenchmen' Keep Up With Leafs," *Montreal Daily Star*, December 8, 1930, 22
9 Ibid
10 Ibid
11 Ibid

Chapter 10

1 Baz O'Meara, "The Passing Sport Show," *Montreal Daily Star*, February 7, 1931, 17; Selke and Green, *Behind the Cheering*, 169
2 Conn Smythe with Scott Young, *If You Can't Beat 'Em in the Alley* (Toronto: Paperjacks, 1982), 99
3 McParland, *The Lives of Conn Smythe*, 101
4 "Les joueurs du Canadien evalues a $217,000, n'ont pas coute une fortune a Catta et Leo," *Le Petit Journal*, March 1, 1931, 22; Baz O'Meara, "The Passing Sport Show," *Montreal Daily Star*, September 12, 1930, 35; "Canadien Perd A Vancouver Par 2 A 0," *Le Petit Journal*, April 7, 1929, 19; "Morenz restera-t-il au milieu de nous?" *Le Petit Journal*, January 23, 1927, 8.
5 e.g., Andy O'Brien, *Headline Hockey* (Toronto: Ryerson Press, 1963), 35. The Leafs

would make their own $75,000 bid for Morenz in the midst of the 1931–32 season, but they too were rebuffed

6 McFarlane, *Clancy*, 69.

7 Charlie Querrie, "25 Years in Sport," *Toronto Daily Star*, March 23, 1931, 11

8 D.A.L. MacDonald, "Canadiens Rally to Defeat Tired Toronto Team, 2-1," *Gazette*, December 10, 1930, 20

9 "Morenz Breaks Up Hard-Fought Game," *Montreal Daily Star*, December 10, 1930, 26

10 D.A.L. MacDonald, "Canadiens Rally to Defeat Tired Toronto Team, 2-1," *Gazette*, December 10, 1930, 20

11 *Montreal Daily Star*, December 10, 1930. He had done the same in a training camp game: Part I, Chapter 2; "Reds Show Up In Good Style Lose By Goal," *Montreal Daily Star*, November 8, 1930, 15

12 L.S.B. Shapiro, "Canadien Victory Marks Champions' Fifth Straight," *Gazette*, December 10, 1930, 20

Chapter 11

1 Recorded in 1930 by Rudy Vallee & His Connecticut Yankees, and several others. Roger Kahn, *Games We Used to Play*, 36, 43; Fischler, *Those Were the Days*, 85

2 Andy O'Brien, *Les Canadiens: The Story of the Montreal Canadiens* (Toronto: McGraw-Hill Ryerson Ltd., 1970), 45

3 "La comete passe sur Ottawa et fait des degats," *Le Droit*, December 12, 1930, 9

4 The original song had been known by the title of *Tyrolienne des Pyrenees*, and was a staple of the Société musicale des montagnards canadiens, and the Choeur montagnard, as well as the Chorale des montagnards (the latter two choirs performed in distinctive costume)

5 Baz O'Meara, "The Passing Sport Show," *Montreal Daily Star*, December 12, 1930, 47; "Watching Flying Frenchmen Fly," *Ottawa Citizen*, December 12, 1930, 12

6 "La Comete Passe Sur Ottawa et Fait des Degats;" *Le Droit*, December 12; "Watching Flying Frenchmen Fly," *Ottawa Citizen*, December 12, 1930, 12, referring to the band as Le Regiment de Hull

7 The music was published in the U.S. in 1917, but the origins of the song are traced back to the 1879 Gilbert and Sullivan comic opera. It is now identified as part of "The Celtic Song" for the Glasgow Celtic Football Club, among others

8 "Watching Flying Frenchmen Fly," *Ottawa Citizen*, December 12, 1930, 12

9 "Hurray! Les Canadiens," *Le Petit Journal*, March 18, 1928, 20. A "bolide" is a racecar

10 Dr. H. Baba, "Pro Hockey Seen Through Visitor's Eyes," *Montreal Daily Star*, January 20, 1931, 27

11 Marc T. McNeil, "From a Rink-Side Seat," *Gazette*, January 25, 1935, 12

12 Fischler and Fischler, *Heroes and History*, 41

13 Doc Holst, "Another Morenz Looms As Future Comet of Ice Hockey World," *Stratford Beacon-Herald,* March 13, 1937, 10
14 Unidentified newspaper article, sourced from the Howie Morenz file at the D.K.(Doc) Seaman Hockey Resource Centre/Hockey Hall of Fame
15 Frayne, *Famous Hockey Players*, 9. See also: Neil D. Isaacs, *Checking Back: A History of the National Hockey League* (New York: W. W. Norton and Company Inc., 1977), 87–88
16 e.g., Earl Seibert, quoted by Paul Patton, "Life in fast lane too much for Morenz," *Globe and Mail,* March 7, 1987, C5; Mark T. McNeil, "Canadiens Again Beat Maroons in Intra-City Tilt," *Gazette,* January 16, 1931, 18; Roy Worters, quoted in Beddoes et al., *Hockey*, 181; Liss, *Goal!*, 36–37; Eddie Shore in Roche, *The Hockey Book*, 105
17 Gzowski, *The Game of Our Lives*, 85
18 "Flatteuse opinion sur Howie Morenz," *La Patrie,* March 24, 1928, 20
19 Ken Dryden, *The Game: A Thoughtful and Provocative Look at a Life in Hockey* (Toronto: Macmillan of Canada, 1983), 219-220
20 "The Fan's Corner," *Globe and Mail,* March 18, 1937, 16
21 Roche, *The Hockey Book*, 184
22 Andy O'Brien, "Howie Morenz . . . a hockey legend," *Montreal Star*, March 12, 1976, B3
23 Chick Appel, "A New Approach to the Much-Told Morenz Saga," *Stratford Beacon-Herald*, December 27, 1960, 14
24 Eddie O'Meara, "Canadiens In Sensational Finish To Nose Out Senators 5 to 4," *Ottawa Journal*, December 12, 1930, 28
25 L.S.B. Shapiro, "Canadiens Defeat Ottawa, 5 to 4, in Dramatic Battle," *Gazette*, December 12, 1930, 20
26 *Ottawa Journal*, December 12, 1930, 28
27 "Canadiens Storming Attack Turns Tide of Seeming Defeat to Victory," *Montreal Daily Star*, December 12, 1930, 47
28 *Fire on Ice* was a stage musical collectively created from an original script by Keith Roulston, with music composed and arranged by John Roby. The work was performed at the Blyth Summer Festival, August 2–22, 1981, after being workshopped at the Toronto Theatre Festival in May 1981. A recording of the Blyth performance with this song remains available through the University of Guelph's Blyth Festival Theatre Archives at the McLaughlin Library, Archival and Special Collections: XZ1 MS A757019 (audio cassettes), and XZ1 MS A751005 (Festival Program).

Chapter 12

1 Eli Baker, "Short Shots on Sport," *Ottawa Citizen*, December 12, 1930, 13
2 Foster Hewitt, *Hello Canada! and Hockey Fans in the United States* (Toronto: Thomas Allen Limited 1950), 38

3 "Morenz avait promis a Joliat d'aller le voir jouer durant les eliminations finales," *L'Illustration Nouvelle*, March 10, 1937, 23
4 *Montreal Herald*, probably 1934, loose undated clipping accessed in the Howie Morenz file at the Hockey Hall of Fame Resource Centre.
5 E.W. Ferguson, "Who's Going to Get April Fooled Tonight?" *Montreal Herald*, April 1, 1931, 9. See also: O'Brien, *Superstars*, 126
6 Robinson, *Howie Morenz*, 13
7 Lloyd Percival, *The Hockey Handbook* (Toronto: The Copp Clark Publishing Co. Limited. 1951), 311, 313–315.
8 Milt Dunnell, "Sports Mill," *Stratford Beacon-Herald*, January 29, 1937, 10
9 Jerry Nason, "At 71, you leave hockey to the boys," *Boston Globe*, March 13, 1973, 29
10 "Chick" Appel, "A New Approach to the Much-Told Morenz Saga," *Stratford Beacon-Herald*, December 27, 1960, 14
11 Leslie Roberts, "The Magnificent Morenz," unidentified newspaper clipping, likely *Stratford Beacon-Herald*, undated.
12 Marc T. McNeil, "Tired Canadiens Are Held to Tie By Americans, 1-1," *Gazette*, December 15, 1930, 24
13 http://mbhockeyhalloffame.ca/people/nick-wasnie. Most sources attribute the slapshot's invention to Bun Cook of the Rangers, according to his own teammate, Alex Shibicky. See: Lance Hornby et al., ed., *Hockey Dynasties: Blue Lines and Bloodlines* (Toronto: Key Porter Books Ltd., 2002), 43
14 "25 years after transplant, woman still defies odds," *St. Cloud Times* (St. Cloud, Minnesota), July 24, 2003, 5B
15 Baz O'Meara, "The Passing Sport Show," *Montreal Daily Star*, December 15, 1930, 27

Chapter 13

1 D.A.L. MacDonald, "Canadiens Held to Scoreless Tie By Chicago Hawks," *Gazette*, December 19, 1930, 20
2 Howie Morenz, "Hockey Flashbacks," *Esquire's First Sports Reader*, March 1935, 44
3 *Gazette*, December 19, 1930, 20
4 Ibid
5 Doc Holst, "Another Morenz Looms As Future Comet of Ice Hockey World," *Stratford Beacon-Herald*, March 13, 1937, 10
6 Bill Westwick, "The Realm of Sport," *Ottawa Journal*, April 17, 1941, 20
7 Joan Finnigan, *Old Sores, New Goals: The Story of the Ottawa Senators* (Kingston, Ontario: Quarry Press, 1992), 149–150
8 King Clancy, "I Meet Morenz" in Roche, *The Hockey Book*, 125
9 McFarlane, *Clancy*, 81
10 Brandt, Bill, "Once in a Lifetime," unidentified magazine article, April 1948, 39, sourced at Library and Archives Canada, Charles Mayer Fonds

11 Trent Frayne, *The Mad Men of Hockey* (Toronto: McClelland and Stewart Ltd., 1974), 66. An alternative version of the story appeared in Frank Graham, "The Life and Death of the N.Y. Americans," *Sport*, 60. If the story was not apocryphal, it may have referred to Clarence Boucher, who played eleven games with the Americans in 1926–27, and thirty-five more in 1927–28

Chapter 14

1 "Rangers Beat Canadiens To Climb Ahead," *Montreal Daily Star*, December 24, 1930, 16
2 Ibid. Some papers credited Albert Leduc with helping: "Les Rangers Triomphent du Canadien," *La Presse*, December 24, 1930, 19; L.S.B. Shapiro, "Rangers Outplay Canadien Six to Score 5 to 1 Win," *Gazette*, December 24, 1930, 15
3 Anna Pavlova (1881–1931) and Vaslav Nijinsky (1889–1950) were ballet contemporaries. Jim Coleman, *Calgary Herald*, February 19, 1971, 47. See also Gzowski, *The Game of Our Lives*, 118
4 L.S.B. Shapiro, "Rangers Outplay Canadien Six to Score 5 to 1 Win," *Gazette*, December 24, 1930, 15
5 Ibid

Chapter 15

1 Marc T. McNeil, "Huge Throng Goes Wild with Joy as Canadiens Win," *Gazette*, March 30, 1931, 18; "Thumb-Nail Sketches of Canadien Players," *Globe*, April 16, 1931, 11. Georges would eventually be acknowledged as the league's fastest skater: *Montreal-Matin*, January 16, 1965, 34
2 There are obvious discrepancies in both the month and the year of Sylvio's birth between the census record and Mouton's book, and discrepancies in the spelling of "Cilviau" as well. The 1921 census also has naming inconsistencies for Leonice/Leonis and the age of their sister Dora
3 Ted Mahovlich, *The Big M: The Frank Mahovlich Story* (Toronto: Sports Publishing Inc., 1999), 168–169
4 Tommy Shields, "Ottawa Incurs Another Defeat In Scoring Fest with Canucks," *Ottawa Citizen*, December 29, 1930, 11
5 "Morenz avait promis a Joliat d'aller le voir jouer durant les eliminations finales," *L'Illustration Nouvelle*, March 10, 1937, 23
6 Fischler, *Those Were the Days*, 151–152

Chapter 16

1 "Le Canadien et le Montreal Se Livre une Sensationnelle," *La Presse*, December 31, 1930, 18

2 Marc T. McNeil, "Crowd of 13,000 Is Attracted to Game at Forum," *Gazette*, December 31, 1930, 16
3 Milt Dunnell, *Toronto Daily Star*, December 21, 1950, on the occasion of Howie Morenz being named the best hockey player of the half-century
4 Bert Perry, "Detours Through the Sport Maze," *Globe*, January 3, 1931, 33
5 "Maroons and Canadiens Play Sensational Overtime Game – Score 1-1," *Montreal Daily Star*, December 31, 1930, 18
6 "Le Canadien et le Montreal Se Livre une Sensationnelle" *La Presse*, December 31, 1930, 18
7 *Montreal Daily Star*, December 31, 1930, 18
8 *La Presse*, December 31, 1930, 18
9 *Montreal Daily Star*, December 31, 1930, 18

Chapter 17

1 Bert Perry, "Maple Leafs Defeat Canadiens, 2-1, Before Record Crowd at Arena," *Globe*, January 5, 1931, 8, with another 1,000 turned away: Baz O'Meara, "Bailey Bags Gol to Cinch Contest," *Montreal Daily Star*, January 5, 1931, 21
2 Morley Callaghan, *Strange Fugitive* (New York: Charles Scribner's Sons, 1928), 163
3 L.S.B. Shapiro, "Canadiens Beaten By Toronto Leafs, 2-1, in Hectic Game," *Gazette*, January 5, 1931, 17
4 Fischler, *Those Were the Days*, 150; Fischler and Fischler, *Heroes and History*, 63–64
5 Lou Marsh, "Leafs Beat Canadiens 2-1 Chair Hurled at Referee," *Toronto Daily Star*, January 5, 1931, 8
6 Borneo, Sumatra, South Africa, and even indigenous America.
7 "La mentalite de certains partisans du hockey," *Le Petit Journal*, January 4, 1931, 20
8 *Toronto Daily Star*, January 5, 1931, 8
9 Baz O'Meara, "*Bailey Bags Gol to Cinch Contest*," *Montreal Daily Star*, January 5, 1931, 21
10 Stanley I. Fischler, *Power Play!: The Story of the Toronto Maple Leafs* (Toronto: Copp Clark Publishing Company, 1972), 38
11 Morley Callaghan, *Strange Fugitive* (New York: Charles Scribner's Sons, 1928), 165
12 Baz O'Meara, "Between the Lines at Toronto Tilt," *Montreal Daily Star*, January 5, 1931, 21

Chapter 18

1 Babe Pratt describing his first dressing room encounter with Howie Morenz in Eric Whitehead, *The Patricks: Hockey's Royal Family* (Toronto: Doubleday Canada Ltd., 1980), 208
2 Dean Robinson, "Morenz," *Stratford Beacon-Herald*, January 8, 1971, 8

3 "The Funniest Guy" in Beddoes et al., *Hockey*, 289
4 Marc T. McNeil, "From a Rink-Side Seat," *Gazette*, January 28, 1935, 14
5 "Le Detroit cause une tres forte surprise en battant le Canadien, 6-2," *La Presse*, January 7, 1931, 20
6 "Detroit Conquers in Speedy Conquest," *Montreal Daily Star*, January 7, 1931, 22
7 Stephen Leacock, "This World Championship Stuff—and Why I Am Out of It," *Short Circuits* (New York: Dodd, Mead and Company, 1928), 212, 216
8 D.A.L. MacDonald, "Canadiens Are Off Color and Bow to Detroit Falcons," *Gazette*, January 7, 1931, 14
9 Leo Dandurand, "Story Behind Fabulous Canucks Recalls How NHL Got Its Start," *Montreal Star*, January 14, 1960.

Chapter 19

1 "Canadiens Get Queer Break from Worters," *Montreal Daily Star*, January 9, 1931, 30
2 "Americans Hot, See Visions of Stanley Trophy," *New York Daily News*, January 9, 1931, 58
3 D.A.L. MacDonald, "Freak Tally Gives Canadiens 2-1 Win Over American Six," *Gazette*, January 9, 1931, 18. See also: "Le Canadien Bat L'American et Monte en Deuxieme Place," *La Presse*, January 9, 1931, 22; W.A. Hewitt, "Sporting Views and Reviews," *Toronto Daily Star*, January 9, 1931, 10
4 *Montreal Daily Star*, January 9, 1931, 305; Howie Morenz, "D'un but a l'autre," *La Patrie*, March 26, 1928, 9
6 *New York Daily News*, January 9
7 Fischler, Stan, *Those Were the Days*, 29
8 *Montreal Daily Star*, January 9, 1931, 30
9 *Gazette*, January 9, 1931, 18
10 *Montreal Daily Star*, January 9, 1931, 30

Chapter 20

1 Marc T. McNeil, "Canadiens Regain Lead by Crushing Toronto Leafs, 6-1," *Gazette*, January 12, 1931, 18
2 Marshall McLuhan, *Understanding Media: The Extensions of Man*, 2nd edition (New York: Signet Books, 1966), 214
3 L.S.B. Shapiro, "Brilliant Effort Marks Canadiens' Recovery of Form," *Gazette*, January 12, 1931, 18
4 Bert Perry, "Leafs Lose Lead to Canadiens in Dazzling Display," *Globe*, January 12, 1931, 10
5 Ibid
6 Milt Dunnell, "Sports Mill," *Stratford Beacon-Herald*, March 10, 1937, 9

7 Barry Meisel, *Losing the Edge: The Rise and Fall of the Stanley Cup Champion New York Rangers* (New York: Simon & Schuster, 1995), 251. See also: Ken Dryden, *The Game* (Toronto: Macmillan of Canada, 1983), 104

8 "Training Optics on Flashing Canadiens," *Montreal Daily Star*, January 12, 1931, 20

9 *Stratford Beacon-Herald*, December 27, 1950, 14

Chapter 21

1 "Canucks Here Again, But Not So Sure of Victory," *Philadelphia Inquirer*, January 13, 1931, 19

2 D'Arcy Jenish, *The Montreal Canadiens: 100 Years of Glory* (Toronto: Doubleday Canada, 2008), 87

3 Stan Baumgartner, "Just a Moment," *Philadelphia Inquirer*, December 2, 1930, 17

4 Robert T. Paul, "Food Means Nothing to Benny Leonard" *Philadelphia Daily News*, November 29, 1930, 18

5 *Philadelphia Inquirer*, December 4

6 "Police Needed To Quell Fight in Boston Game," *Montreal Daily Star*, December 26, 1930, 20

7 e.g., Elmer W. Ferguson, "The Gist and Jest of It," *Montreal Herald*, March 9, 1937, 9

8 Trent Frayne, "How They Broke the Heart of Howie Morenz", *Maclean's*, October 15, 1953), 27

9 e.g., Fischler and Fischler, *Everybody's Hockey Handbook*, 45. See also: Georges-Hebert Germain, *Overtime: The Legend of Guy Lafleur* (Toronto: Penguin Books, 1992), 167, though Germain makes the error of describing Morenz as a player of the "thirties and forties," and an anglophone who was told to speak with a Swiss accent.

10 Manifest, Detroit, October 13, 1934; U.S. Department of Labor, Immigration and Naturalization

11 Frayne, *Famous Hockey Players*, 11. See also: Stephen Cole, *The Canadian Hockey Atlas* (Toronto: Doubleday Canada, 2006), 180-181

12 "Thumb-Nail Sketches of Canadien Players," *Globe*, April 16, 1931, 11 (column 3). At the same time, they suggested that the fourth generation back had been Swiss.

Chapter 22

1 L.S.B. Shapiro, "Canadiens Hailed as History-Making Ice Aggregation," *Gazette*, April 15, 1931, 17

2 D.A.L. MacDonald, "Quakers May Take Bert McCaffrey at Waiver Price," *Gazette*, January 16, 1931, 18

3 E.W. Ferguson, "Morenz and Lepine Star as Speed of Champions Again Defeats Maroons," *Montreal Herald*, January 16, 1931, 8
4 Ibid
5 "Pit Lepine Est Le Heros De La Victoire Decisive Du Canadien Sur Son Rival," *La Presse*, January 16, 1931, 24. See also: Marc T. McNeil, "Canadiens Again Beat Maroons in Intra-City Tilt," *Gazette*, January 16, 1931, 18.
6 "Morenz denies he will quit hockey," *The Gazette*, March 27, 1934, p.12, c.4

Chapter 23

1 Lou Marsh, "Leafs Outplay Canadiens Win Sparkling Game 3-1," *Toronto Daily Star*, January 19, 1931, 8
2 "Bailey Brilliant Scores Two Goals," *Montreal Daily Star*, January 19, 1931, 23
3 Andy O'Brien, *Les Canadiens: The Story of the Montreal Canadiens* (Toronto: McGraw-Hill Ryerson, 1970), 26; Andy O'Brien, *Fire-Wagon Hockey: The Story of Montreal Canadiens* (Toronto: Ryerson Press, 1970), 26
4 *Toronto Daily Star*, January 19, 1931, 8
5 *Montreal Daily Star*, January 19, 1931, 23
6 Ibid
7 "Canadiens at Gotham," *Montreal Daily Star*, January 20, 1931, 26; Baz O'Meara, "The Passing Sport Show," *Montreal Daily Star*, January 20, 1931, 27

Chapter 24

1 "Canadiens at Gotham," *Montreal Daily Star*, January 20, 1931, 26
2 Robinson, *Howie Morenz*, 78
3 "Auto Show Edition 1931," *Montreal Daily Star*, Saturday, January 17, 1931, 29–48
4 Richard Gruneau and David Whitson, *Hockey Night in Canada* (Toronto: Garamond Press, 1993), 94
5 "A Real Tribute to a Great Player," *Montreal Herald*, undated (circa October 1934), sourced from Charles Mayer Fonds, Library and Archives Canada. In 1934 he was involved in a $60,000 lawsuit against a western U.S. skate manufacturer for use of his name without permission: *Gazette*, March 27, 1934, 12
6 L.S.B. Shapiro, "Canadiens Defeat Rangers on Rivers' Goal in Overtime," *Gazette*, January 21, 1931, 18
7 "Les Champions Continuent D'Ameliorer Leur Position," *La Presse*, January 21, 1931, 24
8 "Gustave Desrivieres" in "Canadiens Defeat Rangers, 2-1, In N.H.L.'s Longest Overtime Game," *Globe*, March 29, 1930, 12; "Morenz's Goal in Overtime Defeats Chicago Hawks," *Gazette*, January 31, 1930, 16; "Des Rivieres" in "Flying Frenchmen Beat Maple Leafs," *Globe*, February 5, 1930, 11; "Canadiens Register Decisive Victory," *Globe*, March 19, 1930, 10; "Jules Rivers" in "La Victoire Sourit

Au Canadien Sur Le Boston Par 1 A 0, Hier," *La Patrie*, March 27, 1931, 12; "Riversieres" in "Team Now At Top of Form," *Boston Globe*, April 3, 1930, 27; and finally, "Gus Rivers Just as Mean as When He Was Called Des Rivieres", *The Brooklyn Daily Eagle*, January 21, 1930, 26; "as English as George Hainsworth," in "Thumb-Nail Sketches of Canadien Players," *Globe*, April 16, 1931, 11.

9 "Gus Rivers is Nemesis of Rangers," *Montreal Herald*, January 21, 1931, 8.

Chapter 25

1 "Thumb-Nail Sketches of Canadien Players," *Globe*, April 16, 1931, 11

2 "Leduc Enacts Familiar Role at Ottawa to Bring Canadiens Victory," *Montreal Daily Star*, March 4, 1931, 26

3 Al Parsley, "'Battleship' Leduc Added Color to Bygone Era of Pro Hockey," unidentified newspaper article circa November 1961 found in Charles Mayer Fonds, MG30-C76, volume 12; Library and Archives Canada

4 Douglas How and Ralph Costello, *K.C.* (Toronto: Key Porter Books, 1993), 40–41

5 "Morentze" in "Une Acquisition" *La Patrie*, July 10, 1923, 6; "Morentz" in "Sprague Cleghorn Sera Avec Le Club De Hockey Canadien," *La Patrie*, November 16, 1923, 6; "Avec Le Canadien," *La Patrie*, December 15, 1923, 6; "Le Canadien Remporte Une Grande Victoire Sur Le Saint-Patrick Qu'Il Defait Par 3 A 0, " *La Patrie*, December 31, 1923, 6; "Morenze" in "Le Canadien Engage Morenze de Stratford," *La Presse*, July 9, 1923, 15; "Howie Morenze," *La Presse*, July 10, 1923, 15; "Howie" in "Le Canadien Est Blanchi A Hamilton, Hier Soir, 4 A 0," *La Patrie*, January 3, 1924, 6

6 After using the "Morentz" spelling in "*Le Canadien Joue Samei de Malchance A Toronto*," *La Patrie* December 14, 1925, 6, the paper changed to the English spelling in its description of the opening game at Madison Square Garden in its issue of "*Les Principaux Arisans de la Victoire Hier*," December 16, 1925, 6

Chapter 26

1 "Noted in Passing As Canadiens Win," *Montreal Daily Star*, January 26, 1931, 20

2 Baz O'Meara, "The Passing Sport Show," *Montreal Daily Star*, January 24, 1931, 15; with complementary allusions in "Morenz Is Likely To Be At Old Spot," on the same page

3 "Les Hommes de Cecil Hart Declassent Completement L'American de New York,' *La Presse*, January 26, 1931, 18

4 Unidentified newspaper clipping, March 10, 1937, under the title: "Dressing Room Tributes to Memory of Morenz"

5 Olivier Bauer, *Hockey as Religion: The Montreal Canadiens* (Champaign, Illinois: Common Ground Publishing, 2011), 29, 53–57. Compare: Paul Henderson, *The Goal of My Life* (Toronto: Fenn/McClelland & Stewart, 2007), 108

6 Gerard "Gerry" Gosselin, *Monsieur Hockey* (Montreal: Les Editions de l'Homme, 1960), 115

7 Pindar, in Stephen Amidon, *Something Like the Gods* (New York: Rodale, 2012), v

8 "Les Hommes de Cecil Hart Declassent Completement L'American de New York," *La Presse*, January 26, 1931, 18

9 "'A Chacun Son Merite' = Morenz," *Le Petit Journal*, February 1, 1931, 22; "Morenz Makes Nice Gesture," *Montreal Herald*, January 28, 1931, 7. The accurate attribution of the goal had appeared in "Canadiens Crush Americans by 6-1 in Rugged Tussle," *Gazette*, January 26, 1931, 20

Chapter 27

1 "Canadiens Score 7-1 Victory Over Philadelphia Six," *Gazette*, January 30, 1931, 18

2 "Ottawa Certain To Supply Opposition," *Montreal Daily Star*, January 17, 1931, 50

3 "Canadiens Obtain New Right Winger," *Gazette*, April 7, 1930, 20

4 Baz O'Meara, "*The Passing Sport Show*," *Montreal Daily Star*, February 7, 1931, 17

5 Doc Holst, "Another Morenz Looms As Future Comet of Ice Hockey World," *Stratford Beacon-Herald*, March 13, 1937, 10

6 "Gagnon is Leader in Goal-Getting," *Montreal Daily Star*, January 30, 1931, 30

7 "Gagnon et Joliat Sont Les Heros De La Victoire des Champions du Monde," *La Presse*, January 30, 1931, 30

8 "A Little Voice Tells Morenz He's the Tops in Everything," *Detroit Free Press*, February 12, 1937, 20

9 The 1911 Census reports that William Morenz was 44 years old—and would have been 36 when his son Howard was born: Ontario District 111 (Perth South), Sub-district 5, page 9, lines 4–10

10 Roy MacGregor, *The Home Team: Fathers, Sons & Hockey* (Toronto: Penguin Books, 1997), 311

11 Robinson, *Howie Morenz*, 158. See also: MacGregor, *The Home Team*, 311

12 Associated Press, November 15, 1928, from Providence, R.I., as appeared in *Morning Call* (Allentown, Pennsylvania), November 16, 1928, 36

13 Majors were not required to be five minutes long. The Toronto major had been a four-minute penalty

14 "Hockey: Geoffrion continues family tradition,," *Globe and Mail*, March 4, 2011, S10

15 "Gagnon et Joliat Sont Les Heros De La Victoire des Champions du Monde," *La Presse*, January 30, 1931, 30

Chapter 28

1 Mark C. Gridley, *Jazz Styles: History and Analysis*, 5th ed. (New Jersey: Prentice-Hall, Inc., 1994), 2
2 "Gagnon Gets Brace of Smart Tallies," *Montreal Daily Star*, February 2, 1931, 22
3 Lou Marsh, "Canadiens Meet Ottawa in Play-Off," *Toronto Daily Star*, March 3, 1924, 12
4 Fischler, *Those Were the Days*, 148; Fischler and Fischler, 62
5 Irving Vaughan, "18,000 See Les Canadiens Whip Hawks, 4-2," *Chicago Daily Tribune*, February 2, 1931, 29
6 L.S.B. Shapiro, "18,000 Look On As Canadiens Defeat Chicago Six, 4-2," *Gazette*, February 2, 1931, 18
7 Richard M. Sudhalter and Philip R. Evans, *Bix: Man & Legend* (London: Quartet Books, 1974), 295
8 Leigh Montville, "You said it – they want to bury us," *Boston Globe*, January 7, 1975, 21

Chapter 29

1 "Canadiens Increase Margin to Six in Rough Contest with Toronto," *Montreal Daily Star*, February 4, 1931, 24
2 Randall Poe, "The Writing of Sports," in David L. Vanderwerken and Spencer K. Wertz, eds., *Sport Inside Out* (Fort Worth: Texas Christian University Press, 1985), 552
3 "Glancing Around Between Periods," *Montreal Daily Star*, February 4, 1931, 24
4 D.A.L. MacDonald, "Canadiens Defeat Maple Leafs, 2-1, in Roaring Game," *Gazette*, February 4, 1931, 18
5 "Les Deux Clubs Rivaux se Livrent une Lutte Acharnee," *La Presse*, February 4, 1931, 23
6 *Gazette*, February 4, 1931, 18
7 *La Presse*, February 4, 1931, 23
8 Baz O'Meara, "The Passing Sport Show," *Montreal Daily Star*, February 4, 1931, 25
9 *La Presse*, February 4, 1931, 23
10 Kahn, Roger, "The Life and Death of Howie Morenz," *Games We Used to Play* (New York: Ticknor & Fields, 1992), 36, 43
11 "Le Canadien S'Affirme de Nouveau Superieur a Son Rival, Le Montreal," *La Presse*, February 18, *1931, 22*
12 "L'American compte quatre points en 12 minutes mais le Canadien gagne quand meme, " *La Presse*, February 23, 1931, 18.
13 An expression coined by Leo Dandurand, quoted in Mikael Lalancette, *Georges Vezina: L'Habitant Silencieux* (Montreal: Les Editions de l'Homme, 2021), 333

14 Charles Mayer, *L'Epopee des Canadiens: 40 Ans d'Histoire 1909–1949* (Montreal: Charles Mayer, 1949), 79–80; Howie Morenz Memorial Fund Programme, 14; and a manuscript of Charles Mayer in Charles Mayer Fonds, MG30-C76, volume 12; Library and Archives Canada.

Chapter 30

1 Baz O'Meara, "The Passing Sport Show," *Montreal Daily Star*, October 21, 1930, 27

2 *Montreal Herald*, April 8, 1931, 7

3 Dave Anderson, *Sports of Our Times* (New York: Random House, 1979), 117

4 "Mort de 'Pit' Lepine a l'age de 54 ans," *Montreal Matin*, August 3, 1955, 27. See also: "Notes de Hockey Chez Les Professionnels," *Le Petit Journal*, January 30, 1927, 11; "Les Canadiens Ecrasent New-York Americans Par Le Score de 6 A 1," *Le Petit Journal* , January 25, 1931, 21

5 U.S. Department of Labor, Immigration and Naturalization Service; Entry at Detroit, Michigan, October 13, 1934 [mim1478_67-4763].

6 Al Parsley, "Canadien Hockey Club Pays Fine Tribute at Farewell Banquet," *Montreal Herald*, October 12, 1934, 10

7 "Potins de la Joute," *La Presse*, February 6, 1931, 25. See also: L.S.B. Shapiro, "Roster of Players on Canadien Club," *Gazette*, April 4, 1930, 21; "Played 13 Years with Habitants, Centre Man Was Strong Checker," *Gazette*, August 3, 1955, 20

8 "Canadiens And Maroons In Exciting Draw," *Montreal Daily Star*, February 6, 1931, 35

9 "Old Rivals Show Terrific Tussle," *Montreal Daily Star*, February 6, 1931, 34

10 Jacques Beauchamp, "Le regrette Alfred 'Pit' Lepine peut-etre considere comme l'un des immortels de la ligue Nationale," *Montreal Matin*, August 4, 1955, 23

Chapter 31

1 Baz O'Meara, "The Passing Sport Show," *Montreal Daily Star*, February 7, 1931, 17. Trenholme Park is located in Montreal West

2 "New Hockey Booklet," *Gazette*, February 10, 1931, 18. LeMesurier was a "noted" Montreal cartoonist and advertising illustrator.

3 "Le Gardien des Buts Du Boston Joue Une Partie Absolument Phenomenale," *La Presse*, February 9, 1931, 21; " New Marks Made n Fast Contest, " *Montreal Daily Star*, February 9, 1931, 22

4 "Armand Mondou, le Morenz de la Canado-Americaine," *Le Petit Journal*, January 29, 1928, 22

5 Beddoes et al., *Hockey*, 179–180

6 "New Hockey Booklet," *Gazette*, February 10, 1931, 18. LeMesurier was just 37 years old and soon fell ill. After a 10-month illness, he died on October 27, 1932: *Le Devoir*, October 28, 1932, 7

7 Unidentified newspaper article, likely autumn 1939, author identified as Ralph Adams, titled "Canadiens' Genial Centre Sets Pit Lepine As Example," sourced at Library and Archives Canada, Charles Mayer Fonds.

8 Ibid

9 "New Marks Made in Fast Contest," *Montreal Daily Star*, February 9, 1931, 22

10 Like the bronze cast by former NHLer Gary Aldcorn. Brian McFalone, *Over the Glass & Into the Crowd* (Guelph: MainStreet Press), 19

11 Robinson, *Howie Morenz*, 153.

12 "Glorieux Couronnement d'Une Grande Saison de Hockey," *La Presse*, April 16, 1931, 34. The author has been unable to locate the original or a reproduction.

Chapter 32

1 Roche, *The Hockey Book*, vii–viii. See also: Ross Brewitt, . . . *Last Minute of Play: Tales of Hockey Grit and Glory* (Toronto: Stoddart, 1993), and *Into the Empty Net: Tales of Big League Hockey* (Toronto: Stoddart, 1994), which capture some of the importance of storytelling among the hockey-playing fraternity. Also effective in preserving a few of the significant stories of long ago in a format that is evocative of hockey's storytelling tradition: Paul Quarrington's "The Boston Bruins" in *Original Six* (Toronto: Reed Books Canada, 1996), 86–111, and Dick Irvin, *The Habs: An Oral History of the Montreal Canadians 1940–1980* (Toronto: McClelland & Stewart, 1992).

2 "Hockey's Greatest Players Here Tonight to Show Wares Against Buck Gaudette's Cluster of All-Maine Stars," *Lewiston Daily Sun*, February 12, 1931, 12

3 *Le Messager* (Lewiston, Maine), February 13, 1931, 7

4 "Le Canadien triomphe de l'American, 2-0," *La Presse*, February 16, 1931, 24

5 "Morenz Thrills Gotham Patrons," *Montreal Daily Star*, February 16, 1931, 24

6 Morley Callaghan, *Strange Fugitive* (New York: Charles Scribner's Sons, 1928)

7 Hugh MacLennan, *Two Solitudes* (Toronto: Collins, 1945), at 63-64, 204–206, 237-238, 284-286, 300-301, 311, 334.

Chapter 33

1 *Morenz Memorial Fund Program*, November 2, 1937, 6

2 Maurice "Rocket" Richard and Stan Fischler, *The Flying Frenchmen: Hockey's Greatest Dynasty* (New York: Hawthorn Books Inc., 1971), 48

3 Robinson, *Howie Morenz*, 7

4 *Hamilton Herald*, circa December 20, 1923, as quoted in Sam Wesley and David Wesley, *Hamilton's Hockey Tigers* (Toronto: James Lorimer and Company, 2005), 63

5 "Canadiens Hockey Champions, Taking Hard-Fought Game," *Gazette*, March 26, 1924, 16, referred to Morenz's encounter with Morris in the first period as a "mild melee."

6 "Le Canadien S'Affirme de Nouveau Superieur A Son Rival, Le Montreal," *La Presse*, February 18, 1931, 22
7 As his goals were attributed during his career. Statistical revisions by the NHL since, adding an additional goal for the 1924–25 season, would have put his 200th goal as the third goal by the Canadiens against the Maroons in the 4-4 draw on February 5, 1931, in his 286th game
8 Neither before: Didier Pitre and Newsy Lalonde never scored 200 NHL goals; nor after: Rocket Richard was closest to Morenz, having scored his 200th in game 308 (January 14, 1949)
9 Baz O'Meara, "The Passing Sport Show," *Montreal Daily Star*, January 5, 1931, 21
10 Odie Cleghorn's observations were reported verbatim in both the "Referee Says Both Players To Blame For Socking," *Montreal Herald*, February 18, 1931, 6; "Glancing Around Between Periods," *Montreal Daily Star*, February 18, 1931, 27
11 "Le Canadien S'Affirme de Nouveau Superieur A Son Rival, Le Montreal," *La Presse*, February 18, 1931, 22
12 "Slugging and Fisticuffs At End OF Bitter Struggle," *Montreal Herald*, February 18, 1931, 6

Chapter 34

1 "Bruins Are Tied By Canadiens, 1-1," *Boston Post*, February 20, 1931, 27; see also: *Boston Globe*, February 20, 1931, 31
2 Ibid
3 Ibid
4 C. Michael Hiam, *Eddie Shore and That Old Time Hockey* (Toronto: McClelland and Stewart, 2011), 57, 62
5 Howie Morenz, "D'Un But A l'Autre," *La Patrie*, March 31, 1928, 20
6 Roche, *The Hockey Book*, 105–106
7 Ibid, 193
8 "Flying Frenchmen Deadlock Bruins," *Montreal Daily Star*, February 20, 1931, 34
9 "Nick Wasnie's Backhand Shot For Tying Goal on Garden Ice," *Boston Globe*, February 20, 1931, 31
10 David McNeil, *In the Pressure of the Moment: Remembering Gerry McNeil* (Vancouver: Midtown Press, 2016), 39, 119–124
11 Howie Morenz, "D'Un But A l'Autre," *La Patrie*, March 26, 1928, 9
12 Paul Patton, "Life in fast lane too much for Morenz," *Globe and Mail*, March 7, 1987, C5
13 "16,500 Look On As Canadien Six And Boston Tie, 1 To 1," *Gazette*, February 20, 1931, 18
14 Ibid

Chapter 35

1 The phrase "laying down" was common in Howie Morenz's time, and remains so: e.g., Beck A. Taylor and Justin G. Trogdon, "Losing to Win: Tournament Incentives in the National Basketball Association," *Journal of Labor Economics*, 2002, vol. 20, issue 1, 23–41
2 Gzowski, *The Game of Our Lives*, 118
3 Roche, *The Hockey Book*, 103
4 Mike Rodden, "On the Highways of Sport," *Globe and Mail*, March 10, 1937, 21
5 Mike Rodden, "On the Highways of Sport," *Globe and Mail*, April 14, 1931, 10. See also: William Brown, *The Montreal Maroons* (Montreal: Vehicule Press, 1999), 98
6 Roche, *The Hockey Book*, 194–195; Ed Fitkin, *The Gashouse Gang of Hockey* (Toronto: W. M. Baxter Publishing Co., 1950), 100; and Stan Fischler, *The Rivalry: Canadiens vs. Leafs* (Toronto: McGraw-Hill Ryerson, 1971), 11–12
7 E.W. Ferguson, "Canadiens Silence Scandal-Mongers as They Beat Americans," *Montreal Herald*, February 23, 1931, 6. See also: "L'American compte quatre points en 12 minutes mais le Canadien gagne quand meme," *La Presse*, February 23, 1931, 18;
8 *Montreal Herald*, February 23, 1931, 6
9 Andy O'Brien, *Rocket Richard* (Toronto: Ryerson Press, 1961), 104
10 "Canadiens Rally Magnificently To Down Amerks, 6-4," *Gazette*, February 23, 1931, 18
11 Declan Hill, *Fix: Soccer and Organized Crime* (Toronto: McClelland and Stewart, 2008), 7

Chapter 36

1 "Howie Morenz se rend a l'hopital," *Le Petit Journal*, March 1, 1931, 1
2 "Larochelle Sortira de l'hopital," *La Presse*, November 28, 1931, 30; "Larochelle et Mondou Pratiquent Au Forum," *La Presse*, December 3, 1930, 22; "Wildore Larochelle Hurts His Shoulder," *Montreal Daily Star*, November 26, 1930, 28; "Larochelle Ready To Take Position," *Montreal Daily Star*, November 28, 1930, 38
3 "Le Canadien Joue en Champion et Bat le Detroit Par Le core Decisif de 5 a 0," *La Presse*, February 27, 1931, 32
4 "Scoring Leaders Try Hard But Can't Get Any Goals," *Montreal Herald*, February 27, 1931, 10

Chapter 37

1 Lou Marsh, "Leafs Come From Behind Twice to Tie Candiens in Overtime, *Toronto Daily Star*, March 2, 1931, 10

2 "Canadien et Toronto font joute nulle, 5-5," *Le Petit Journal*, March 1, 1931, 21
3 Ibid
4 *Toronto Daily Star*, March 2, 1931, 10
5 *Boston Herald*, March 25, 1931, 30
6 *Toronto Daily Star*, March 2, 1931, 10
7 *Le Petit Journal*, March 1, 1931, 21
8 *Toronto Daily Star*, March 2, 1931, 10
9 Ibid
10 L.S.B. Shapiro, "Hectic Scenes as Canadiens Battle Leafs to 5-All Tie," *Gazette*, March 2, 1931, 19
11 *Toronto Daily Star*, March 2, 1931, 10
12 Dean Robinson, "Morenz," *Stratford Beacon-Herald*, January 8, 1971, 8
13 *Gazette*, March 2, 1931, 19. See also: G.D. Lawrence, "On the Sidelines" *Montreal Herald*, March 6, 1931, 8. The *Herald* suggested an alternative: that Morenz had been kept in the penalty bench for three minutes and 30 seconds instead of just two. That view is supported by Rosaire Barrette in *Leo Dandurand Sportsman*, 163–164
14 *Toronto Daily Star*, March 2, 1931, 10. See also: *Montreal Daily Star*, March 2, 1931, 22; Bert Perry, "Leafs Batttle Canadiens to Draw In Season's Most Turbulent Game," *Globe*, March 2, 1931, 14–15. Reports differed as to whether it was off Morenz's skate, stick, or leg: "Victime De Revoltantes Injustices, Le Canadien Fait Neanmoins Joute Nulle A Toronto," *La Presse*, March 2, 1931, 18
16 *Gazette*, March 2, 1931, 19
17 *Le Petit Journal*, March 1, 1931, 21

Chapter 38

1 Trent Frayne, "How they Broke the Heart of Howie Morenz," *Maclean's*, October 15, 1953, 24; appears in Frayne, *Famous Hockey Players* (New York: Dodd, Mead & Company, 1973), 12–13
2 Registry of MacVicar Memorial Presbyterian, Montreal Annex, Quebec, June 21, 1926. Mary Louise was born on January 23, 1908, and turned 18 on January 23, 1926.
3 Recherche de Benoit Melancon, UMontreal
4 Germain, Georges-Hebert, *Overtime: The Legend of Guy Lafleur* (Markham, Ont.: Viking, 1990, 222. See also: Roy Macgregor, *Wayne Gretzky's Ghost and Other Tales from a Lifetime in Hockey* (Toronto: Vintage Canada, 2012), 51, regarding a young Paul Kariya: "The focus is hockey, and it leaves very little room for anything else."
5 Tod Hartje with Lawrence Martin, *Behind the Red Line: An American Hockey Player in Russia* (Toronto: Maxwell Macmillan Canada, 1992), 45
6 Bobbie Bouton and Nancy Marshall, *Home Games: Two Baseball Wives Speak Out* (New York: St. Martin's/Marek, 1983), 247

Chapter 39

1 "Morenz Injured In First Johnny Gagnon Absent As Rangers Nose Out Win," *Montreal Herald*, March 6, 1931, 8. See also: "Rangers Improve in Play-Off Race," *Montreal Daily Star*, March 6, 1931, 34
2 "Affaibli Par l'Absence de Gagnon et de Morenz, Le Canadien Est Vaincu," *La Presse*, March 6, 1931, 20
3 *Montreal Herald*, March 6, 1931, 8
4 Ted Allan and Sydney Gordon, *The Scapel, The Sword* (Boston: Little, Brown and Company, 1952), 324; Roderick Stewart, *The Mind of Norman Bethune* (Toronto: Fitzhenry & Whiteside, 1977), 112
5 *Montreal Herald*, March 6, 1931, 8

Chapter 40

Quotes from "Monsieur Joliat." Macdonald, William Pugsley, *Paul Marchand and Other Poems* (Toronto: Pine Tree Publishing Co., 1933), 41–46

1 Howie Morenz, "D'Un Bout a l'Autre," *La Patrie*, April 3, 1928, 10
2 McAllister, *Hockey Stars Today and Yesterday*, 68
3 "Joliat Acclaimed By Fans at Forum," *Gazette*, April 18, 1947, 16
4 "Joliat Est Le Heros de la Victoire du Canadien," *La Presse*, March 9, 1931, 20
5 McAllister, 68
6 *Le Messager* (Lewiston, Maine) February 13, 1931, 7
7 Unidentified newspaper article, written from Ottawa, post-1947; in the extensive LAC files of Charlie "Three Stars" Mayer's clipping archive.
8 "Le Canadien l'emporte sur le Providence, hier soir, par 8 a 4 devant une foule considerable," *La Presse*, November 6, 1930, 20

Chapter 41

1 The Canadiens defeated Victoria 4-2 in their first elimination game, with Morenz scoring the opening goal, the winning goal, as well as the insurance goal.
2 e.g., Richard M. Lapp and Alec Macaulay, *The Memorial Cup: Canada's National Hockey Championship* (Madeira Park, B.C.: Harbour Publishing, 1997), 17–18
3 Tim Burke, "'Morenz Greatest' Echoes in Toe's," *Gazette*, February 16, 1978, 23
4 E.W. Ferguson, "The Always Modest Morenz," *Montreal Herald*, February 21, 1931, 10
5 33 goals and 18 assists of the team's 116 goals and 65 assists in 1927–28
6 Jean Beliveau 1955–56: 47 goals, 48 assists, 95 points—42.79% of 222 team goals; Bernie Geoffrion 1960–61: 50 goals, 45 assists, 95 points—37.4% of 254 team goals; Guy Lafleur 1977–78: 60 goals, 72 assists, 132 points—36.7% of 359 team goals; Maurice Richard 1944–45: 50 goals, 23 assists, 73 points—32.8% of 228 team goals.

7 "Nick Wasnie's Goal Brings Canadiens Win Over Chicago," *Gazette*, March 11, 1931, 18. See also: "Le Canadien Gagne en Depit du Jeu Phenomenal de Gardiner, du Chicago," *La Presse*, March 11, 1931, 22

Chapter 42

1 E.W. Ferguson, "Star Leaves Hospital With Ankle Recovered And Is Anxious To Go," *Montreal Herald*, March 12, 1931, 8

2 Inaugurated in 1910, the trophy was made of solid silver and served as the trophy successively emblematic of the National Hockey Association title (1910–17), the National Hockey League title (1921–27), the NHL's Canadian or International Division winner (1928–38), and eventually the Stanley Cup runner-up (1939–50). The trophy was retired in 1950. Morenz eventually won it with the Canadiens seven times

3 Harry Cross, "New Garden Opens Formally Tonight," *New York Times*, December 15, 1925, 23. By further sleight of hand, the National Hockey League recognized that win as belonging to the 1924 season: e.g., Charles L. Coleman, *The Trail of the Stanley Cup, 1927-1946*, v.2 (Sherbrooke, P.Q.: Progressive Publications, 1969), xxvii

4 Baz O'Meara, "The Passing Sport Show," *Montreal Daily Star*, March 14, 1931, 15

5 Ibid

6 Even in 1924 Morenz might have had some competition from Georges Vezina's two shutouts and an even 1.00 goals against average

7 Horace Lavigne, "Battant Le Vancouver A Son Propre Jeu Le Canadien Se Classe Pour La Finale Avec Le Calgary," *La Patrie*, March 21, 1924, 6

8 Morenz would eventually win the Hart three times: 1928, 1931, and 1932, the first NHL player to do so, and the only member of the Montreal Canadiens to do so, ever

9 "Le Montreal Joue Une Excellente Partie Pour Vaincre Le Canadien, 3-0," *La Presse*, March 13, 1931, 30

10 Ibid. A generation later, Frank Selke similarly described the Canadiens without Richard as a team without its soul: Selke, 142

11 Baz O'Meara, "The Passing Sport Show," *Montreal Daily Star*, March 14, 1931, 15

12 Trent Frayne, *It's Easy All You Have to Do is Win* (Toronto: Longmans Canada Limited, 1968), 55. Also as quoted in *The Thrill of Victory: Best Sports Stories from the Pages of Maclean's* (Toronto: Viking Canada, 2003), 11

13 e.g., Bernard Pozier, "Gardien Blue-Blanc-Rouge," in *Les poètes chanteront ce but* (Trois Rivières, Québec: Écrits des forges 1991, 2004), 67

14 Roch Carrier (translated Sheila Fischman), *Our Life with the Rocket: The Maurice Richard Story* (Toronto: Penguin Canada, 2001), 58

Chapter 43

1 "Morenz Is Likely To Get Into Game," *Montreal Daily Star*, March 14, 1931, 15
2 Fischler, *Those Were The Days*, 73; Fischler and Fischler, 41–42
3 Armand Jokisen, "En Blanc et en Noir," *L'Illustration Nouvelle*, March 10, 1937, 21
4 Hugh MacLennan, *Two Solitudes* (Toronto: Collins, 1945), 285
5 Claude Larochelle (translated by Dan Rosenburg), *Guy Lafleur: Hockey's #1* (Quebec: Lotographie Inc., 1978), 119
6 Marc T. McNeil, "Canadien Draw With Ottawa, 3-3, In Final Combat," *Gazette*, March 16, 1931, 18.
7 E.W. Ferguson, "Canadiens Go Easily In Game With Ottawa," *Montreal Herald*, March 16, 1931, 7

Chapter 44

1 "Morenz Met Cude Hors de Combat Lorsqu'Il l'Atteint Au Menton Avec Le Disque," *La Presse*, March 23, 1931, 22
2 "Le Champion d'Aujourd'hui, Howie Morenz, A Developpe Le Lancer Appele 'Bean Puck'," *Le Petit Journal*, January 18, 1931, 23
3 "Cannonball" in Leslie Roberts, "The Magnificent Morenz"; unidentified newspaper clipping, likely *Stratford Beacon-Herald*, undated; Jim Coleman in *Calgary Herald*, February 19, 1971, 47. "Torpedo" in "Morenz Gets Goal in Lengthy Tilt," *Montreal Daily Star*, March 16, 1931, 28. "Thudding" in "New Marks Made in Fast Contest," *Montreal Daily Star*, February 9, 1931, 22. "Travelling like a bullet" in "Morenz Injured in First Johnny Gagnon Absent as Rangers Nose Out Win," *Montreal Herald*, March 6, 1931, 8; "Noted in Passing Between Rounds," *Montreal Daily Star*, February 6, 1931, 35; "Canadiens Again Beat Maroons in Intra-City Tilt," *Gazette*, January 16, 1931, 18; "Canadiens Beat Weakened Leafs With Speedy Last-Period Display," *Globe*, December 10, 1930, 8.
4 Frayne, 16
5 Stephen Cole, *The Canadian Hockey Atlas* (Toronto: Doubleday Canada, 2006), 180
6 Dink Carroll, "Playing the Field" column, *Gazette*, April 4, 1944, 14
7 Dan Diamond, ed., *Hockey Hall of Fame: The Official Registry of the Game's Honour Roll* (Toronto: Doubleday Canada, 1996), 68
8 Neil D. Isaacs, *Checking Back: A History of the National Hockey League* (New York: W. W. Norton and Company, 1977), 194. Ed Giacomin described the anxiety of facing a knuckler: Stephen Cole, *The Last Hurrah* (Toronto: Penguin Books, 1995), 140
9 Quoted by M.J. Rodden in "On the Highways of Sport," *Globe*, December 29, 1930, 12

10 Joseph C. Nichols, "Players of the Game: Howie Morenz—Speedy Centre of the Canadiens," *New York Times*, April 6, 1931, 28. See also: Bill Brandt, "Once in a Lifetime," *Sport*, vol. 4, no. 4 (April 1948), 39, 101

11 "Maroons Defeat Canadiens, 2-1, in Thrilling Contest," *The Gazette*, January 8, 1930, 16. See also: "Le Champion d'Aujourd'hui, Howie Morenz, a Developpe Le Lancer Appele 'Bean Puck,'" *Le Petit Journal*, January 18, 1931, 23

12 Quoted by Elmer W. Ferguson, "The Gist and Jest of It," *Montreal Herald*, March 11, 1937, 9

13 *Le Petit Journal*, January 18, 1931, 23

14 "Cude Shows Grit after Being Hurt," *Montreal Daily Star*, March 23, 1931, 24

15 L.S.B. Shapiro, "Canadiens Held to 4-All Deadlock by Philadelphia Six," *Gazette*, March 23, 1931, 21

16 "Canadiens et Philadelphie Font Joute Nulle de 4 A 4," *Le Petit Journal*, March 22, 1931, 25, suggested that Morenz was not credited with an assist on the goal, but *Montreal Daily Star* and L.S.B. *Gazette* report that he was.

17 Morenz repeated the feat in 1931–32, making him the leading goal scorer for the Canadiens for seven consecutive seasons. This uninterrupted streak remains unmatched, even by players as dominant as Rocket Richard, Jean Béliveau, and Guy Lafleur.

PART III: PLAYOFF SEASON

Chapter 1

1 "Bruins Rally to Win, 5 to 4," *Boston Globe*, March 25, 1931, 15

2 Ibid

3 "Bruins Win Out in 'Death' Period," *Boston Post*, March 25, 1931, 18; "Malgre Une Avance de Trois Points, Le Canadien Se Fait Rattraper et Perd la Premiere," *La Patrie*, March 25, 1931, 12

4 "Phillips blesse a une jambe ne pourra jouer de la saison," *La Presse*, March 26, 1931, 33. The photograph was eventually published as "Picture Reveals Interference in Stanley Cup Game," *Montreal Daily Star*, March 28, 1931, 34. It had originally appeared as "Shore Whacking Home Goal In Third Period After Taking Pass-Out From Clapper," in *Boston Globe*, March 25, 1931, 20

5 *Boston Globe*, March 25, 1931, 15

6 L.S.B. Shapiro, "Canadiens Refuse to Protest Bruins' Overtime Victory," *Gazette*, March 26, 1931, 18. See also: "Malgre Une Avance de Trois Points," *La Patrie*, March 25, 1931, 13

7 *Boston Globe*, March 25, 1931, 15

8 L.S.B. Shapiro, "Bruins Rally to Down Canadiens in Amazing Game," *Gazette*, March 25, 1931, 20

9 E.W. Ferguson, "Mantha Boys Most Clannish Family in Hockey Today, " *Montreal Herald*, March 28, 1931, 10

10 Ibid. Elmer Ferguson eventually peddled a more fanciful and better-known version than the truthful one, e.g., Elmer W. Ferguson, "The Gist and Jest of It," *Montreal Herald*, March 9, 1937, 9; and then "The Calvert Sports Column," January 20, 1953, *Globe and Mail*, 14; repeated in George Sullivan's *Faceoff*, 116. During Morenz's time there were two playoff games between the Canadiens and Bruins in Boston that the Bruins won 1-0 on goals by Weiland (March 19 and 21, 1929), but both were on passing plays in regulation time. The description of Weiland jumping and batting down the puck in the Calvert Sports column version does echo part of what had happened on March 24, 1931.

Chapter 2

1 Baz O'Meara, "G. Mantha's Goal Puts Teams Even," *Montreal Daily Star*, March 27, 1931, 40

2 Ibid. The *Star* is the only report that attributes the shot on Morenz to Barry. All others say it was Darragh's.

3 "Mantha Scores for Canadiens and Evens Series With Bruins," *Globe*, March 27, 1931, 10

4 *Montreal Daily Star*, March 27, 1931, 40

5 Joseph C. Nichols, "Players of the Game: Howie Morenz—Speedy Centre of the Canadiens," *New York Times*, April 6, 1931, 28

6 J.W. Mooney, "Canadiens Win Second Game, 1-0," *Boston Post*, March 27, 1931, 42

7 E.W. Ferguson, "Near Riot as Habitant Outsmart Mighty Bruins to Tie Play-Off Series," *Montreal Herald*, March 27, 1931, 10

8 Victor O. Jones, "Canadiens Tie Up Series, Winning 1-0," *Boston Globe*, March 27, 1931, 40

9 *Montreal Herald*, March 27, 1931, 10. See also: "Georges Mantha compte l'unique point de la joute sur une passe de Lepine dans la premiere periode," *La Presse*, March 27, 1931, 33

10 Ibid

11 L.S.B. Shapiro, "Canadiens Outplay Boston to Capture Second Contest, 1-0," *Gazette*, March 27, 1931, 16

Chapter 3

1 E.W. Ferguson, "Younger Mantha Puts Champions in Front in Race," *Montreal Herald*, March 30, 1931, 8

2 Ibid

3 Victor O. Jones, "Canadiens Make It Two Straight," *Boston Globe,* March 29, 1931, 37. See also: J.W. Mooney, "Canadiens Clinch in Overtime Game," *Boston Post,* March 29, 1931, 19
4 "Georges Mantha est le heros de la troisieme joute," *Le Petit Journal*, March 29, 1931, 25
5 George Mantha Again Scores Winning Goal," *Montreal Daily Star*, March 30, 1931, 27
6 "Geo. Mantha Again Breaks Up Contest," *Montreal Daily Star*, March 30, 1931, 26
7 "George Mantha Is Star as Canadiens Beat Boston, 4 to 3," *Gazette*, March 30, 1931, 18
8 *Montreal Daily Star*, March 30, 1931, 26. See also: "Canadiens Score in Overtime To Defeat Boston Bruins, 4-3," *Globe*, March 30, 1931, 10; Horace Lavigne, "Le Canadien prend le devant sur le Boston apres un dur match," *La Patrie*, March 30, 1931, 12. A diagram of the goal published in *Le Petit Journal*, "Le Point Victorieux," March 29, 1931, 25, shows a somewhat different sequence of events.
9 Marc T. McNeil, "Huge Throng Goes Wild With Joy As Canadiens' Win," *Gazette*, March 30, 1931, 18.
10 Ibid

Chapter 4

1 Horace Lavigne, "Le Canadien succombe devant la condition du club Boston," *La Patrie,* March 31, 1931, 12
2 E.W. Ferguson, "Boston Man-Power Factor As Series Is Forced to Limit," *Montreal Herald*, March 31, 1931, 6
3 J.W. Mooney, "Bruins Win 3 to 1 to Even Up Series," *Boston Post,* March 31, 1931, 21
4 R.A.C. Ballantyne, "Little Joy Among Fans as Canadiens Bow before Bruins," *Gazette,* March 31, 1931, 20
5 Victor O. Jones, "Bruins Win 3-1, Tying Up Series," *Boston Globe*, March 31, 1931, 21. See also: "Champions Flater under Heavy Pace," *Montreal Daily Star*, March 31, 1931, 30
6 "Les deux clubs rivaux sont maintenant egaux avec deux voctoires et deux defaites, chacun," *La Presse*, March 31, 1931, 24
7 "Bruins Defeat Canadiens, Necessitating Fifth Game," *Globe*, March 31, 1931, 10
8 *Boston Post,* March 31, 1931, 21
9 *Boston Globe*, March 31, 1931, 21
10 *Gazette,* March 31, 1931, 20
11 *La Presse*, March 31, 1931, 24
12 *Montreal Herald*, March 31, 1931, 6

13 *Boston Post*, March 31, 1931, 21
14 *Montreal Herald*, March 31, 1931, 6

Chapter 5

1 J.W. Mooney, "Canadiens Win Playoff Final," *Boston Post*, April 2, 1931, 21. *La Patrie* reported it differently.
2 Ibid
3 "Boston Raps Calder and Ion and Insinuates Nasty Things," *Montreal Daily Star*, April 3, 1931, 18, in the reprint of an article from the *Boston Herald*, April 2, 1931.
4 "Wildor Larochelle compte le point decisif sur une passe de Burke et donne la victoire a son club," *La Presse*, April 2, 1931, 26
5 Horace Lavigne, "Larochelle donne la victoire aux champions," *La Patrie*, April 2, 1931, 10
6 L.S.B. Shapiro, "Canadiens Triumph Over Bruins, 3 to 2, to Capture Series," *Gazette*, April 2, 1931, 20
7 Victor O. Jones, "Canadiens Win, Taking Series," *Boston Globe*, April 2, 1931, 23
8 *La Presse*, April 2, 1931, 26
9 "Comment of Big Figures in Big Series," *Montreal Daily Star*, April 2, 1931, 36

Chapter 6

1 Baz O'Meara, "Mondou Unable to Make Chicago Trip," *Montreal Daily Star*, April 3, 1931, 18
2 M.J. Rodden, "On the Highways of Sport," *Globe*, April 2, 1931, 10
3 L.S.B. Shapiro, "Canadiens Defeat Chicago, 2 to 1, in Stanley Cup Game," *Gazette*, April 4, 1931, 18
4 Charles Bartlett, "Invaders Whip Home Team at Its Own Game," *Chicago Daily Tribune*, April 4, 1931, 21
5 "Les hommes de Cecil Hart l'emportent sur le Chicago par 2 a 1 dans une dure partie," *La Presse*, April 4, 1931, 48
6 *Chicago Daily Tribune*, April 4, 1931, 21
7 Ibid
8 *Gazette*, April 4, 1931, 18. See also: Douglas Hunter, *War Games: Conn Smythe & Hockey's Fighting Men* (Toronto: Viking, 1996), 46–47
9 Charles Bartlett, "Chicago Seeks Tie Tonight in Ice Cup Series," *Chicago Daily Tribune*, April 5, 1931, 27
10 Ibid

Chapter 7

1 Baz O'Meara, "Black Hawks on Even Terms for Stanley Cup," *Montreal Daily Star*, April 6, 1931, 23

2 "Tiring Canadiens Lose Overtime Battle, 2-1, To Chicago Black Hawks," *Globe*, April 6, 1931, 8
3 "Leduc et Mondou Encore Sous Observation Et Morenz Subit le Traitement Electrique," *La Patrie*, April 7, 1931, 12
4 "Gottselig donne la victoire aux Hawks apres un match furieux," *La Patrie*, April 6, 1931, 10
5 "Chicago Six Beats Canadien, 2 to 1," *New York Times*, April 6, 1931, 28
6 Baz O'Meara, "Howie Morenz May Not Play Again," *Montreal Daily Star*, April 6, 1931, 24; Frank Orr, *The Stanley Cup: The World Series of Hockey* (Toronto: Longman Canada, 1976), 77, suggested that Morenz had been bothered by the shoulder injury throughout the playoffs
7 *La Patrie*, April 7, 1931, 12

Chapter 8

1 "Morenz Improved; Is Likely to Play," *Montreal Daily Star*, April 7, 1931, 30. See also: "Leduc et Mondou Encore Sous Observation Et Morenz Subit le Traitement Electrique," *La Patrie*, April 7, 1931, 12
2 "Team in Workout Shows Old Sparkle," *Montreal Daily Star*, April 8, 1931, 38. See also: E.W. Ferguson, "Canadiens Near Rangers' Record for Cup Matches in the Present N.H.L.," *Montreal Herald*, April 8, 1931, 6
3 "Canadiens to Rely on Extreme Speed," *Montreal Daily Star*, April 9, 1931, 38
4 "Le Chicago Aura Size Joueurs Bien En Forme A Opposer Au Canadien," *La Presse*, April 9, 1931, 28 while in the same article *La Presse* anticipated Lepine starting at centre.
5 "Leduc Est Le Seule Unite Du Canaiden, Incertaine De Jouer Contre Les Hawks," *La Patrie*, April 9, 1931, 12
6 "Le Canadien perd en trois minutes une partie qu'il avait bel et bien gagnee," *La Presse*, April 10, 1931, 30
7 "Hawks Take Advantage by Beating Canadiens in Lengthy Struggle," *Globe*, April 10, 1931, 8
8 E.W. Ferguson, "Jaded Canadiens Weaken and Lose in Long Overtime," *Montreal Herald*, April 10, 1931, 6
9 Horace Lavigne, "Les Hawks balaient une avance de deux points et gangnent," *La Patrie*, April 10, 1931, 12
10 *Globe*, April 10, 1931, 8
11 *La Presse*, April 10, 1931, 30
12 G.D. Lawrence, "On The Sidelines," *Montreal Herald*, April 10, 1931, 6
13 *La Presse*, April 10, 1931, 30
14 "Third Period Rally Flusters Hartmen," *Montreal Daily Star*, April 10, 1931, 36
15 L.S.B. Shapiro, "Chicago Defeats Canadiens, 3 to 2, in Overtime Game," *Gazette*, April 10, 1931, 18. See also: "Hawks Whip Canadiens, 3 to 2, in Overtime,"

Chicago Daily Tribune, April 10, 1931, 29; "13,000 See Chicago Defeat Canadiens," *New York Times*, April 10, 1931, 30

Chapter 9

1 E.W. Ferguson, "Hawks Can Take Stanley Cup by Victory Tonight," *Montreal Herald*, April 11, 1931, 10
2 Stephen Amidon, *Something Like the Gods: A Cultural History of the Athlete from Achilles to LeBron* (New York: Rodale, 2012), 37
3 "In Flanders Fields," authored by Dr. John McCrae
4 E.W. Ferguson, "Canadiens Are Favored Face Hawks With Better Team Than In Chicago Games," *Montreal Herald*, April 9, 1931, 6. "Ed is one of the most ardent Canadien rooters . . ."
5 Howie Morenz, "D'un Bout a l'Autre," *La Patrie*, April 2, 1928, 11
6 L.B.S. Shapiro, "Canadiens Rally To Defeat Hawks In Fourth Game, 4-2," *Gazette*, April 13, 1931, 22. Other versions of the goal appear in "Les Canadiens Whip Hawks, 4-2; Even Series," *Chicago Tribune*, April 12, 1931, Part 2, 1
7 Ibid
8 E.W. Ferguson, "Champions in Amazing Feat to Beat Hawks," *Montreal Herald*, April 13, 1931, 6
9 Morenz, *La Patrie*, April 2, 1928, 11
10 Marc T. McNeil, "Huge Hockey Crowd Mirrors Action on Ice in Emotions," *Gazette*, April 13, 1931, 22. See also: "Gagnon et Lepine comptent 2 points chacun et donnent la victoire au Canadien," *La Presse*, April 13, 1931, 22
11 "Glancing Around the Forum as Canadiens Defeat Hawks," *Montreal Daily Star*, April 13, 1931, 26. According to Wil Larochelle, in "Marty Burke Eulogizes Great Player, Fine Pal," *Stratford Beacon-Herald*, March 10, 1937, 9; and Cecil Hart, *Morenz Memorial Fund Program*, November 2, 1937, 22, Morenz was as magnificent a leader in the dressing room as on the ice.
12 *Montreal Herald*, April 13, 1931, 6
13 G.D. Lawrence, "On the Sidelines," *Montreal Herald*, April 13, 1931, 6
14 Horace Lavigne, "Le Canadien egale les chances et triomphe de Chicago," *La Patrie*, April 13, 1931, 12
15 "Gagnon and Lepine in Starring Role," *Montreal Daily Star*, April 13, 1931, 26.
16 Ibid, 29

Chapter 10

1 L.S.B. Shapiro, "Canadien Defeat Chicago, 2 to 0, to Keep World Title"
2 "Noted as Canadiens Win Stanley Cup," *Montreal Daily Star*, April 15, 1931, 41
3 Baz O'Meara, "The Passing Sport Show," *Montreal Daily Star*, April 14, 1931, 35
4 "Canadiens Win Stanley Cup By Blanking Black Hawks In Fifth Game of Series," *Globe*, April 15, 1931, 17

5 "Morenz Connects For Great Goal," *Montreal Daily Star*, April 15, 1931, 38
6 L.S.B. Shapiro, "Canadien Defeat Chicago, 2 To 0, To Keep World Title," *Gazette*, April 15, 1931, 18. Others credited the steal solely to Morenz: "Canadiens Beat Hawks, 2 – 0, To Retain Crown," *Chicago Tribune*, April 15, 1931, 26; "Canadiens Win Stanley Cup by Blanking Black Hawks in Fifth Game of Series," *Globe*, April 15, 1931, 17
7 "Morenz Scores Goal Finally on Great Play," *Montreal Daily Star*, April 15, 1931, 41
8 Leo Dandurand, "Details inedits sur le grand Howie," *Le Petit Journal*, March 14, 1937, 51
9 L.S.B. Shapiro, "Canadien Defeat Chicago, 2 to 0, to Keep World Title," *Gazette*, April 15, 1931, 18
10 *Globe*, April 15, 1931, 17
11 *Gazette*, April 15, 1931, 18
12 "Le Canadien champion mondial de hockey deux ans de suite," *La Presse*, April 15, 1931, 1
13 G.D. Lawrence, "On the Sidelines." *Montreal Herald*, April 15, 1931, 8
14 "Morenz Connects for Great Goal," *Montreal Daily Star*, April 15, 1931, 38, to "Morenz Scores Goal Finally on Great Play," *Montreal Daily Star*, April 15, 1931, 41. See also: the version of the goal adopted by D'Arcy Jenish, *The Montreal Canadiens: 100 Years of Glory* (Toronto: Doubleday Canada, 2008), 76
15 R.A.C. Ballantyne, "Excited Throng See Canadiens Win Stanley Cup," *Gazette*, April 15, 1931, 18
16 Andy O'Brien, "Uni a Morenz dans la gloire," *Perspectives*, no. 13, March 31, 1962, 15–17 (in English at "Playoff Moment with Morenz" in *Weekend Magazine*, March 31, 1962, volume 12, no. 13, 12–13).

Epilogue

1 "Noted as Canadiens Win the Stanley Cup for Fifth Time," *Montreal Daily Star*, April 15, 1931, 38
2 "When Morenz Scored, John W. Downey Died," *Montreal Daily Star*, April 15, 1931, 40; "Dies on Hearing of Morenz Goal," *Ottawa Journal*, April 15, 1931, 25; "Le Point de Morenz Fait Une Victime," *La Patrie*, April 16, 1931, 12
3 *Montreal Daily Star*, April 15, 1931, 25
4 "Here and There with Canadien in Cup Final," *Ottawa Journal*, April 15, 1937, 25
5 Ibid
6 L.S.B. Shapiro, "Champion Hockey Players Honored at Public Banquet," *Gazette*, April 16, 1931, 16
7 "Pres de 500 Sportsmen Fetent Joyeusement Les Champions du Monde," *La Presse*, April 16, 1931, 34; Mikael Lalancette, *Georges Vezina: L'Habitant Silencieux* (Montreal: Les Editions de l'Homme, 2021), 254–255

8 Leslie Roberts, "It's Always Open Season," *Maclean's*, May 1931, 8. See also: "Canadiens Are Acclaimed, Receive Admirers' Tribute," *Montreal Daily Star*, April 16, 1931, 39
9 *National Hockey League Guide 1937*, 71
10 Fischler, *Those Were the Days*, 148; Fischler and Fischler, *Heroes and History*, 62–63
11 Hugh MacLennan, "Fury on Ice," first published in *Holiday Magazine*, 1954, reproduced in David Gowdey, *Riding on the Roar of the Crowd: A Hockey Anthology* (Toronto: Macmillan of Canada, 1989), 4, 10.
12 Armand Jokisen, "En Blanc et En Noir," *L'Illustration Nouvelle*, March 10, 1937, 21
13 Ken Campbell, "Howie Morenz" in *Hockey News: A Century of Montreal Canadiens* (Owen Sound, Ontario: Transcontinental Media G., 1999), 27
14 "Howe Morenz Est Mort A l'Hopital Hier," *L'Illustration Nouvelle*, March 9, 1937, 1
15 John LeBlanc, "10,000 Fans at Morenz Rites," *Stratford Beacon-Herald*, March 12, 1937, 1
16 Baz O'Meara, "Memories of Morenz," *Howie Morenz Memorial Fund Programme*, November 1937, 36
17 Horace Lavigne, "Sur la tombe de l'unique Morenz," *Howie Morenz Memorial Fund Programme*, November 1937, 56
18 Tommy Munns, "Scanning the Sport Field," *Globe and Mail*, March 12, 1937, 19
19 Gerard "Gerry" Gosselin, *Monsieur Hockey* (Montreal: Les Editions de l'Homme, 1960), 115
20 Ted Mahovlich, *The Big M: The Frank Mahovlich Story* (Toronto: Sports Publishing Inc., 1999), 228
21 "Howie Morenz Played the Game," *Stratford Beacon-Herald*, March 10, 1937, 4
22 *Morenz Memorial Fund Program*, November 2, 1937, 33

The Statistical Record

1 Charles Mayer, *L'Epopee des Canadiens de Georges Vezina a Maurice Richard* (Ottawa: Charles Mayer, 1949), 81; Manuscript, Charles Mayer in Charles Mayer Fonds, MG30-C76, volume 12; Library and Archives Canada.
2 *Morenz Memorial Fund Program*, November 2, 1937, 22
3 e.g., Claude Mouton, *The Montreal Canadiens: A Hockey Dynasty* (Toronto: Van Nostrand Reinhold Ltd., 1980), 270
4 Charles L. Coleman, *The Trail of the Stanley Cup, v.2, 1927–1946* (Sherbrooke, Quebec: National Hockey League, 1969), 691, credits Morenz with 273 regular-season goals
5 Adding five assists for the 1924–25 season, and dropping one for the 1933–34 season
6 However, not all of Morenz's Stanley Cup playoff scoring gets recognized in official NHL statistics, which can reduce his total by as much as 10 points: e.g.,

Andrew Podnieks et al., *Kings of the Ice: A History of World Hockey* (Richmond Hill, Ontario: NDE Publishing, 2002), 106

7 Those 20 points also represented 17.4% of the Canadiens' end-of-season scoring total: "Hockey Standings," *Gazette*, January 29, 1937, 14

Acknowledgments

THIS BOOK IS the product of contributions from many individuals and institutions. The staff and resources of Library and Archives Canada; Biblioteque et Archives nationales du Quebec; the Perth County Archives in Stratford, Ontario; and the Hockey Hall of Fame Resource Centre in Toronto, Ontario, were welcoming, encouraging, and sometimes intrigued enough to anticipate and answer some research queries on their own. So too were my fellow members of the Society for International Hockey Research—of which I would like to single out two by name: David McNeil and Jean-Patrice Martel. The public library staff in Boston, Massachusetts; Halifax, Nova Scotia; Lewiston, Maine; New York, New York; Ottawa, Ontario; Philadelphia, Pennsylvania; and Westmount, Quebec; each provided much appreciated "local" guidance about accessing relevant resources which, even now, remain off-line. Particular thanks are due to the Archives and Special Collections Archive of the McLaughlin Library at the University of Guelph for both preserving, and then facilitating access to, its recording of "Fire on ice" from the 1981 Blyth Festival performance. I also want to credit Robert Murray for the photograph of Andre J. Fortier's statue rendering of Howie Morenz outside the Bell Centre in Montreal.